A BASIC DICTIONARY OF ISLAM

Also by Ruqaiyyah Waris Maqsood

Teach Yourself Islam

Living with Teenagers

For Heaven Sake

The Challenge of Islam (for boys)

The Love of Islam (for girls)

The Muslim Marriage Guide

The Muslim Prayer Encyclopaedia

The Beautiful Commands of Allah

The Beautiful Promises of Allah

Basic Dictionary of Islam

A BASIC DICTIONARY OF ISLAM

Ruqaiyyah Waris Maqsood

Goodword
BOOKS

Dedicated to
my dear friend and brother,
A.S.K. Joommal
in appreciation of all his support,
and in admiration of his life-time's
work dedicated to attacking and
eradicating all that masquerades as Islam,
but is patently false.

First published 1998

Reprinted 1999, 2000

Distributed by
AL-RISALA
The Islamic Centre
1, Nizamuddin West Market,
New Delhi 110 013
Tel. 4611128, 4625454
Fax 4697333, 4647980
e-mail: skhan@vsnl.com
website: www.alrisala.org

Printed in India

'Abasa. The title of the 80th surah of the Qur'an, meaning 'he frowned.' This is a Makkan surah of 42 verses, and takes its name from an incident when the blind companion Abdallah b. Shurayh (known as Ibn Umm Maktum) interrupted the Prophet and was treated with impatience because the Prophet was busy with Walid b. Mughirah, one of the important Quraysh chiefs whom he hoped to convert. The Prophet frowned and turned away from him, but should have made time for him. In later years he often greeted him with the words: 'Welcome to him on whose account my Sustainer rebuked me!' The revelation came from Allah as a rebuke. It is such an important passage for those to consider who try to present the Prophet as a superhuman being, beyond rebuke. The Prophet was humble, and fully human, as we are. The blind man went on to be one of the most famous of Muslims and several times served as the prayer leader in Madinah while the Prophet was away in warfare.

Abbas. (d. 32/653). One of the Prophet's uncles. The Prophet's grandfather, Abd al-Muttalib, remarried in his old age, and his two late-born sons—Abbas, some three years older than the Prophet, and Hamzah, about the same age, were the Prophet's playmates. Abbas married Umm Fadl, whose half-sister Zaynab was the Prophet's fifth wife, and whose sister Maymunah was the Prophet's twelfth wife. Abbas became a merchant who made a large fortune, and had the right of supplying drink to pilgrims in Makkah. Despite his wife Umm Fadl being one of the earliest Muslims, he was opposed to Islam so long as the Prophet lived in Makkah. However, after the death of Abu Talib he became the Prophet's protector and defended his cause at the assembly of Aqabah. He fought against the Prophet at the Battle of Badr however, and was taken captive. Some say the Makkans had forced him to fight on their side; it is also suggested he was a secret Muslim but kept quiet about it. He finally joined the Muslims openly before the fall of Makkah, and was therefore referred to as 'the last of the Muhajirun'. He retained the right to supply water to the pilgrims. He fought in the Battle of Hunayn, and largely financed the campaign against the Byzantines. He was one of those who washed the Prophet's body when he died. When Umar was Caliph, Abbas gave his house to enlarge the mosque at Madinah. He died in Madinah in either 32 or 34 AH. The Abbasid caliphs descended from his son Abdallah.

Abbasids. A dynasty of caliphs taking their name from the Prophet's uncle Abbas, since their founder was one of his descendants. The dynasty ruled from 132/750-656/1258, and as a rival caliphate in Cairo from 659/1261-923/1517. Al-Mansur established his capital in Baghdad. Abbasid power declined after the Buyids entered Baghdad in 334/945. The last Abbasid caliph, al-Musta'sim, was murdered by the Mongols when they sacked Baghdad in 656/1258.

Abd. The 'root' of the Arabic word for servant or slave. Commonly used as part of a name by Muslims in conjunction with one of the names of God, as for example in Abdallah (Servant of Allah) Abd al-Karim (Servant of the Generous One), Abd al-Rahim (Servant of the Compassionate One) etc. 'Al' means 'the'. When a Muslim gets called Abdul, you can now see that this is incomplete. Muslims without knowledge of Arabic sometimes make this mistake.

Abdal (sing. badal). Lit. 'substitutes' or 'replacements'; used to designate a rank in the Sufi hierarchy of saints. The abdal are so called because each is replaced on his deathbed by the next.

Abd al-Hamid II (1258/1842-1336/1914). the 36th Ottoman Caliph, whose reign was occupied mainly with the Turkish wars against Russia and Greece. After the Young Turk Revolt (1326/1908), he was deposed and sent into exile. The last Caliph of all Islam.

Abd al-Malik (26/646-86/705). The 5th Umayyad caliph, the son of Marwan. He had to defeat the anti-caliph Abdullah ibn Zubayr, the Prophet's nephew, and revolts of the Kharijites. During his reign the Dome of the Rock was built in Jerusalem, an Islamic gold coinage was issued, and the garrison of Wasit was built in Iraq.

Abd al-Muttalib. The Prophet's grandfather, a man of outstanding piety and nobility, a chief of the Quraysh clan Hashim. His real name was Shaybah, and he was the son of Hashim and the heiress Salmah of Yathrib. At the age of fourteen he was taken to Makkah by his uncle al-Muttalib, and people thought he was a new servant, hence his nick-name. He was famous for having had a vision in which the lost source of the Zam-zam well was rediscovered and put back into use again for the pilgrims coming to Makkah. When the Prophet's mother died he took the six-year old into his care and cherished him, until he himself died two years later. He had already noted the exceptional qualities of his grandson, and loved him dearly. He had a very large family, most of whom became Muslims, especially Abbas, his five daughters by his wife Fatimah of Makhzum, and Hamzah and Safiyyah, the children of Halah. His son Abu Lahab was a bitter enemy of Islam.

Abd al-Rahman III (c276/889-350/961). The greatest of the Umayyad Andalusian caliphs. He consolidated Cordoba and waged war against the Christian rulers of Spain. Cordoba became one of the great capitals of the Islamic West.

Abd al-Uzza ibn Abd al-Muttalib. See Abu Lahab.

Abdallah. The Prophet's father. Abdallah's father (Abd al-Muttalib) had sworn that if he had ten sons he would sacrifice one of them to God, but when Abdallah was chosen by lot he was granted a vision in which he was told to sacrifice 100 camels instead. Abdallah grew up to be a merchant, travelling to many distant cities. He married his cousin Aminah, but shortly after she became pregnant he was taken ill and died. Thus he never saw his son who was to become the Prophet of Islam.

Abdallah ibn Mas'ud. was one of the earliest Muslims. He claimed to be the 10th. He was the first to recite the Qur'an openly in Makkah, and was tortured by the Quraysh. He was one of the best reciters of Qur'an. In the Battle of Badr, he killed Abu Jahl, who had once struck him in the face. He found him, nearly dead, and beheaded him. He was regarded as a member of the Prophet's family, for he and his mother stayed there for long periods. He was also called Ibn Umm Abd—the son of the mother of the slave. Caliph Umar sent him to Kufah as adviser to the Governor, Ammar ibn Yasir. He was the authority for 848 hadiths. He died in Madinah in 32 AH, and was one of the ten to whom the Prophet promised Paradise in his life-time.

Abduh. Muhammad Abduh (1849-1905) was one of the most significant modernist figures in C19 Egypt. He was educated at the al-Azhar university in Cairo, and became a teacher there. He spent some time in exile in France, and taught in Beirut. His lectures there formed his book 'Risalat al-Tawhid' (The Theology of Unity), an explicit attempt to write a modernist Islamic theology. In 1888 he returned to Egypt and became a judge (mufti); in 1897 he was the chief mufti of Egypt. He was concerned with the decay of Islamic society, and the deteriorating status of Islam. He saw the dangers of the increasing separation of Islamic spheres of influence and areas controlled by the modern sense of human reason. His efforts to bring the two together were his main platform, and the emergence of a new, learned class which would revitalize Islam. He argued against blind acceptance of traditional tafsir and pressed for making Qur'an commentary available for ordinary people. His commentary 'Tafsir al-manar' was therefore minus the theological speculations, the detailed grammatical discussions and the obtuse scholarship which characterised past works. He emphasized the search for knowledge, the use of the intellect, the need for education and political independence—all ideas to be found in the Qur'an.

Abortion. The termination of pregnancy. Islam allows birth control that prevents pregnancy (see birth control), and some scholars allow abortion for valid reasons up to the sixteenth week of pregnancy when the mother generally feels the foetus inside her 'quicken,' and it is assumed that the child's soul has entered its body. However, this is a debatable assumption. Modern ultrasound equipment shows the full development of the foetus as a separate living entity from its conception. (One then enters the complicated sphere of the nature of an unborn person in its stage of existence as male sperm plus unfertilised egg). It is certainly the case that a foetus has developed enough to be regarded as fully human by the sixth week, when its sensory and motor nerves are functioning, and the foetus reacts to painful stimuli. One hadith of the Prophet indicates six weeks as an important moment in the development of the foetus: 'When forty-two nights have passed over that which is conceived, Allah sends an angel to it who shapes it, makes it ears, eyes, skin, flesh and bones; then the angel says: 'O Lord, is it male or female?' and your Lord decides what He wishes, and the angels record it.' In modern support of this, it is true that ultra-sound scanners can now detect in the sixth week whether the foetus is male or female.

All Muslims reject the deliberate termination of a life once started, as the child has the right to a chance of life in the same way as any other person. When a mother seeking abortion declares that she has the right to do as she likes with her own body, she is forgetting the rights of the separate living person with its own body that is temporarily within her. She is usually thinking of the difficulties and problems that arise from an inconvenient pregnancy. Islam allows birth control, but not the killing of a conceived new human being.

However, if the life of the mother is put in real danger by the pregnancy, and it becomes a matter of choosing between the two, then most scholars would allow the abortion on the grounds that the existing and functioning life of the mother takes precedence over that of the unborn child (whose separate and functioning existence is still only potential, since it cannot exist apart from the mother at that stage).

Ablaq (lit. 'piebald'). It is a technical term to designate Islamic architecture in which two colours or tones are used alternately. Ablaq masonry figured largely in Mameluke architecture.

Abraha. An Ethopian (Abyssinian) Christian king, the ruler of Yemen at the time of the Prophet's birth. Abraha was the Christian viceroy of the Yemen, which was ruled by the Abyssinians, in the C6 CE. He became jealous of Makkah's commercial success and attempted to invade the city. He had realised that the Ka'bah was crucial to the success of the Quraysh, and to deflect pilgrims to south Arabia and attract more trade for himself, he built a magnificent Christian temple in San'a. When his hopes were disappointed, he set out against Makkah with a large army that included an elephant, hence that year was called the Year of the Elephant. This elephant stopped in its tracks as they drew in sight of Makkah, and refused to move any further. According to surah 105:3 the army was totally destroyed by flying creatures (tayr), which could be translated as bird or insect. Many commentators repeat that swarms of birds dropped stones on the army, which destroyed it. Others suggest that *'hijarah min sijjil'* could mean 'stone-hard blows of pre-ordained chastisement', and that it was an extremely virulent outbreak of an airborne disease either smallpox or typhus, that destroyed the army. Whatever the nature of the doom, the people of Makkah were miraculously saved by this unexpected rescue. Abraha himself died on his return to San'a.

Abraham. See Ibrahim.

Abraham's father. See Azar.

Absence. When a husband is away from a wife for a long period of time, this is disapproved in Islam. An Islamic marriage establishes certain rights and duties on both parties, one of which is marital companionship. Caliph Umar asked his daughter Hafsah how long a woman could tolerate the absence of a husband, and she replied 'four months.' Therefore, on the basis of this, a man may be absent from home (for military service or work etc.) for four months maximum, unless his wife freely agrees. If he is away longer, he has not committed a sin, but is in breach of his duties to his wife, and she may apply for a divorce.

Abu Bakr. (d. 634; Real-name Abdallah ibn Uthman (Abu Quhafah) but given the nickname 'Father of the little camel' because of his fondness for them). He was the son of Uthman (Abu Quhafah), son of Amir, son of 'Amr, grandson of Taim, son of Murrah. He was a man of considerable wealth, but spent his fortune to help the Prophet at the time of the boycott and later. He earned the title as-Siddiq (the Witness to the Truth) when people were ridiculing the Prophet for his account of the Ascent to Heaven on Laylat ul-Miraj, but Abu Bakr defended him by saying that he always spoke the truth, and if he said it was truth, then it was. He married four times; from Qutaylah he had a son Abdallah and a daughter Asma; from Umm Ruman he had a son Abdal Rahman and a daughter Aishah; from Asma bint Umays (the widow of Ja'far ibn Abu Talib) he had a son Muhammad; and from Kharijah bint Zayd he had a daughter Umm Kulthum. Abu Bakr was the Prophet's closest friend, a merchant, and the first adult male to become a convert to Islam. His daughter Aishah became the Prophet's third wife when she was just a child. He was a gentle, quiet man, easily moved to tears of compassion, or when faced with nobility and beauty. He had the ability to interpret dreams, and was frequently called on to do so. The Prophet once said of him that he was not unique in the number of his prayers, or fasts, or spiritual discipline, but he was superior in that the spirit of Islam had settled in his heart. The Prophet elected him to take his place leading the prayers in Madinah when he became too ill, and despite Aishah's fears that he might be too gentle in temperament to lead the Muslims, he was elected the first Caliph after the Prophet died. His rule lasted only two years (532-634) and was disturbed by the efforts of various tribal leaders to oust him (the Riddah Wars). As Caliph, he was known as As-Siddiq (the Witness to the Truth) and Amirul Muminin (Ruler of the Believers), the first of the 'Rightly-guided Caliphs' or Khulafa ar-Rashidun.

Abu Dawud (202/817-275/889). Full name Sulayman ibn al-Ashath abu Dawud al-Sijistani. One of the six chief compilers of Islamic traditions in Sunni Islam. His most important work was the Kitab al-Sunan.

Abu Hanifa (c80/699-150/767). Full name Abu Hanifa al-Nu'man ibn Thabit. He was one of the most important jurists and theologians of early Islam, living and teaching in Kufa. Toward the end of his life he was imprisoned in Baghdad, where he died. His views were collected and recorded by his disciples. The Hanafi School of Law is dominant in India, Pakistan and much of the Middle East. See Madhhab.

Abu Lahab. ('Father of Flame') Real name Abd-ul Uzza, a son of Abd al-Muttalib and uncle of the Prophet, who with his wife violently opposed Islam. In the early years, he subjected the Prophet to all sorts of abuse and torment, and the revelation of Surah 111 refers to him. A famous story concerned his wife deliberately strewing the Prophet's way with sharp thorns. One day, he missed the thorns, and discovered that she was ill. He visited her and did household chores for her, and thus repaid her hostility with kindness. When he became the chief of the clan Hashim after the death of Abu Talib, the tension was one of the major considerations that led to the Hijrah. Abu Lahab perished just after the Battle of Badr when Umm al-Fadl (one of the early women converts, the wife of Abu

Lahab's brother Abbas—cracked him over the head with a wooden post for attacking a Muslim slave in their house.

Abu'l-'As. The son of Khadijah's sister Halah. He married the Prophet's daughter Zaynab. See Zaynab bint Muhammad.

Abundance. See Kawthar.

Abu Sufyan b. Harb. A chief of the Quraysh. Originally a bitter enemy of Islam and the Prophet, leading the army against the Muslims in the battles of Badr, Uhud and al-Khandaq, he became converted towards the end of the Prophet's life after his daughter Ramlah (Umm Habibah) married him. He was a close friend of Abbas and became increasingly impressed by the Prophet's gentleness and generosity towards his enemies and captives. He tentatively embraced Islam shortly before the capture of Makkah. The Prophet granted asylum to all who took refuge with him, and in the end pardoned virtually the entire population. Abu Sufyan then fought with the Muslims instead of against them. His son Mu'awiyah became the fifth Caliph. His wife Hind bint Utbah was a fiery oppponent of Islam, famous for mutilating the body of Hamzah.

Abu Sufyan b. Harith. The son of the Prophet's senior uncle, Harith b. Abd al-Muttalib. He was about the same age as the Prophet, and very like him in looks. He was the Prophet's milk-brother, as he was also suckled by Halimah of Bani Sa'd. He was a talented poet. He was one of the closest companions of the Prophet until he received his call to be Messenger of Allah. At this point Abu Sufyan turned against him, and remained hostile until just before the Fall of Makkah, at which stage he came to the Prophet with his son and asked to be forgiven. The Prophet, deeply upset, at first could not see him, and he threatened to take his son into the desert to die. He was then forgiven and became a staunch Muslim.

Abu Talib. An uncle of the Prophet, and the father of Ali and Ja'far. When the Prophet was orphaned, Abu Talib took him into his care, and although he never became a Muslim himself, he protected the Prophet courageously throughout his life. The Prophet loved him dearly, and always regretted that he rejected Islam. He died suddenly in 619, shortly after the death of Khadijah. Abbas heard him whisper something, and witnessed that at the last he had declared the faith. Of his wife, Fatimah bint Asad, the Prophet said that she cherished him more than her own children.

Abu Ubaydah ibn al-Jarrah. One of the first to accept Islam, the day after his friend Abu Bakr. In the

Battle of Badr he had to choose between faith in Allah or confronting his own father. He chose Allah, and killed his father—a very distressing experience. In the Battle of Uhud two metal rings were driven into the Prophet's face—Abu Ubaydah tugged them out with his own teeth, losing two of his own teeth in the process. He was sent by the Prophet as Governor of Najran in 9 AH, Umar made him Commander of the Syrian campaign, and later he became Governor of Syria. Caliph Umar recalled him when plague broke out, but he refused to desert his people and died at the age of 58. He was one of the ten to whom the Prophet promised Paradise in their lifetimes. See al-'Ashara al-Mubashshara.

Abyssinia. See Ethiopia.

Accountability. Allah requires absolute justice. When people have wronged others, the injured parties will have their wrongs righted on Judgement Day. Even if the wrongdoers hurt, neglected, cheated, abandoned or abused people secretly, they will see it in their records, and be required to atone for it. However, Allah is always compassionate. 'If He punished everyone as they truly deserved, no-one would be left alive' (4:110; 6:54; 39:53).

'Ad. An ancient tribe frequently mentioned in the Qur'an. The prophet sent to them was Hud. He was badly treated, and the people of 'Ad were swept away by a violent storm (7:65-69; 11:52-58; 26:128; 41:15-16; 46:21; 54:19; 69:6).

Adab. Correct behaviour, inward and outward; inner courtesy manifesting as graciousness in right action. Excellent manners.

Adam. The first Prophet. He and his partner Hawwah (Eve) were the first created beings, intended to be the khilafahs (or vicegerents) of Allah on earth. They did not 'fall' to this position, but were created for this purpose. They were equal partners, being created from a single soul (4:1). The angels were concerned that physical beings with freewill would cause chaos, and Shaytan the chief Jinn refused to honour Adam (15:28-31). His pride and disobedience were the origin of evil. On being rebuked by Allah, he determined to prove his point by tempting them into disobedience, and thus became the enemy of humans. Adam and Hawwah originally lived in a state of innocence and happiness, described as a 'garden,' in which they were set one limit—

a tree whose fruit they were forbidden to eat. Shaytan deceived them by falsely suggesting it was the 'tree of life' (20:120) and tempted them to try to live for ever on earth—a wishful desire to avoid death, and lack of faith in life after death. In Islam, it is not suggested that they originally inhabited a mythical state of Paradise, or that there was such a thing as a 'tree of life' or 'tree of the knowledge of good and evil.'

The humans lost their innocence through disobedience; and, in hoping to be free of dependence upon Allah, they lost the real meaning and purpose to life itself. Adam and Hawwah fell for Shaytan's temptations and were driven out of their garden (2:35-39; 7:19-25; 20:120-122). However, when they realised this loss, it brought tawbah; they turned back to Allah for forgiveness, and were reunited and forgiven at Mount Arafat—an event remembered in the wuquf or 'stand' during the Hajj. Allah taught that all humans who repent of sins and turn back to belief will be forgiven, and only those determined to reject Him will be punished in Akhirah.

Islam differs radically from Christianity in that it has no doctrine of inherited original sin; every individual human faces Judgement Day for their own decisions and actions, and not those of their parents, and forefathers. Consequently there is no need of a 'saviour' or for God to incarnate Himself in order to sacrifice Himself. See also Forgiveness, Amal, Crucifixion.

Adha. See Eid al-Adha.

'Adhab. The torment, suffering or affliction inflicted by Allah or a human ruler in order to punish unbelief, doubt of the divine mission of the prophets, and rebellion against God. (Used of the 'Ad, Firawn, Lut, the Thamud, etc.).

Adhan. The public call or summons to prayer. In Muslim countries a man called the Muezzin (Muadhdhin) goes up the minaret and calls loudly so that Muslims can leave what they are doing and go to the mosque to pray. The first caller was the Prophet's Abyssinian friend Bilal. The words of the Adhan are: 'Allahu Akbar! (four times) Ash-hadu an la ilaha il-Allah (twice) Ash-hadu anna Muhammadar rasulullah (twice) Hayya alas-salah (twice) Hayya alal falah (twice) Allahu Akbar (twice) La ilaha illallah (once).

In English, these words mean: 'God is the Most Great! I bear witness that there is no God but Allah. I bear witness that Muhammad is the Prophet of Allah. Come to prayer! Come to success! God is the Most Great! There is no God but Allah!

In the Adhan for the dawn prayer the phrase 'It is better to pray than to sleep!' is added—'assalatul khairum min an-naum.'

Just before the prayers actually start a second call to prayer is given to the congregation, called the iqamah.

al-Adiyat. The title of surah 100, meaning 'the War horses' or 'Chargers'; it is a Makkan surah of 11 verses, and the title refers to a verse about early Arab raiding practice. Whenever people surrender to their appetites, like madly storming battle chargers, they forget God and their responsibilities towards Him.

Adl. Justice, in every sphere of life. The aim of Islam is to establish a way of life on earth in which every person and creature enjoys full rights, not only economically but in every sense. The mean or balance between two extremes, hence 'justice' in human affairs; a person who possesses the high moral qualities necessary to hold public or judicial office. It also refers to the absolute justice of Allah.

Adnin. Arabic name for the Garden of Eden.

Adoption. This is not formally allowed in Islam. Orphans may be fostered, and it is a great act of merit to rear an orphan—but no child should ever not know its true parentage. No matter how close foster-children, they are not blood relatives and never can be. Someone may marry a foster-brother, for example, but not a real brother. See Yatim.

Adultery. This is the sin of cheating on one's husband or wife. Islam requires all sexual activity to be within the bounds of a marriage partnership, and condemns sex before marriage, or sex with any person outside the marriage (adultery or homosexuality). It is part of the agreement that marriage partners should always do their best to satisfy their husbands or wives, and not deny them sexual satisfaction so long as they are not ill or in pain. Adultery is regarded as a shameful thing, and the theft of a marriage partner's honour as the worst sort of theft there could be. As marriage is a contract, it can be ended honourably if it goes wrong. But adultery is punishable in Islamic law by 100 lashes (17:32; 24:2-3, 4-10). The infliction of this hadd punishment was taken very seriously. It should only be administered after the act of adultery was physically observed by four reliable witnesses, who could identify each adulterer with absolute certainty. If perjury was committed, perhaps out of malice, then the one who gave false testimony should be lashed and his or her testimony never again accepted in the future. In some societies adultery is considered so shameful it is punished by death—the practice that was considered normal at the time of the Prophet, and in the Old and New

Testaments. The Prophet preferred mercy, but is known to have reluctantly condoned some executions—however, this was not the penalty laid down in the Qur'an. The Qur'an recommended that sexually promiscuous people should only marry each other.

'Aff. The characteristic of Allah to be merciful. See Forgiveness, Compassion, Maghfirah.

al-Afghani (1254/1838-1314/1897). One of the major C19 reformers of Islam in Egypt. Despite his name, Jamal al-Din al-Afghani was born and raised in Iran. He travelled to India and Afghanistan, and became famous for his violent dislike of British imperialism. He gained political notoriety and was expelled from Istanbul and later Cairo, where he made anti-British speeches. He was an active campaigner against imperialism, and returned to India where he first associated with then wrote against the followers of Sayyid Ahmad Khan charging him with selling out to the British. Later, in Paris, he joined Muhammad Abduh and they published an Islamic newspaper 'the Strongest Link'—'al-Urwa al-Wuthqa'. He died from cancer in Istanbul. He taught that Islam could restore its vitality by reclaiming the rational sciences from the West—Muslims should obey the injunction to seek as much knowledge as possible.

Afrad (sing. fard). It means literally the 'single ones,' and refers to hadiths where the second link in the isnad contains no more than a single name of a tabi.

Agha Khan. Agha is the Turkish word for 'chief' or 'head'; Khan is the Turkish and Persian word for 'chief' or 'lord'. the combination was used by the Imams of the Nizaris, a branch of the Isma'ilis. The title was given to the Shah of Persia in 1233/1818. The present Agha Khan is active as a peacemaker for the UN.

Aghlabids. An Islamic dynasty which ruled from Qayrawan between 184/800-296-909; founded by Ibrahim ibn al-Aghlab, who was made Amir of Ifriqiya by Caliph Harun al-Rashid, in return for an annual tribute. Aghlabid control eventually reached as far as Malta and Sicily. The Aghlabids were overthrown in Africa by the Fatimids.

A.H. This is the abbreviation for 'Anno Hejira', or 'the year of the Migration', the year in which the Prophet left his home town of Makkah, which had consistently rejected his call to Islam, and moved to Madinah, a town to which he had been invited as ruler. Muslims take all future dates from this year, the first year of the success of Islam.

Ahlan wa sahlan. The greeting of welcome, 'you are with your parents and at home, the equivalent of saying 'make yourself at home, you are welcome.'

Ahl al-Bayt. The 'People of the House,' the immediate family and descendants of the Prophet. See Prophet's family.

Ahl al-Kitab. The People of the Book, those to whom a scripture was revealed by God through the prophets—the Jews and Christians.

Ahl as-Suffah. The 'People of the Bench;' the poor and needy amongst the Companions of the Prophet, who lived on a verandah in a courtyard next to his house in Madinah. See Suffah.

Ahl-i-Hadith. A reformist movement in search of a redefinition of the nature of Iman (faith). It was started at the end of the C19, taking its cue from Shah Waliullah and Muhammad ibn al-Wahhab. Like the Deobandis they are critical of Sufism. They believe in an individalistic approach. Their different style of beard and different form of prayers led to their being banned from some mosques in Pakistan.

Ahmad Khan (1817-1898). Sir Sayyid Ahmad Khan was an Indian rationalist and reformer who argued that religion should conform to human nature, and all elements of supernaturalism should be declared false. He wrote the first major explicitly modernist commentary on the Qur'an, directed towards making all Muslims aware of the fact that Western influence in the world required a new vision of Islam, for Islam as it was actually practised and believed in by most of its adherents would be seriously threatened by modern advances in thought and science. His major life involvement was in Muslim education, and he devoted his later years to the development of the college at Aligarh. Education was the only way that Muslims would recapture their earlier status in the world. Aligarh was a Muslim theological college accepting Sunni, Shi'ite and Hindu, and was aimed at the liberalisation of Islamic law in the light of modern demands, ideas, a scientific world view, and a pragmatic approach to politics.

Ahmad ibn Hanbal. (d. 855). The originator of the Hanbali School of Law, which grew out of his selection of Hadith entitled al-Masnad. Hanbalis prevail in Saudi Arabia and other Gulf States. See Madhhab.

Ahmadiyyahs. A sect which most Muslims do not recognise as being Muslim, because its followers have added non-Muslim beliefs to the Qur'an and sunnah, the most important of which is that Jesus survived his crucifixion, and travelled to Kashmir where he married and produced offspring. Jesus' supposed burial-place is in the Rozabel, Srinagar. Ahmadiyyahs claim that their founder, Ghulam Ahmad, was one of his descendants, and was also a prophet—which denies the Islamic belief that Muhammad (pbuh) was the last prophet. Ahmadiyyahs are very active in Pakistan, and also in the UK where they have efficient publishing and missionary activities. They are also known as Qadianis, because Ghulam Ahmad came from the city of Qadian.

al-Ahqaf. The Sand-Dunes; the title of surah 46 from the word in v. 21. It includes the conversion of some jinns of Nakhlah in vv. 29-30. It is a Makkan surah of 35 verses, the title referring to the place where the 'Ad tribe lived.

Ahwal (sing. hal). Lit. 'status.' It is a technical term in Sufism, referring to spiritual states of esctasy or illumination achieved by the help of Allah, as one progresses along the Sufi path.

al-Ahzab. The title of surah 33, the 'Parties' or 'Groups,' usually translated as 'the Confederate Clans' from the references to the War of the Confederates in vv. 9-27; it is a Madinan surah of 73 verses. The clans were those who joined the Makkans to besiege Madinah in the Battle of Khandaq. Some verses deal with the Prophet's marriage to Zaynab bint Jahsh.

Aishah. One of the 'Mothers of the Believers', and is widely known as 'the Prophet's Beloved'. This daughter of Abu Bakr married the Prophet when she was a child, possibly six years old. Other traditions suggest she was in her teens. Certainly their physical relationship did not start until she entered her teens. She was either only eighteen or twenty-eight when the Prophet died. Famous for her quick wit and retentive memory, she was one of the chief sources of information about the Prophet, in particular about his private life and practices, and was frequently used as a 'check' against which reported sayings could be verified; she is known to have corrected many wrongly reported sayings. She never bore the Prophet a child, which caused her sadness. He gave her the kunya name 'Umm Abdallah', referring to her beloved little nephew. Her integrity as a Muslim was tested on one occasion when she was left behind by the camel caravan in the desert and was returned safely by a young tribesman. Jealous rivals accused her of adultery, and a

Quranic revelation was given especially to vindicate her innocence (Surah 24:11-19). The Prophet died in her arms and was buried in her room. She continued to be involved in Muslim politics until she died some 40 years later, on one occasion leading an army into battle (the Battle of the Camel) against Ali, because she felt he should have done much more to bring the killers of Caliph Uthman to justice. Most scholars agree that she died in 50 AH/672 CE at the age of 67, esteemed as a great scholar and recorder of hadith.

Ajal. Lit. 'appointed time,' 'moment of death' or 'lifespan.' All things, including human beings, have their ajal, determined by Allah.

Akhbar (sing. khabar). News, message, information. In hadith terminology it means 'report.'

Akhirah. The Hereafter, Life after Death. This is one of the key fundamental beliefs of Islam, and provides one of the motivations for being Muslim. The fact of life after death is taken as axiomatic, but the form(s) it will take are not known to humanity. 'In Heaven I prepare for the righteous believers what no eye has ever seen, no ear has ever heard, and what the deepest mind could never imagine' (Surah 32:17, and hadith qudsi). Descriptions of conditions in Paradise and Hell are given in detail in the Qur'an, but most scholars take the principle that these are to be interpreted metaphorically, since the Qur'an itself states that 'We will not be prevented from changing your forms and creating you again in forms you know not.' (56:60-61). The Qur'an reveals that a person's future life will depend very much on three things—what they believe, how they have lived, and the mercy of Allah. All one's deeds during lifetime are recorded in each person's 'book' by two recording angels, and will provide the basis of judgement. All judgement is entirely individual, and no one will be able to excuse or 'buy off' the fate of another—which will be entirely dependent on Allah's mercy.

It is worth pointing out that Muslims who suppose their future state in the life to come is entirely dependant on the balance of their good and bad deeds, are not understanding the teaching that Allah may choose to forgive any number of sins, great and small, as He wills. It is not for us to judge or condemn others—We do not know the mercy of Allah, or His decisions. Muslims who occupy their time trying to accumulate 'good points' by endless repetition of phrases and other ritual practices, would do far better to examine their moral and ethical standards, and the good deeds they do to and for others.

Akhlaq. Conduct, character, attitudes and ethics.

Akhwan al-Muslimun. See Muslim Brotherhood.

al-A'la. Title of surah 87, the 'Highest'—a name of Allah which appears in the first verse. It is a Makkan surah of 19 verses glorifying Allah.

Alawis. A minority sect of Shi'ism, found mainly in Syria, where their greatest influence is at Aleppo. They have been politically dominant since 1971, but were persecuted and marginalised by the Crusaders, Mamelukes and Ottomans after the fall of Shi'ite rule. Their doctrines come from the teachings of Muhammad ibn Nusayr an-Namari d. 850, a contemporary of the tenth Imam. They accept the pillars of Islamic belief as symbolic but not binding.

Alamut. The 'nest of the eagle,' the name of a castle in the Elburz mountains near the Caspian Seas, which was the headquarters of Assassins, an extremist branch of the Isma'ilis. Their leader was Hasan al-Sabbah. The castle fell to the Mongols in the C13.

al-Alaq. Title of surah 96, the 'Blood Clot' or Germ-cell. A Makkan surah of 19 verses. It refers to Allah's creation of humanity. The first five verses of this surah were the very first to be revealed to the Prophet by the angel Jibril, in a cave on Mount Hira, in 610.

Alcohol. Forbidden in Islam as 'khamr', a substance that intoxicates or poisons the mind. Alcohol was drunk as much by the tribesmen of the Prophet's time as it is today, with similar social problems. However, the ban on alcohol was spread over a long time. It commenced with the comment that both good and evil came from the same plant (the date palm)—Surah 16:67 and 2:218; followed later by the request that one should not come to prayer while alcohol was in the body—Surah 4:43—(which effectively banned it for Muslims since prayer was a daily requirement), and ending with the order not to drink it at all—Surah 5:93-94. When this clear order came, all devout Muslims who still had any alcohol threw it away, and a good practising Muslim does not drink it, to this day. In some Muslim societies, possession of alcohol can bring harsh penalties (e.g. Saudi Arabia).

Alhambra. Lit. 'the red.' A complex of buildings in Granada,

Spain, one of the glories of Muslim architecture.

Ali. (Caliph from 656-661) The Prophet's cousin (son of Abu Talib) and husband of his daughter Fatimah. He was known as the Lion of God (Asadullah), and showed his loyalty and courage when he became a convert and defender of the Prophet at the age of ten, and declared his willingness to serve him even if all others turned against him. The Prophet's lieutenant in all his battles, and father of the Prophet's grandchildren, many felt he should have been the first Caliph after the Prophet's death, but he accepted the leadership of the 'elders' Abu Bakr, Umar and Uthman before he took his turn twenty-four years later. His later battles included the Battle of the Camel against Aishah in 656, and the Battle of Siffin against Mu'awiyah. His partisans formed the 'Shiat Ali' (now called Shi'ites), and continued to favour the leadership of the Prophet's family line. He died violently, murdered whilst at prayer in the mosque at Kufa. He had foreseen the event and the identity of the assassin, and asked for clemency for him.

Ali al-Hadi (c212/827-214/868). The tenth Shi'ite Imam, also called 'the Pure One' (al-Niqi). He was born in Madinah and became Imam at the age of seven. The Abbasid caliph al-Mutawakkil placed him under house arrest in Samarra in 233/848, and he remained so for 20 years until he died. He and his son, the 11th Imam Hasan al-Askari, are buried in Samarra.

Ali al-Rida (c148/765-203/818). the eighth Shi'ite Imam. He lived at the time of the civil war between the two sons of the Abbasid Harun al-Rashid. The victor, al-Mamun, nominated al-Rida as his successor, but he died two years later, possibly poisoned. He is buried at Mashhad.

Ali Zayn al-Abidin (36/658-94/712). The fourth Shi'ite Imam, son of Husayn, the son of the Prophet's son-in-law Ali. After the Battle of Karbala, in which Husayn was slaughtered, he was rescued by Husayn's sister Zaynab, and lived an isolated and pious life. Shi'ite historians believe he was murdered by the Umayyad caliph. He is buried in Madinah.

Alif Lam Mim. Arabic letters which occur at the start of surahs, 2, 3, 29, 30, 31, and 32. The meaning has never been conclusively explained. One suggestion is that the letters represent the words Allah, Latif (Gracious) and Majid (Glorious). Another suggestion is that they represent 'Ana'llahu a'lamu'—'I am the God who knows.' See al-Muqatta'at.

'Alim. (pl. 'Ulama). A learned man, particularly of Islamic legal and religious studies.

Al-Imran. The House of Imran. Title of surah 3, a Madinah surah of 200 verses derived from verses 33 and 35, referring to the common origin of the long line of Prophets. This surah relates the stories of Zachariah, John the Baptist, Mary and Jesus, all of whom belonged to the House of Imran.

Allah. The Muslim term for God, the Almighty One, the Compassionate, the Merciful, the Source from which all things seen and unseen emanate and return. In the revelation, Allah refers to Himself in many Names which all reveal His qualities. One term never used was 'Abb' or 'Father'—so common in the Jewish and Christian tradition. Since this was never used once over the whole 23 years, it must have been deliberate—presumably to avoid Muslims continuing the error of thinking of God in human paternal terms. His names include Creator (al-Badi), Controller (al-Muqit), Knower of all hidden things (al-Batin). See Beautiful Names.

Allah Ta'ala. Allah, the Most High, the Lord of all the worlds; the One, the Existent, the Creator; the First without beginning and the Last without end.

Allahu Akbar. This is the cry 'Allah is the Most Great', used in Muslim prayers and as an expression of loyalty towards God or encouragement to Muslims in many circumstances. See Adhan.

Almohads. (al-Muwahiddun—those who believe in the Oneness of God). A Berber Muslim dynasty active from 1121-1296, rivals of the Almoravids. They were founded by Muhammad ibn Tumart of Sus. By 1163 they had entered Andalusia, and ruled most of Spain and all of North Africa. The last great Almohad was Yaqub (1184-99). Almohad rule in Andalusia gradually disintegrated but lingered in Africa until 1269 when they were replaced by the Hafsids in Tunisia and the Moravids in Morocco.

Almoravids. (al-Murabitun—from the concept of 'ribat' or religious fortress). A Berber dynasty in North Africa converted in the third century AH by the 'marabout' Ibn Yasin, and led originally by Yusuf bin Tashifin, who founded Marrakesh in 1062. They subdued all Morocco and Central Maghreb, ruling from 1076-1147, and drove back the advancing Christians in Spain. They deposed the Andalusian Amirs and became the masters of Muslim Spain from 1090-1145. The Almoravids were originally pious and austere, but degenerated to luxurious excess, and were defested by new 'purists', the Almohads.

Amal. This is the concept of 'action'. To be a Muslim one must have both 'iman' (faith) and 'amal' (action). One's faith is worthless unless it translates into a good way of life; one's actions are worthless unless one has faith. Atheists might well say that the second statement is not true, but every human being would agree that pious belief is meaningless if one lives as a hypocrite, and does not put the beliefs into action.

Amal al-Hasanah. Good deeds. Those actions which result in the creation of *husn* (beauty). When a people conduct themselves in accordance with Allah's law, every act helps to bring about *husn* in their own personality, and makes it balanced and correctly proportioned. These deeds also help to maintain balance and proportion in the general social order, and the well-being of the world in which we live.

al-Amal as-Saliha. Actions that are Salih.

Amal as-Sayyiah. Evil deeds; those which upset the balance of the personality and result in social disorder and distress.

Amana. Trust in God (4:58; 33:72). See Trust. Istikhara.

al-Amin. 'the Trustworthy', a title given to the Prophet when he was a young man by the people of Makkah, in recognition of his outstanding honesty and upright character.

Aminah bint Wahb. The mother of the Prophet. She had a short and sad life, marrying her cousin Abdallah and being widowed whilst pregnant with her only child. She spent the rest of her life in the household of Abdullah's brother Harith. The infant Prophet was given to the custody of a Bedouin wet-nurse (Halimah), and brought back to Aminah when he was weaned. Aminah died when the Prophet was only six years old. Her half-sister Halah, married Abdallah's father at the same time as her marriage, and their children were Hamzah and Safiyyah. These two, and Harith's son Abu Sufyan, were the Prophet's closest playmates.

Amir (Ameer). Lit. 'One who Commands'. Leader, commander, head of a community, source of authority in any given situation.

Amir al-Mu'minin. 'Commander of the Faithful,' a title of respect given to the Caliph. Umar was the first to bear this title.

Amr. Divine planning. In English there is only one word to denote the creation of any thing, but the Qur'an indicates two stages—the Divine Plan for that entity and the actual process of bringing it into being. Allah plans and directs His energy,and then the intended thing assumes its physical form.

Amr Allah. 'At God's command'—the statement of acceptance of the Divine Will for us. Often used to refer to a person's acceptance of imminent death.

Amr ibn al-As. A Quraysh companion of the Prophet, a politician converted in his middle age before the capture of Makkah. He died in c42/663 when he was over 90. He was converted in Abyssinia under the influence of the Christian Negus. He was sent to Oman where he converted the rulers. In 12 AH (633) Abu Bakr sent him with an army to Palestine, and he was present at the Battle of Yarmuk and the capture of Damascus. His real fame was due to his conquest of Egypt. He founded al-Fustat, which was later called Cairo and where he built the first mosque in Egypt. He felt himself wronged when Uthman recalled him in favour of Abdallah ibn Sa'd and opposed him—along with Abi Talhah and al-Zubayr. He was associated with Mu'awiyah at the Battle of Siffin, where it was his idea to place leaves of the Qur'an on the soldier's lances.

al-Anam. Title of surah 6, 'the Cattle'; a Makkan surah of 165 verses, the title referring to a verse about cattle used in pagan sacrifices. Revealed towards the close of the Makkan period, an exposition of God's oneness and uniqueness.

Anas ibn Malik. One of the most prolific recorders of hadiths. After the hijrah, his mother Umm Sulaym gave him to the Prophet as a servant, when he was around 10 years old. He grew up as a member of the household, and remained in the Prophet's service until he died. He supported the rival caliph Abdallah ibn al-Zubayr. He died at Basra at a very advanced age—between 97-107 years.

Anbiya. The plural form of Nabi.

al-Anbiya. Title of surah 21, 'the Prophets'; a Makkan surah of 112 verses, referring to the many prophets that preceded Muhammad. Stressing the oneness, uniqueness and transcendence of God, the basis of all prophetic revelation. See Prophet, Nabi.

al-Andalus. An Arabic word probably derived from Atlantic rather than Vandalicia (land of Vandals). It referred to Spain and Portugal, which became Muslim after 91/710.

al-Anfal. Title of surah 8, 'the Spoils'; a Madinan surah of 75 verses. Its title refers to the questions arising from the spoils taken at the Battle of Badr.

Angels. A separate order of beings created by God. They are said to be created of light as humans are said to be created of earth. They are regarded as being so close to God that since they continually serve Him they have no freewill as such. Their functions are barely imagined, but it is known that they are continuously present in all aspects of life on earth, particularly close at moments of prayer; that they serve to bring messages and warnings, being 'protecting friends' (41:30-32) and particular angels are assigned to each individual to keep the record of their deeds (82:10-12). Certain named angels are Jibril the Messenger frequently spoken of in the Qur'an as the Holy Spirit, Israfil (the caller of souls on Judgement Day), Azrail (the angel that takes souls at death), Munkar and Nadir (the questioners of souls), Mikail (protector of holy places and life-sustainer in times of trouble), Malik (the keeper of Hell), and Ridwan (the keeper of Paradise).

It is impossible for humans to perceive angels as they really are—they belong to the realm of al-Ghayb. They are the means by which the spiritual realm of Allah can have an effect on the physical world of matter. When they are sent with messages to humans, they may assume human shape, but this is not their real form. They are often represented as having wings, but this presentation is by no means consistent. Attempts to depict or draw angels is forbidden in Islam.

Anger. Anger was disapproved by the Prophet, who always advised against hasty action. If people felt angry when standing, they should sit down; if sitting, they should lie down. However, anger was always justified when against tyranny and oppression, and it is not Islamic to simply ignore these problems and allow injustice to flourish without trying to do something about them.

Animals. Animals are wonderful creations of Allah, and should always be treated with respect. Allah made it clear that although we may be largely unaware of their life-cycles, they were all created in communities, like we are. In other words, even an ant on which we might stamp has its own family, its own desires and needs and urge for life. (27:18-19)

Our relationship with animals should always be kind and compassionate, and with concern for their welfare as important living things on our planet. Such things as fox-hunting, bear-dancing, badger-baiting, and cock or dog-fighting, as so-called 'sport' are totally forbidden and no Muslim should take part in, watch, or encourage such things. (See Hunting) So is the exploitation of animals for luxury use, although Muslims are encouraged not to waste animal products that result from the natural death of the animal. Cruel experimentation with animals to further the cause of science is also disapproved, especially such things as pinioning rabbits in order to insert drops of noxious substances in their eyes, etc. It is even more disapproved when such experimentation is being done merely to create cosmetics, or try out substances which have harmful effects.

al-Ankabut. The Spider, title of surah 29, a Makkan surah of 69 verses derived from v. 41 where the spider's house is a symbol of false beliefs and hopes. The predatory spider feels so confident, but in the end its web is flimsy, and easily swept away. Those who trust in other helpers than Allah are as the spider whose web is the flimsiest of houses.

Ansari. (Plural: Ansar) Anyone of the companions of the Prophet Muhammad from the inhabitants of Madinah who embraced and supported Islam. They helped the Muslims who had emigrated from Makkah leaving all their possessions behind, by taking them into their own homes and caring for them.

Anza. A spearheaded stick, used by the Prophet when praying. He stuck it into the ground in front of him, slightly to the right, to cut his praying-area off from the world.

al-'Aqaba. Lit. 'the steep,' a mountain pass to the north of Makkah just off the caravan route to Madinah, where the Messenger of Allah met in secret with the first Muslims from Madinah in two successive years. They pledged to follow the Messenger, and in the second or Great Pledge of 'Aqaba, to defend him and his companions as they would their own wives and children. This led to the hijrah.

al-Aqib. A name of the Messenger of Allah, meaning 'the Last.'

Aqida (pl. aqaid). Doctrine, dogma, faith, belief, creed.

Aqiqah. The ceremony of cutting the hair of a new baby seven days after birth and donating its weight in silver or gold to charity. Parents of bald bodies usually give a gift too. Some parents also offer the meat of an animal or two as the basis for a feast, and to distribute to the needy. Others give the equivalent of this in cash. It is not a compulsory practice, but a pleasant tradition. See Birth Ceremonies.

Aql. The intellect, the faculty of reason.

al-Aqsa. This is the mosque in the old walled city of Jerusalem with the silver dome. Built in 715 by Caliph Walid on the site of the place where traditionally the Prophet commenced his ascent through the Heavens on the Night of Ascent (Laylat ul-Miraj. It is built on the site of the old palace of King Solomon, over the site of his stables. One of the assassins of St. Thomas a Becket is buried there, and in the Crusader period it was the headquarters of the Knights Templar. In 1951 King Abdallah of Jordan was assassinated there.

Al-Aqsa Mosque in Jerusalem

Arabesque. A decorative flourish in writing or art, often involving leaf or other plant shapes; a common feature in Islamic art.

Arabic. Some Muslims regard Arabic as a special sacred language because 'it is the language spoken by God,' the language in which the Qur'an is revealed. This is a misguided reverence to the language—Allah can speak in any and every language, and gave revelations to people of many different races and tongues prior to the Qur'an. For example, most of the Prophets referred to in the Qur'an (such as Musa, Sulayman) probably received their revelations in some form of Hebrew. Isa received his revelation in Aramaic, a Hebrew dialect. Allah knows best about those revelations granted to the prophets of other parts of the world.

The real importance of learning Arabic, or reciting the prayers in Arabic are twofold. Firstly, it preserves the exact original of the Qur'anic text—all translations differ, and depend on the linguistic skills of the various humans who take on the task, plus their personal ability and insights into spiritual understanding. Therefore, no translation is as authoritative as the original Arabic.

Secondly, when salah prayers are said in Arabic, it enables all Muslims throughout the earth to join together in prayer, no matter where they have travelled to. See Necklace.

al-Araf. (i) The partition between Heaven and Hell (7:44). (ii) The title of surah 7, 'the Ramparts,'

Arafat Mountain

'Battlements' or 'Heights' between Heaven and Hell; a Makkan surah of 206 verses, picking out an expression used in vv. 46-48. It expounds the need for continued prophetic guidance.

'Arafa. A plain 15 miles to the east of Makkah on which stands the Jabal ar-Rahmah, the Mount of Mercy, where it is said Adam was re-united with Hawwah (Eve) after years of wandering following their expulsion from the Garden of Adnin (Eden). One of the essential rites of the Hajj is to stand on 'Arafa between the times of 'asr and maghrib on the 9th of Dhu'l-Hijjah. See also 'Asr, Du'a, Dhu'l-Hijjah, Hajj, Maghrib.

Arafat Mountain. The small mountain in the plain of Arafat, a few kilometres from Makkah, the place where Adam and Hawwah were re-united, and prayed together before God, and were forgiven their sins. Now the scene of the climax of the Hajj pilgrimage, the Wuquf on the 9th Dhul-Hijjah when pilgrims gather to pray and ask for forgiveness.

Architecture. Islamic architecture is notable for it sense of space and purity. The most common features of mosques are: an entrance porch, a spacious carty and (which becomes full of worshippers for Eid prayers) a fountain or a tank for ablutions, or where wudu may take place. Archways, pillars and domes, minarets to call the faithful to prayer (see minaret). Open carpeted space inside a prayer hall mihrab to show the direction of Makkah (see Mihrab). Minbar on which to give the sermon (see Minbar) beautiful lights and chandeliers, beautiful tiling, stone work, woodwork and stained glass.

Many people are impressed by the atmosphere of severance and prayer inside a mosque, and also surprised at the functional uses—as a discussion place, youth club, school, place to rest, and so on.

The prayer-hall seems so open and spacious because there are no chairs as pews to sit on; the congregations are usually huge, and the people sit and pray in orderly lines, on the carpet or floor.

Arif. 'One who knows,' the gnostic. In Sufi terminology, it means knowledge of the self, and that everything comes from Allah. The Sufi does not see anything but he sees Allah in it, before it, and after it.

Ariyya. Loan for use—putting another temporarily and gratuitously in the possession of the use of a thing, whilst the right of ownership is retained; used in particular reference to the allocation to poor families of the produce of certain date palms by the owner of a date grove.

Arkan. A pillar. See Five Pillars.

Arqam. Al-Arqam ibn Abi'l-Arqam, of the clan Makhzum, was one of the earliest converts to Islam and companions of the Prophet. Although the Makhzum were bitterly opposed to the Prophet, he made his house near the Ka'bah on the hill of Safa available for the Prophet's assemblies. He migrated to Madinah and inhabited a house in the Banu Zuraik quarter. He took part in all the major battles and was a particular friend of Sa'd ibn Abi Waqqas. He died in c 54-55 AH aged over 80.

The house of al-Arqam remained a place of veneration until the time Caliph Mansur, and was lived in for a time by Khazuran, the mother of Harun al-Rashid.

Arranged marriages. Since most Muslim societies do not approve of free mixing between the sexes after puberty, Muslim parents regard it as a duty to arrange the best possible marriage for their children. They inquire carefully into the character and background of any intended partner for their children. In some societies marriage is encouraged as soon as the youngsters are tempted to become sexually active, and this can mean brides as young as ten years old. This is illegal in many countries, but sexual promiscuity is usually rife in those countries—and this is considered dishonourable in Islam. If a youngster is married off by parents against his or her wishes, this is an abuse of Islam. The Prophet insisted that prospective spouses should at least see each other, and grant their consent to their parents' plans. Marriage is a contract; if it fails, the couple are free to divorce, and remarriage is up to the individual and not necessarily arranged by parents.

Arranged marriages to relatives, such as cousins, is

Art of Islam

Islamic plates, bowls, tiles and other objects and utensils may be beautifully decorated with motifs from nature, or calligraphy if the object is to be treated with respect.

common in some Muslim societies, but it is not particularly encouraged in Islam. it can lead to terrible unhappiness if the marriage fails for any reason, and the couple are unable to be divorced because of the trauma it would cause the wider family. It is true that the Prophet did marry one cousin, but she was his seventh choice and had been previously married to someone else.

Arranged marriages should be alert to the possibility of disaster, and be compassionate.

Art in Islam. All pictorial representation of God, spirit beings, the Prophet or his close companions or previous prophets is forbidden in Islam. So is any form of statuary that could lead to idolatry, arising from the ancient revealed law that humans should not make graven images and bow down to them. Some scholars take the point of view that all statues should therefore be forbidden; others see no harm in such things as ornaments and toys such as dolls or any statues that do not suggest worship. Statues of kings and politicians are disapproved of (although very common in some so-called Islamic societies). The schools vary in their opinions. The extreme point of view about art-work is that it should not be done at all; other scholars forbid depictions of the human figure or animals, but allow scenic views; the most moderate point of view considers all art on fabric such as paper, cloth, or wood to be allowed, so long as it keeps the first rule given above, and does not encourage lust, pornography or nationalism. Photography and pictures on TV or Video follow the same rulings.

There are examples of art work depicting angels or the Prophet (usually without showing his face) in Muslim Museum collections and books, particularly from Persia.

The miniatures found in some Islamic works are presented solely and expressions of Islamic artistry. They in no way resemble, nor were they intended to resemble, any individual person. They contain no shadow and no third dimension. As two-dimensional space, they follow the laws of natural perspective, of number and geometry. The scenes depicted are often symbolic representations of ideas related to the spiritual path. Finally, in adherence to the prophetic Tradition that "God is Beautiful and He loves beauty," the art of the miniature was developed in many places of the Islamic world to propagate the religion by enhancing and beautifying the source works of Islam.

Ascension of the Prophet. See Laylat ul-Miraj.

Ascetic. See Zahid and Zuhd.

Ashab. Companion. The title given to the earliest converts of

Islam; those who were the Prophet's early associates before the Hijrah from Makkah.

Ashab al-Kahf. The 'people of the cave'—the term used in the Qur'an for the youths who in the West are called the 'Seven Sleepers of Ephesus' (18:9f). They were loyal to the One True God and concealed themselves in a cave, where God put them and their dog (al-Rakim) to sleep. They woke 309 years later. Many legends grew up about them. (There is another Afsus—the old Arabissus in Cappadocia, now called Yarpuz, where 13 male corpses by the name of al-Rakim were preserved in a cave. The Arab geographer Ibn Khurd'adhbah regarded this as the genuine cave of the story).

Ash-hadu-an. The opening words of the declaration of faith, the Shahadah.

Al-'Ashara al-Mubashshara. The 'Ten' to whom Paradise was promised. All the lists naming them include Abu Bakr, Umar, Uthman, Ali, Talhah, Zubayr, Abd al-Rahman ibn Awf, Sa'd ibn Abi Waqqas and Sa'id ibn Zayd. In some lists the Prophet himself is the first; in other lists he is not named, and the tenth is Abu Ubaydah ibn al-Jarrah.

al-Ash'ari (d. 935 CE). He was originally a Mu'tazili, but he abandoned their form of rationalism in favour of the ultimate transcendency of Allah—which meant that absolute piety on the part of any believer would still not be a guarantee of entry into Heaven. He did retain their dialectic methodology, which came to form the basis for Sunni dogma. He opposed all theological speculation.

Ashraf. pl. of sharif. 'Nobles, descendants of the Prophet.

Ashraf al-Mursaleen. The most honoured of the prophets. One of the titles given to the Prophet Muhammad.

Ashurah. The 10th day of Muharram, the first month of the Muslim lunar year. It is considered a highly desirable day on which to fast. The commemoration of Musa (Moses) leading his people to freedom from Pharaoh. The Prophet always fasted on this day, and many Sunni Muslims follow this practice. Shi'ite Muslims, who emphasize devotion to the Prophet's family, celebrate Ashurah as the anniversary of the death of his grandson Husayn at Karbala. They hold processions, passion plays, and occasionally blood-letting, cutting themselves with knives and flogging themselves with chains (now generally banned). Sunnis do not regard Husayn's death as any more special than that of any other noble martyr. There is no need to mourn for him if he died in the faith!

Asiyah. The wife of a Pharaoh, the queen who discovered the infant Musa (Moses) in a basket in the River Nile, and raised him as her own son. When Musa became chosen as a prophet, he was persecuted by the Pharaoh, but neither he nor his step-mother Asiyah would abandon the faith. The Prophet considered her to be one of the greatest of women.

Asma. Daughter of Abu Bakr, half-sister of Aishah. Famous for two things; firstly the hadith that a girl arriving at puberty should cover her whole body except face (or head) and hands, and secondly for her help to the Prophet during his escape from Makkah. She became known as 'She of the Two Girdles' — Dad-un-Nitaqayn — when she split her girdle and used one half in order to tie the provisions on his camel when he left on the Hijrah.

al-Asma' al-Husna. The Beautiful Names of Allah. See Beautiful Names.

Asr. (Salat ul-asr) the mid-afternoon prayer, which may be performed from late afternoon until a short while before sunset.

al-Asr. The Flight of Time; the title of surah 103, a Makkan surah of 3 verses. All humanity is in a state of loss unless they find the true faith and act accordingly.

Astaghfiru'llah. 'I ask Allah for forgiveness.'

Athar. A report transmitted by a Companion or Successor of the Prophet.

Atonement. The doctrine of one person (or sacrifice, or deity) being able to cancel out the sins of another. This doctrine is rejected in Islam—each individual is judged on his or her own life, actions and intentions. See Crucifixion.

A'udhu bi'llahi min ash-shaytan ir-rajim. 'I seek protection in Allah from Satan the outcast.' (See Shaytan). A prayer said when commencing salah.

Averroes. (Abul Walid ibn Rushd, d. 1198). An Arab philosopher of Spain, known for his work on Aristotelian philosophy, and for harmonising the Qur'an with philosophy and logic.

Avicenna. See Ibn Sina.

Awliya (pl. of wali). In some places these are recognised as 'holy men' who have special powers, and to whose graves people sometimes make special pilgrimages and offer special prayers. However, Islam does not recognise any powers, miraculous or otherwise, of any dead person, no matter how saintly he or she was during life. Visiting such tombs in order to ask these dead saints to exercise their supposed powers is not of Islam, but is based on superstition. One may, of course, remember great saints with respect, and pray *for* their souls.

Aws. Son of the Arab heiress Qaylah, a founder of one of the tribes of Yathrib/Madinah.

Ayah. pl. ayat. Lit. 'a sign', a phrase of Qur'an. A 'sign' or 'symbol' in the sense that the created order and all it contains are identified as signs of Allah's power and mercy. There are 6,666 ayat in the Qur'an.

Ayat al-Kursi. The verse of the Throne (2:255).

Ayat Muhkamat—messages that are clear in themselves and self-evident.

Ayat Mutashabihat—passages in the Qur'an which are figurative or allegorical, and need interpretation.

Ayat an-Nur. The verse of Light (24:35). 'God is the light of the heavens and the earth; His light may be compared to a niche in which there is a lamp; the lamp is in a crystal; the crystal is, as it were, a glittering star kindled from a blessed olive tree neither of the east nor of the west. Its oil would burst into flames even though fire had never touched it. Light upon Light!' (24:35)

Ayatollah. Leading Shi'ite imam. Means literally 'sign of God'.

Ayatollah Khomeini. The leader of the people's revolution against the Shah of Persia in 1978.

Ayyub. A prophet who lived in the Petra region of Jordan, (called Job in the Bible, from the 'land of Uz'; al-Uzza was the chief goddess of Petra). He was famous for his patience and fortitude. He was a wealthy tribal sheikh struck down by various misfortunes instigated by Shaytan, but who refused to falter in his faith in Allah (6:84; 21:83-84; 38:41-42).

Azar. This is the name given in the Qur'an to the father of the Prophet Ibrahim (Abraham) (6:74). In the Bible his name is given as Terah, and early Muslim geneologists call him Tarah or Tarakh. In the Jewish Talmud he was sometimes called Zarah, and the Christian historian Eusebius called him Athar. It is not impossible that the Qur'an name Azar is the pre-Islamic Arabicized form of Athar or Zarah. Prophet Ibrahim was forbidden to pray for him since it was clear he would persist in his idol worship. Some commentators believe that the word 'Azar,' which is not Arabic, is a term of abuse rather than a proper name.

al-Azhar. Lit. 'the brilliant' or 'the radiant.' the full name is al-Jami al-Azhar, the title of Islam's most famous university. Founded by the Fatimids in Cairo after the conquest of Egypt in 358/969. Originally it promoted Isma'ili doctrine and scholarship, but became orthodox Sunni when the Ayyubids took over in Egypt.

al-Aziz. (i) The Almighty. One of the Names of Allah. See Beautiful Names. (ii) The title of the Egyptian noble to whom the Prophet Yusuf was sold as a slave, and whose wife tried to seduce him. See Surah 12.

Azrail. The angel that takes souls at death.

Ba'ath. The word for resurrection. See Akhirah.

Bab as-Salaam. The 'Door of Peace;' the name of one of the entrances to the sacred shrine in Makkah, and of one of the entrances to the mosque of the Prophet in Madinah.

Babies. Babies should be cherished by Muslims as gifts of God, and have the right to a caring mother and father (see Abortion). In some cultures boy babies are preferred to girls, but this is un-Islamic—it is God Who chooses which sex these living souls shall be and any human parent who resents that choice or tries to alter it, is ungrateful and arrogant. The Prophet was aware of the dependency of women in his time, and particularly praised those who raised girls and cared for them. It is particularly wrong to misuse the knowledge of the sex of an unborn baby given through ultrasound equipment as a basis for aborting females.

Backbiting. Nasty talk and slander, forbidden in Islam. The Prophet declared that nasty talk behind someone's back was like eating their flesh. It is conduct unbecoming in a Muslim.

Badana. (Plural, Budn); a camel offered as a sacrifice.

Badl (pl. abdal). A 'substitute body.' Those exalted persons who by the perfection of their servitude to Allah remain in constant contemplation of His Presence; it is sometimes attested of them that they have been seen at the Ka'bah while others confirmed their presence elsewhere, hence the term 'substitute.'

Badr. A place about 95 miles to the south of Madinah near to the coast where in 2/624 in the first battle between 300 outnumbered Muslims led by the Messenger of Allah overwhelmingly defeated 1,000 idol worshippers of Makkah. (3:13)

Bagh. Indian word for garden.

Bahirah. A Christian monk (traditionally associated with the shrine of the prophet Harun (Aaron) at Petra on the road to Bosra) who recognised that the young Muhammad was destined to be the Prophet of Islam.

al-Balad. Title of surah 90, 'the City'; a Makkan surah of 20 verses. It underlines the idea that humanity has a choice whether to follow the difficult path of generosity, or be miserly towards others.

Bani. Lit. 'Sons'. A tribe.

Bani al-Asfar. The Byzantines.

Bani Isra'il. The tribe of Isra'il.

Baqa'. subsistence; the highest station in Sufism, in which the soul is said to subsist in Allah, after experiencing annihilation of self. See fana'.

al-Baqarah. 'The Cow'. The title of surah 2, derived from verses 67-73. A total of 286 verses covering a vast range of topics. It was the first to be revealed in Madinah, and is the longest surah in the Qur'an.

al-Baqi'. The cemetery of the people of Madinah where many of the family of the Messenger of Allah, and his Companions, are buried. The Prophet used to visit it frequently, to pray for his departed loved ones.

Barakah. A sense of blessedness, peace and joy. An awareness of the blessings of Allah; frequently a powerful atmosphere felt at certain shrines, sanctuaries, and places where people pray or feel moved by beauty and awe.

Baraka'llahu fi'k. 'May the blessing of Allah be on you.'

Barelvis. Sunni Muslims who follow the interpretations of Islam of Maulana Ahmad Raza Khan (1856-1921) of Bareily in India. He was a Hanifi scholar of Ahl-i-Sunnat, the followers of the Prophetic traditions and the Prophet's companions. The Barelvi movement is a radical movement which does not accept the views of the Deoband ulema or the Ahl-i-Hadith, which were all influenced by Wahhabism. The Wahhabis who regarded the Prophet as an ordinary human being (albeit inspired), tried to stop the honouring of saints' graves in Indo-Pakistan; the main thrust of the Barelvi movement is its overwhelming love for the Prophet.

Basarat. Allah's characteristic of being able to see all things. See Omnipresence, Omniscience, Witness.

al-Basri (d. 728). He was considered to be the earliest Sufi. He was born in Madinah, the son of a freed slave, and later settled in Basra, Iraq. Many Sufi tariqas claim connection with him, and through him to Imam Ali and the Prophet.

Barzakh. The barrier between this world and the next. The place or state in which people will be after death and before judgement.

Batil. Ideas and actions that are destructive. It includes all thinking and conduct that leads to destructive results.

Batin. The inner or esoteric aspect of a text, doctrine or religion. It also refers to the inner, spiritual state of the believer. See Zahir.

Bay'a. An oath of allegiance.

Bayt al-Dhulma. The House of Darkness. One of the names given to the grave. The grave (qabr) is also known as Bayt al-Ghurba (House of the Stranger); Bayt al-Wahda (House of Solitude); Bayt al-Turab (House of Dust); Bayt al-Dood (House of Worms); and Bayt al-Fitnah (House of Trial). All these titles refer to the experience of life between this world and the world to come.

Baytullah. The Sacred House. Arabic names for the Ka'bah shrine in Makkah—the House of God.

al-Bayt al-Haram. The 'Sacred House,' the Ka'bah shrine.

Bayt al-Mal. Lit. 'the House of Wealth.' The treasury of the Muslims where income from zakat and other sources is gathered for re-distribution.

Bayt al-Maqdis. The Sacred House. The mosque in Jerusalem on the site of the rocky outcrop at top of the hill of Zion; the Dome of the Rock, the gold domed mosque adjacent to the al-Aqsa mosque. The rock is believed to be the site of the Holy Altar of the Jewish Temple to the One True God in Jerusalem. When Caliph

The Dome of the Rock

Umar went to the site many years after the defeat of Jerusalem by the Romans, he found it in ruins—it had long been forbidden to Jews, on pain of death. Umar began to clear the site with his own bare hands, and the Temple area became the third most holy place of Islam. The word 'maqdis' comes from the root-word 'quds' meaning 'holy.' The place is also called al-Quds.

al-Bayyinah. Title of surah 98, 'The Clear Proof'; a Madinan surah of 8 verses.

Beast. See Dajjal.

Beautiful Names, The. (Ar. Al-Asma' al-Husna). According to tradition, Allah has many Beautiful Names. These names are all descriptive of the attributes of Allah, such as the Sustainer, the Most Gracious, the Most Merciful, the King, the Holy. The Source of Peace, the Giver of Faith, the Preserver of Safety etc.

ad-Dar The Distresser; *al-'Adl* The Just; *Al-'Afuw* The Forgiving; *al-Ahad* The One; *al-Akhir* The Last; *al-'Ali* The High One; *al-'Alim* The Knowing; *al-Awwal* The First; *al-'Azim* The Great; *al-'Aziz* The Mighty, and also the Precious; *al-Badi* The Originator; *al-Ba'ith* The Raiser, *al-Baqi* The Enduring; *al-Bari* The Producer; *al-Barr* The Beneficent; *al-Basir* The Seeing; *al-Basit* The Expander; *al-Batin* The Inner; *al-Fattah* The Opener, *al-Ghaffar* The Forgiving; *al-Ghafur* The Pardoner; *al-Ghani* The Self-Sufficient; *al-Hadi* The Guide; *al-Hafiz* The Protector; *al-Hafiz* The Guardian; *al-Hakam* The Judge; *al-Hakim* The Wise; *al-Halim* The Kindly; *al-Hamid* The Praiseworthy; *al-Haqq* The Truth; *al-Hasib* The Accounter; *al-Hayy* The Living; *al-Jabbar* The Irresistible; *al-Jami* The Gatherer; *al-Kabir* The Great; *al-Karim* The Magnanimous, the Generous, the Noble; *al-Khabir* The Well-Informed; *al-Khaliq* The Creator; *al-Latif* The Gracious; *al-Majid* The Glorious; *al-Malik* The King; *al-Matin* The Firm; *al-Mubdi* The Founder; *al-Mudhill* The Abaser; *al-Mughni* The Enricher; *al-Muhaymin* The Vigilant, the Guardian; *al-Muhsi* The Counter; *al-Muhyi* The Giver of Life; *al-Mu'id* The Restorer; *al-Mu'izz* The Honourer; *al-Mujib* The Responsive; *al-Mu'min* The Giver of Peace; *al-Mumit* The Slayer; *al-Muntaqim* The Avenger; *al-Muqaddim* The Bringer Forward; *al-Muqit* The Maintainer, the Determiner, He Who Brings to Pass; *al-Muqsit* The Just; *al-Muqtadir* The Prevailer; *al-Murshid* The Guide; *al-Musawwir* The Shaper; *al-Muta'ali* The Self-Exalted; *al-Mutakabbir* The Superb; *al-Mu'ti* The Giver; *an-Nafi* The Propitious; *an-Nasir* The Helper; *an-Nur* The Light; *al-Qabid* The Seizer; *al-Qadir* The Capable; *al-Qadir* The Powerful; *al-Qahhar* The Victorious; *al-Qahir* The Wise; *al-Qawi* The Strong; *al-Qayyum* The Self-Subsistent; *al-Quddus* The

Holy; *al-Wadud* The Loving; *al-Wahhab* The Bestower; *al-Wahid* The One; *al-Wakil* The Steward; *al-Wali* The Protector; *al-Waliy* The Patron; *al-Warith* The Inheritor; *al-Wasi* The Vast; *ar-Rafi* The Exalter; *al-Rahim* The Compassionate; *ar-Rahman* The Merciful; *ar-Raqib* The Watchful; *ar-Ra'uf* The Gentle; *ar-Razzaq* The Provider; *as-Sabur* The Forbearing; *as-Salam* The Peace; *as-Samad* The Eternal; *as-Sami* The Hearer; *ash-Shahid* The Witness; *ash-Shakur* The Appreciative; *at-Tawwab* The Accepter of Repentance; *az-Zahir* The Evident; *Dhu'l-Jalal wa'l-Ikram* The Lord of Majesty and Generosity; *Malik al-Mulk* Possessor of the Kingdom.

Bedouin. Nomadic Arab tribespeople who herd sheep and goats throughout the Middle East.

Begging. Asking for money without working for it. The Prophet disapproved of begging and taught his followers that it was better to earn money by any honest means, no matter how simple, than to beg from others—unless there was no alternative.

Bektashiyya. A Turkish Sufi order whose practices include some elements drawn from Christianity. Named after the 7th/13th century Sufi Hajji Bektash. It is limited to Anatolia in Turkey, and is a strongly Shi'ite order. The order gained influence under the Ottomans but was suppressed by Ataturk of Khurasan (d. 1338).

Bid'a. An innovation, a practice that has been added to Islam without the authority of Quranic revelation or the sanction of the Prophet. Any Muslim religious leader should be able to justify their teaching easily from these two sources, and any person being required to do something outside these sources has the right to challenge the practice. Some extreme Muslims take a ridiculous attitude over bid'a, insisting on trying to imitate the way of the Prophet very closely in some details—however, they ignore the fact that modern facilities were unknown at the time of the Prophet, and should therefore look at the principle behind the action rather than the detail of the action itself. For example, it is not bid'a to use knife and fork, modern toilet, modern technological equipment and so forth. It is bid'a to make things compulsory in Islam that the Prophet left to personal choice—for example, growing beards, wearing turbans etc.

Bid'a hasanah. A 'good innovation'—but still denied as valid by most jurists.

Bigotry. see Tashdid.

Bila kayfa. 'Without knowing how'—referring to the practice of accepting the anthropomorphic terms for Allah in the Qur'an, without questioning what they mean in reality. (e.g. 'Our souls are in God's hands—does God have hands?)

Bilal. An Abyssinian slave, who became one of the first Muslims. He was tortured by his master Umayyah by being staked out in the sun with a large rock on his chest, but his freedom was purchased by Abu Bakr. He had a very fine voice, and became the first Muezzin or Caller to prayer. Two of his most famous calls to prayer were when the Prophet was first granted permission to make pilgrimage to the Ka'bah after the Treaty of Hudaybiyah and at Mount Arafat on the Prophet's Farewell Pilgrimage. On the first of these two, the Quraysh had refused permission for the Prophet to enter the Ka'bah. Bilal climbed up on to its roof and gave the call to prayer from there. See Adhan, Muezzin.

Bilqis. The name given by Muslims to the Queen of Sheba (I Kings 10:1-13 in the Bible; 27:20-45 in the Qur'an—where her name is not given). She was summoned to visit King Sulayman b. Dawud, and was very impressed by him. She was a female ruler, and it is significant to note that she was not asked to give up ruling her kingdom, but she was asked to accept Islam. According to some Jewish and Ethiopian traditions, she bore a son to Sulayman, and his descendants became the Emperors of Ethiopia, bearing the title of 'Lion of Judah.' The last of them was Haile Selassie. See Saba.

Birr. Virtuous and pious deeds. It basically means 'extensiveness, largeness,' and applies to any conduct that expands individual personality in a good way, and leads to the greater happiness of society in general.

Birth ceremonies. Muslim babies are welcomed into the family of Islam by having the call to prayer whispered into their ears shortly after birth. The tahnik is the folk-ceremony of touching the baby's lips with something sweet, symbolising the hope that it will develop a sweet nature. The aqiqah is the tradition of shaving the baby's head, usually on the seventh day, and giving the equivalent in gold of the weight of the hair to charity. (Parents of bald babies usually make a gift anyway!) A sacrifice may be made, perhaps to the value of two animals for a boy and one for a girl, though this is not compulsory. The baby should be given a Muslim name, but not a name denoting qualities the child may not actually have (i.e. 'beautiful one' or 'sweet-natured one'). As soon as possible, a boy baby is circumcised (the khitan), and as soon as the child has learned the alphabet in Arabic and can recite a little of the Qur'an, a party known as the 'Bismillah' may be held to celebrate.

Birth control. This is not forbidden to Muslims, so long as the form of control is one that prevents conception (for example, the withdrawal method, the condom, the pill) and is not a form of abortion after conception. However, if God's will is for a child to be born, he or she will be. Any form of birth control has to be with the consent of both parents, not just one of them.

Bismillah ir-Rahman ir-Rahim. 'In the name of Allah, the Compassionate, the Merciful.' The phrase with which Muslims begin all actions and endeavours, such as eating or starting a journey. It is also the preface of every Surah of the Qur'an except the 9th.

Black Cloth. See al-Kiswah.

Black Stone (al-Hujr al-Aswad). A stone set in one corner of the Ka'bah. Tradition states that it came from Heaven and was originally white; this may well refer to its meteoric origin—'white' or star-like as it fell through the atmosphere, and then found as a black lump. Originally set in the shrine by Ibrahim, during repairs at the time of the Prophet the tribal leaders argued over who should have the honour of replacing it. They agreed that God should provide the answer with the next man who came along—this turned out to be the Prophet, who solved the problem by inviting representatives of all tribes to lift it on his cloak.

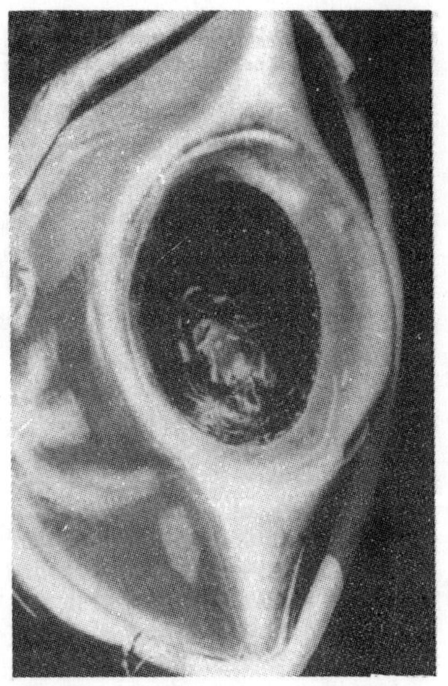

The Black Stone set in the Ka'bah

Blood sports. Cruelty to animals is forbidden in Islam. However, it is accepted that it is the nature of some creatures such as dogs and hawks to hunt naturally, and these may be trained to hunt with skill and efficiency. Things like fox-hunting, badger-baiting, cock-fighting, stag-hunting and so on are totally forbidden.

Boabdil. (Abu Abdallah Muhammad bin Ali)—the last Muslim ruler of Granada, Spain.

Bohras. Originally Hindus who became Musta'li Ismaili Muslims. They do not recognise the Agha Khan as their spiritual leader, but follow an absolute preacher, the

Da'i Mutlaq, who lives in Bombay. They have centres in Gujarat and East Africa, and are by inclination traders.

Buraq. Lit. 'the lightning.' The name given in Islamic tradition to the creature which transported the Prophet in a flash to Jerusalem on the Laylat al-Miraj.

Burdens. The Qur'an teaches that a person's journey through life is full of tests, problems, losses, sufferings, and so forth. Allah assures all people that He loves them, and knows and understands all their burdens. On no soul will be placed a burden greater than it can bear. (1:286; 7:42; 23:62) Unbelievers will face enormous burdens (16:25). When it comes to facing the Judgement Day, no person will be able to, or expected to, bear the burden of another (6:164; 17:15; 29:12-13; 35:18; 39:7; 53:38).

Burhaniyya. A popular Sufi order in Egypt, especially in Cairo, also called the Dasuqiyya. The founder was Burhan al-Din Ibrahim (c644/1246-687/1288). The present day order characterizes itself as Shadhili.

Burial. Muslims should be buried in simple graves without expense and ornamentation. Usually they just have a marker, perhaps bearing the name and dates of the deceased. Before burial Muslims are washed carefully, shrouded in white cloths (two are recommended for a man, five for a woman). A special prayer (the salat ul-janaza) is recited, and the deceased are taken to a burial ground where they may be laid to rest on their right sides with their faces turned towards Makkah. It is considered more respectful to walk in procession than ride in a car, and to carry the deceased personally rather than in a coffin. Coffins are disapproved, as a waste of wood and other materials. Muslims are encouraged not to mourn with ostentation, but to praise God and remember that the deceased will go to the reward he or she has earned.

Burial Alive. This horrendous practise, mainly of girl babies, was prevalent amongst pre-Islamic Arab tribes, and was absolutely forbidden by Allah (6:137). Also, children were occasionally offered as a sacrifice to their gods and idols. This was also forbidden—Allah requires a just and noble life, not sacrifices of animates.

Burj. A tower or bastion.

Burnus. A hooded cloak.

Burqa. An all-covering garment worn by some Muslim women in various societies. In Afghanistan and northern Pakistan the 'shuttlecock burqa' can be seen, so-called from its shape. It has a little grid where the eyes are. In

Iran, an all-covering black cloth is worn, and in Saudi Arabia a covering garment of a different design. None of these garments is specifically Muslim, and the amount of cover worn by a woman cannot indicate the quality of her Islam. See Hijab.

Buruj. Lit. 'towers.' The term used in the Qur'an for the twelve signs of the zodiac.

al-Buruj. The Great Constellations; the title of surah 85. It includes the one descriptions of the Qur'an as a 'well-guarded tablet'—lawh mahfuz.

Buyids. An Islamic dynasty which flourished in Persia and Iraq between 320/932-454/1062. They were Zaydi Shi'ites, but were very tolerant of other branches of Islam. They held sway in Baghdad from 334/945 until conquered by the Seljuks in 447/1055.

Byzantines. The Greek Christians, with their capital of the new Roman Empire at Byzantium (previously Constantinople, now Istanbul). The Byzantine and Persian Empires had been in conflict for centuries, and in the early 7th century the Persians conquered parts of Syria and Anatolia. In 613 they took Damascus; in 614, Jerusalem, and in 615-616, Egypt. The total destruction of the Byzantine Empire seemed imminant. The Muslims tended to sympathise with the Byzantines (who were Christians), but the Quraysh tended to support the Persians (who were polytheists). The prophecy of Byzantine victory given in 30:1-4 was greeted with derision, but by 626 the Persian armies had indeed been defeated.

Calendar. The Muslim calendar is a lunar one, consequently the feast days are eleven days earlier each solar year. Year 1 is taken to be the first year of the Prophet's migration from Makkah to Madinah, in the year 622. To calculate a Muslim year, you take 622 from the year in the calendar, and multiply it by 33/32.

Caliph. (Khalifah), a successor to the Prophet. Someone who rules, or bears responsibility, on behalf of the Prophet, and beyond him, on behalf of Allah. The first four Caliphs were the Prophet's Companions Abu Bakr (632-634), Umar (634-644), Uthman (644-656) and Ali (656-661). These four were known as the Rashidun or Rightly Guided. Following them, the caliphate went to Mu'awiyah, the son of Abu Sufyan, the first of the Umayyad Caliphs. His successors were challenged by the descendants of the Prophet through Ali. The Umayyad family won the day, but many of the caliphs of this line were corrupt and betrayed pure Islamic principles. Other famous family lines of caliphs include the Abbasids, the Fatimids, Safavids, Mughals, Almohads, Almoravids, and Ottomans.

Calligraphy. The art of beautiful writing. Since pictorial art is discouraged in Islam, great emphasis is placed on ornamental calligraphy. Writers of the Qur'anic texts were expected to be extremely pious and devout people themselves. The main types of Islamic calligraphy are Kufic and Naskhi. Of all the arts, Muslims respect calligraphy the most, and the use of the pen is one of the major skills. Muslim architects use calligraphy as decoration on their buildings, and artefacts. The Kufic style was so angular and ornamented that only a practised eye could read it; Naskhi was more cursive, and easier to understand.

A picture made of calligraphy

Camel. It is a silly story that the camel has a superior smile because it alone knows the hundredth name of God! The Prophet had a famous camel, al-Qaswah, who was allowed to choose where the Prophet should make his home in Madinah. The beast stopped by a date-drying ground, which was instantly granted to the Prophet by the owner and became the site of the mosque where Prophet is now buried. Al-Qaswah also carried the Prophet into many battles, and took him right to the Ka'bah when he captured Makkah.

Camel, battle of. The battle fought near Basra between Aishah, Talhah and Zubayr against the forces of Ali in 36/656. Aishah was defeated and her companions killed; Aishah was returned safely to Madinah where she made up her differences with Ali. The battle was so called after the camel from which she led her troops.

Canned food. Some canned food carries a statement in Arabic that it has been prepared in the Islamic way. Governments where this is done appoint agents to supervise the slaughter of animals whose meat is to be canned, and it is halal. Even if this is not the case, we need not ask about the details which we do not know. If we have no reason to doubt the correctness of a statement, we should accept it at its face value, and pray over it.

Capital punishment. Putting an offender to death, a penalty for many offences before the coming of Islam. In the Qur'an it is limited only to cases of murder (2:178) and active treason. In Islam, after trial and sentence, the fate of the murderer lies in the hands of the victim's family. They are entitled to choose equal and just revenge, or to take diyyah instead. The Prophet commented that the very best practice was to forgive the murderer, if they had it in their heart to do so, and to leave the punishment to Allah (17:33; 5:68). The case of the death sentence issued by Iran against the writer Salman Rushdie was highly controversial, and was never officially commended by Muslim leaders of other societies.

Celibacy. Choosing to live without a sexual relationship. This practice was regarded by Christian monks and nuns as a form of piety and purity. However, this was never revealed by Allah to any of the Prophets, and is not approved in Islam. It is regarded as a form of ingratitude for one of God's compassionate gifts to humanity, and is thought of as a dangerous practice anyway since it can result in strange character and emotional aberrations.

Chador. (Lit. 'tent') A sheet-like garment used by Muslim women in some societies (e.g. Iran) to completely cover themselves. It is not necessarily of black fabric—these are matters of tradition and not of Islam.

Charbagh. A 'fourfold garden,' formal geometric Persian garden layout introduced into India by the Emperor Babur; often used in Indian architecture to embellish the surrounds of a saint's tomb.

Charms. see Ruqya.

Chattri. A domed kiosk, also a Rajput cenotaph, which frequently takes this form.

Cheating. Being dishonest in order to gain advantage. Totally forbidden in Islam. If a Muslim cannot be honest he or she has already left Islam.

Children. Should always be welcomed and loved by Muslims. The Prophet forbade any cruelty to children, and also disapproved of spoiling them. Children should always be cared for, and trained towards good lives. A good parent saw to their education as far as possible, training in a trade or means of earning a living, and perhaps arranged their first marriage wisely.

Chishti (Mu'in al-Din Muhammad Chishti—1142-1236). A Sufi saint to whose tomb at Ajmer the Mughal Emperor Akbar made pilgrimage. His dargah is much visited to this day.

Chishti. (Salim). A Sufi saint whose dargah is at Fatehpur Sikri. He was a contemporary of the Mughal Emperor Akbar, who appreciated his prophecy that he would shortly have three children when all his wives failed to produce any. For his sake, he built up the city of Fatehpur Sikri, which is still a centre of pilgrimage.

Chishti Order. The most influential Sufi Order in India and Pakistan; it takes its name from Khwaja Abu Ishaq Shami Chisti (d. 966). The order has been adulterated by elements of Hinduism and Buddhist customs and practices.

Chishstiya see Sufism, Chishti.

Choice, a Prophet's. Aishah recorded that the Prophet once told her that no prophet was taken by death until he had been shown his place in Paradise, and then offered the choice of whether to live on or to die. Shortly before the Prophet's death, he went to the cemetery of al-Baqi with his freedman Abu Muwayhibah, and after praying and greeting the 'people of the grave', he told him he had been offered the treasures of this world and immortality on earth, or meeting his Lord in Paradise. Abu Muwayhibah begged him to choose this world, but he said he had already chosen the presence of Allah. Later, when he lay very ill in Aishah's arms, he lost consciousness for around an hour, and she thought he was passing away; but he opened his eyes suddenly. She felt he had returned after a vision of the Hereafter, and was joyful because she thought this meant he had chosen to remain with them. Then she heard him murmur his last words: 'O Allah, with the supreme companions'. He had made his choice, and died peacefully in her arms.

Chowk. Indian word for courtyard or open space.

Christians. The followers of the Prophet Isa (Jesus) the Christ or Masih (Messiah). True Christians are recommended in the Qur'an for their noble, charitable and compassionate lives (5:85-88), and their devotion to God (2:62). However, Muslims believe that Jesus never claimed to be the Son of God, except in the sense that we are all God's children. For example, the Gospels themselves record that he resisted the temptation to call himself Son of God, and stated that 'you should worship the Lord your God, and Him only shall you serve.' (Matt. 4:10). Muslims regard true Christians as those who follow the teachings of Isa as prophet of Islam, and not the Trinitarian Atonement-Saviour theology, which they feel are mystery-cult Baalistic doctrines added to Isa's message later. Those doctrines are condemned as shirk. Christians are urged to respond to the call of Islam (4:171; 5:75, 80). See Crucifixion.

Christmas celebrations. Some Muslims marry Christians, or live alongside Christian people. Christmas is the festival held on December 25th in most Christian societies to celebrate the birth of the Prophet Isa, (who, of course, they think of as being the Son of God). Other Christians celebrate this festival on other dates, for example, January 6th. The actual date of Isa's birth is unknown. 25th December was chosen by the Church because it was already a midwinter festival, the Birthday of Sol Invictus, the Rising Sun. Hence some Christian groups, for example the Jehovah's Witnesses, refuse to celebrate on what is really a pagan occasion from the times of jahiliyyah. Many Muslims do not know what attitude to take if they are living in a Christian society. Should they regard it as shirk and have nothing to do with it? It is worth remembering that many of the first Muslims were Christians originally (e.g. Salman, Ubaydullah, etc.). One of the Prophet's companions, Asma, once asked him if it was appropriate for her to be kind and dutiful to her non-Muslim mother. He ordered her to be so. Islam urges maintaining good relations with people. There is no harm in giving Christian friends (or relatives) gifts—the Prophet did not instruct his followers not to do so. A Muslim could suggest that Christians wishing to give gifts to Muslim children or friends could keep the gift back until the next Eid. If this would be offensive, simply explain to the Muslim child receiving the gift that it has no religious value. Obviously no Muslim can celebrate the notion of God becoming incarnate, or being born as a human being; however, there is no harm in respecting a day that commemorates the birth of a great prophet.

Christian Sects. At the time of the prophet, Arab Christianity was split into rival camps weakened by persecution and war against each other. The three main groupings were Greek Orthodox (detested by the Arabs), Monophysite (or Jacobite) and Nestorian. The Monophysites believed that Isa was the Divine Word made flesh, and had only one nature (monophysis), his divine nature. Abraha of San'a was a Monophysite. The Nestorians believed that Isa united in himself two natures—human nature inherited from his human mother Mary (see Maryam) and divine nature inherited from the Holy Spirit.

The Monophysites were active missionaries and had baptized large numbers of Arab converts. Most tribes had a priest and deacon (priest's helper).

Almsgiving and fasting were regularly practised, and monasteries (see Rahbaniyah) were open day and night to travellers, who were given food and drink. Monophysite women were veiled when out of doors.

Nestorians were also active, and established schools in many towns. They prayed with their faces to the ground, turned towards the East. Their monastery at Hira was established in the fifth century and during the Prophet's youth, King Nu'man of Hira became a Christian.

The Arab chief Harith went to Constantiple to ask for a Monophysite bishop and was granted one. He and his son Nu'man were captured by the Greeks and exiled to Sicily.

The amazing rapidity of the Muslim advance after the death of the Prophet was aided enormously by the cooperation of local Christians (Monophysites), who were disgusted with Byzantine (Greek) cruelty, oppression and doctrine. The Muslims were welcomed by them as true believers and deliverers.

Circumcision (Khitan). The removal of the foreskin of the penis. This is a widespread custom in Islam, but it is not asked for in the Qur'an. It was practised in pre-Islamic Arabia, and tradition teaches that the Prophet Ibrahim was commanded to circumcise himself and his family, when he was in his 80th year. (Genesis 17:10). It is usually done when the infant is around a week old, or a little later if the baby is weak (2:124). In Turkey boys may be circumcised as late as nine or ten, but this is generally regarded as wrong practice. Female circumcision is a cruel tradition in the Sudan and lower Egypt that predates both Islam and Christianity, and has nothing to do with either. See Khafd.

Circumcision of adult converts. This is not required in Islam. Even circumcision for newborn boys is only recommended, and not compulsory. If a child born in a Muslim family remains uncircumcised until his death, he has not committed a sin. However, it is more hygienic and recommended to be circumcised. If an adult male becomes a Muslim, it is up to him whether he wishes to have this operation or not; it does not affect his status as a good Muslim either way.

Circumcision of women. See Khafd.

Cleanliness. (Taharah). Muslims regard personal cleanliness as of prime importance. Bodies and clothing should always be as clean as possible. Before salah (prayer) a ritual cleanliness is required (wudu) which involves putting on clean clothes after taking either a full bath or shower, or the washing of certain parts of the body. A full bath is always required after sexual intimacy, after menstruation, after childbirth, and after contact with a dead body. The Prophet particularly recommended special cleanliness of hands, mouth, hair and private parts. See Wudu, Ghusl, Istanja, Taharah, Najasah.

Clothing—rules of modesty. Modest dress is required for both male and female Muslims. Muslim men should always be clean and smart, and covered at least from navel to knee. They should not wear clothing that emphasises their private parts, or is aggressive and threatening. Muslim women usually cover everything except hands and face. Clothing is not in any set style, but certain societies have very strong traditions. It is not correct Islam for any lady to be forced to wear a particular garment, and it is certainly an abuse of Islam when women are oppressed for showing their faces. The correct rule for Muslim men when confronted by improperly dressed women is to look away, not to approach, rebuke or abuse them. The question of hijab (head-covering) is under much discussion these days—it was certainly the normal modest dress in the society in which the Prophet lived, and was the sunnah of the ladies of his household. Some modern scholars argue that what is important is not the garment but the modesty. And where normal modest dress has now abandoned the headscarf just as modest male dress has now abandoned 'flowing robe,' a fuss need not be made about this piece of cloth. Other Muslim ladies feel that the headscarf is very much the symbol of their choice of Islam as their way of life, and wear it happily and with pride. See Hijab.

Co-education. There is no harm in a group of people, men and women, or boys and girls, to be present together in a classroom when a teacher is giving a lesson, provided that everyone behaves properly according to the Islamic standards of propriety. However, it is discouraged where young men and women can mix unsupervised socially, such as in the playground at break time.

Compassion. One of the chief characteristics of Allah; every surah but one commences with the phrase: 'In the name of Allah, the Compassionate, the Merciful.' Compassion is the combination of love and mercy, which Allah feels towards every one of His creations. He knows all their weaknesses and limitations, and sees their struggles. The hadith qudsi give many examples of His compassion: 'O Son of Adam, so long as you call upon Me and ask of Me, I shall forgive you for what you have done.'

The Prophet expressed it in these lovely words: 'Be forgiving, and control yourself in face of provocation; give justice to the person who was unfair and unjust to you; give to the one who did not help you when you were in need, and keep fellowship with the one who did not care about you.'

Concubines. A concubine was a woman owned by a particular man, who could use her not only as a servant but also to satisfy his sexual desires on her. Some Muslims have believed that Allah allowed both slavery and concubinage, but in fact both are absolutely contrary to the spirit of Islam.

Allah categorically prohibits any sexual relations between a man and a woman unless they are legally married to each other. The only difference was that a dowry (mahr) had to be paid for a free woman, whereas an owned slave ('one whom your right hand possesses') had no dowry. The freedom conferred upon the bride by the very act of marrying someone who had been her 'owner' was considered to be equivalent to a dowry. (33:50) 'Ma malakat aymanukum' (those whom your right hands possess) really denoted women who had been captured in holy war, and who subsequently embraced Islam (4:25). This passage made it crystal clear that Muslims could only enjoy sexual relations with female slaves if they married them properly.

Some maintain that the Prophet himself had concubines—namely the Christian Maryam Qibtiyah and Rayhanah the Jewess—but in view of the Qur'anic injunctions it is certain that the Prophet married these ladies. Maryam was the mother of his son Ibrahim—who died in infancy like Khadijah's sons by him.

Consciousness of God (taqwa). This is the prime quality of a Muslim, without which he or she cannot properly be called Muslim. Once the presence of God becomes real to an individual, it alters the whole of the way that person lives, and becomes the prime motivation for their life.

Conversion by the sword. Something Muslims are often accused of by the West, without much factual evidence. It is obviously impossible to truly convert anyone by force. The cruel battle leaders and politicians named in history (e.g. Ghenghis Khan) are not in any way representative of Islam, and if any individual did try to convert people by force, this was an abuse of Islam and completely misguided. Allah requests tolerance, for people of different religions to live without feeling threatened by Muslims. Allah clearly stated: 'Let there be no compulsion in matters of faith' (2:256), and the Prophet said: 'He is not one of us whose neighbour cannot feel safe from his harm.' It appears to have been far more characteristic of certain Christian leaders to try to convert by the sword (or other devices), not Muslims. The true Muslim principle when conquering a territory was always to offer people the chance of becoming Muslim, or of declaring peaceful allegiance and paying a tax. See Crusades.

Converts. Many people who convert to Islam from Christianity or Judaism say they feel they are 'coming home'; their discovery of Islam frequently provides the answer to many of the problems that have worried them about the faiths they have grown up in. The feeling is known as fitra or reversion. Muslims claim that Islam is the religion of natural reason, therefore all children are born Muslims. It is as they grow up that they take up the religion of their parents.

Corporal punishment. Muslims do not approve of cruelty, but sometimes it is necessary to punish a child or adult who apparently cannot be made to accept sociable behaviour in any other way. Thus, corporal punishment is not forbidden in schools, and is carried out in some societies for social ills such as drunkenness and debauchery and theft. See Hudood.

Courage. One of the prime qualities of a Muslim. Strong belief in God and the life to come gives Muslims the courage to face up to all adversities and tragedies.

Cowardice. See Jubn.

Creation. God Alone is the Creator of our universe, and all the other universes that we know not of. Allah is totally different in kind from anything that He has created. Muslim scholars keep an open mind towards all scientific theories regarding Creation, bearing in mind that what is regarded as most likely to be true today may well be completely disproved tomorrow—such as the theory that the sun went round the earth, or that the earth was the centre of the universe. If God is true, all true science should be entirely in keeping with His principles. (see First Cause)

Crime. All forms of criminal activity are forbidden to a Muslim. One cannot commit theft, dishonesty and so forth and still regard oneself as Muslim. Honesty and honourable living are key characteristics of Islam, and all Muslims should be entirely trustworthy. However, Islam is well aware of human weakness, and when criminality is discovered, Muslims try to judge with fairness and compassion.

Crucifixion. The penalty of nailing or tying a person to a cross until they are dead. Christian belief is centred on the crucifixion of Isa (Jesus) as reported in the New

Testament of the Bible. This death was seen as a sacrifice, whereby Jesus—the God-Man and third person in the Holy Trinity—was able to release those who believed in him from the clutches of 'original sin' (the sinful nature of humanity derived from the failings of Adam and Eve), the only way in which they could be released.

The Qur'an denies the crucifixion of Jesus (4:157), thus attacking the major doctrine of Christianity. Islam does not accept the idea of one person inheriting, or being punished for, the sin of another; consequently Muslims, like Jews, feel no need of an atoning saviour (6:164; 17;15;35:18; 39:7; 53:38).

There are many fanciful legends circulated amongst Muslims that explain how Jesus avoided death at the hands of the Romans, who were acting in collusion with the Jewish priests. These suggest that God substituted a person who closely resembled Jesus at the last moment. In some accounts, that person was the traitor Judas Iscariot. However, none of these legends finds the slightest support in the Qur'an or authentic traditions.

The Qur'anic phrase 'wa lakin shubbiha lahum'—'it only appeared to them as if it had been so' really implies that in the course of time, under the influence of Trinitarian beliefs common in the ancient world (especially Mithraism) the legend of the dying and rising sacrificed God-man became applied to Jesus.

The Qur'an, moreover, does not imply that Jesus was taken up bodily to heaven in his lifetime (as some Muslims popularly believe). The expression 'God exalted him unto Himself' uses the verb rafa'ahu, which elsewhere always means 'honour' or 'exalt.' It denotes raising a person to a position of special grace—a blessing in which all prophets partake. See 3:55; 19:57—where it is applied to the Prophet Idris.

Crusades. The attempts between 1095-1291 of various armies (supposedly Christian) to recapture Jerusalem from the Muslims who had ruled there since Caliph Umar's occupation in 638. During the ninth century Islam had spread rapidly into European side of the Mediterranean, and the Papacy felt seriously under threat. The Seljuk Turks made Byzantine territories unsafe for pilgrims, so in 1095 the Emperor Alexander Comnenus and Pope Urban II appealed for military aid. There were 8 major crusades. The First Crusade was initially led by Peter the Hermit; his entire army was captured by the Turks. A huge military force of 150,000 Normans, Franks, Venetians and Genoese then captured Jerusalem in 1099 and indulged in one of the worst civilian massacres in history. Muslims and Jews, women and children, were slaughtered indiscriminately for a week. The Crusaders tried to force Latin Christianity on the Eastern Orthodox priests, and persecuted them also. Baldwin was crowned King of Jerusalem in 1100. The Second Crusade began when Zangi of Mosul captured Odessa in 1145. It was led by King Louis VII of France, and failed to capture Damascus. Zangi's son Nureddin recaptured the kingdom surrounding Jerusalem. His deputy, Saladin (Saleh al-Din Yusuf ibn Ayyub—ruler of Egypt and Syria) made a truce with the Christians, but when this was broken, he destroyed the Crusader army at the Battle of Hattin near Galilee and captured Jerusalem, without harming Christians there or their holy places. The Fall of Jerusalem started the Third Crusade, led by Emperor Frederick Barbarossa of Germany in 1189. King Richard the Lionheart of England joined the French and German armies at the siege of Acre, where once again the capture ended in a civilian massacre. Richard, however, negotiated a peace treaty with Saladin (he married his sister) which gave Christians the coastal regions and permitted access to their shrines in Jerusalem. Pope Innocent III called the Fourth Crusade to attack Muslim Egypt in 1198, but the Crusaders were diverted into attacking Constantinople. (This move destroyed all possible cooperation between Eastern and Western Churches). 1212 saw the Children's Crusade, (the belief that 'pure children' could succeed where soldiers failed); it ended with their deaths or enslavement. The Fifth Crusade in 1219 ended with the capture of Damietta on the Nile, and a truce with Egypt. In 1229 Emperor Frederick II's truce returned Jerusalem to European control for ten years. King Louis IX of France led the Seventh Crusade to Egypt in 1248, and the Eighth to North Africa in 1270. However, by the time the Crusades ended the East was entirely under Muslim Ottoman rule. The power and prestige of the Papacy had been enhanced at the cost of the Eastern sects, and the barbarous behaviour of 'Christian' soldiers towards civilians lost them the tolerance of the Muslims, who were to retaliate in later years with equal savagery and persecution. The Crusades gave rise to two powerful religious orders—the Knights Hospitaller (who gave shelter to pilgrims), and the Knights Templar (who protected pilgrims on the way). The Templars were later accused of heresy and banned; it is suspected they had converted to a form of Islam. The city of Jerusalem was still in Muslim hands when the British partitioned it in 1948.

Dahr. Time; the pre-Islamic notion of an impersonal, pre-ordained fate.

Da'i. A caller to the Truth. One who calls is a mad'u. See Dawah.

Da'if. 'Weak'. A da'if tradition is one in which there is some defect either in the chain of transmission, or in the proper understanding of the transmitter, or its contents are not in perfect agreement with Islamic beliefs and practices. It is in fact a tradition of weak or less reliable authority.

Dajjal. The Anti-Christ. In Muslim tradition, an evil creature who will rule the earth for forty days before Judgement Day. It will be defeated by the return of Isa (Jesus), who will destroy it before the end of the world.

Dala'il al-Khairat. A collection of Duroods for blessing the Prophet. This particular collection, and others like it, contain phrases and things that are totally unacceptable from the Islamic point of view, and really should not be used. All that is required of a Muslim is to ask Allah to grant peace and blessings to the Prophet. There is no such thing as the minimum or maximum number of times this should be done. Suggesting otherwise is nothing more than a burdensome nonsense.

Dancing. There is no rigid rule concerning dancing, like many other activities. Decent dancing, which does not arouse unacceptable emotions, and does not make the woman's body an object of exciting desires, and does not involve pulling close to oneself a member of the opposite sex, is permissible. Many communities have perfectly acceptable folk-dancing. The Prophet and Aishah watched some Abyssinians' folk-dancing in the mosque at Madinah.

Dar. Arabic for 'abode' or 'home'. In the Qur'an the term is used with reference to both the life of this world (dar ad-dunya) and the life to come (dar al-akhirah). The term is often used as a name for a Muslim home, shop, madrassah, etc.—as, for example, in Dar as-Salaam (House of Peace); Dar ul-Islam (abode of Islam); Dar al-Taqwa (place of Awareness of god).

The expression Dar al-Harb, (place of War) is frequently used to refer to those areas of the world as yet untouched by Islam.

Dargah. The Indian word for the burial place of a Muslim saint.

Dar al-Islam. The 'house' or 'dwelling-place' of Islam. It has two main meanings; the hearts of true believers, or places where Islam is practised. It is also frequently used as the name of a particular building dedicated to Muslim scholarship.

Darud. A blessing on the Prophet Muhammad; prayer often recited at the end of salah. See Dala'il al-Khairat.

Mosque in Bhopal, India.

Dawah. Invitation, call, preaching. The duty of Muslims to invite others to find the shariah, the 'straight path' of Islam. The call should always be done with wisdom, gentleness, tact and good manners. Aggressive and arrogant preaching can hardly qualify as dawah, since it only appeals to the zealots who preach in that way and those already their followers—it drives others *away* from Islam.

Dawud. The Arabic name of the shepherd-prophet David, the slayer of Goliath (Jalut), and successor of Talut (Saul) as king of the tribes of Israel from c1000 BCE. He captured Jerusalem and made it his capital, after ruling for 6 years from Hebron. His revelations from Allah were known as the Zabur. His most famous son was the Prophet Sulayman (2:247-251; 6:84; 21:78-80; 34:10-11; 38:17-26).

Day of Khaybar. See Khaybar.

Day of Resurrection. Muslims believe that the whole of humanity will be resurrected at a time when God wills. Those who think it impossible for God to recreate human bodies forget the miracle of their first creation. Surah 75 states that God can re-create us, even to our individual fingerprints. However, our resurrection bodies will probably bear no resemblance to our earthly bodies, in any case ('I will create you in forms you know not of'—Surah 56:61). At this time, each individual will be shown his or her 'book' revealing all good and evil aspects of their lives, and will face judgement. Fortunately for us, however, God does not judge like human beings; although always just and fair, He is also Supreme Compassion and Understanding, so no believer need lose hope, or feel certain that he or she will be condemned.

Day of Siffin—see Siffin.

Death. Muslims believe that God knows the time of our deaths from our conception in the womb, or even before. Muslims should not worry about 'how long they have got', but make sure they live every day available to them in the best possible way, making the fullest use of its opportunities to love God and do good works. Since they believe in a scheme of things not limited to the physical world, Muslims are not frightened by the prospect of death, but accept that life on earth is one of God's gifts, and that He may recall our souls when He pleases. We should always be grateful for what we have—even if our circumstances do not seem favourable, and make the very best use of all the time we are granted. Death is simply regarded as the passing from one sphere of life to another, which, insha Allah, will be better for us. Death is always by God's leave (3:145); every person will have a 'taste' of it (3:185; 21:25; 29:57); there may be a second death later (37:59); the first death is not the end of al tings (45:24-26); sincere people will not flee from it (62:6-8); our forms after death will all be chaged. (56:60-61).

Death of the Prophet. The Prophet became ill with fever and violent headaches at the age of 63. When he realised that his death might be imminent, he requested permission to be moved to the room of his beloved Aishah. His weakness grew, and he requested Abu Bakr, Aishah's father, to lead the prayer in his place. He died with his head in Aishah's lap, and she recorded his last words as being: 'Nay, but I have chosen the most exalted companions, in Paradise.' He was buried in Aishah's room in Madinah.

Deen. See Din.

Degrees of Islam. The Prophet suggested that there were several levels or degrees of Islam. The most basic level was that of those who did submit to it, but without real faith in their hearts. In surah 56:7-40, humanity was divided into three groups—those of the right, those of the left, and the foremost. Those of the right had succeeded and found salvation; those of the left had failed in their tests and not believed. The foremost, also called the 'slaves of God' (56:6, 89:29) were those 'brought near to God'. Other revelations have a category of the 'righteous'—a category between the foremost and those of the right.

The Prophet indicated that the heights of Islam were not attained by matters such as praying and fasting to a superlative extent, but were a matter of the heart. He once said of Abu Bakr: 'He surpasses you—not through much fasting and prayer, but by virtue of something rooted in his heart.' (Tirmidhi).

The difference between one degree and another are vaster in the next world than this; 'Truly, the Hereafter is greater in degrees and greater in hierarchic precedence.' (17:21)

The Prophet spoke of the supreme degree in one of the hadith qudsi: 'My slave ceases not to draw near Me with the devotion of his (or her) free will until I love him; and when I love him, I am the hearing with which he hears, and the sight by which he sees, and the hand with which he takes hold, and the foot on which he walks.'

Deluge. The Flood at the time of the Prophet Nuh (Noah) is not presented in the Qur'an as an event that wiped out the whole world (7:64; 11:40). It was only the people to whom Nuh delivered his message and who called him a liar who were drowned. Hence, the deluge affected the territory of Nuh's people, not the whole world—as was suggested in the Old Testament of the Bible. The deluge spoken of in the Bible, and in the myths of Sumeria and Babylonia, may represent an inundation, during the Ice Age, of the huge basin which is today covered by the Mediterranean Sea, caused by the Atlantic Ocean breaking through the land barrier at Gibraltar. Alternatively, archaeologists have found a huge layer of sedimentary mud in the region of Ur, and suggest the Flood was a massive inundation of the Tigris—Euphrates river vallies.

The Qur'an sites the resting place of Nuh's Ark on Mt. Judi, near Ararat in Turkey (11:44). Ararat, the Assyrian Urartu) at one time included the whole area to the South of Lake Van.

Deobandis. These are a break-away group of Sunni Muslims, who follow strictly the ulama of Deoband. They have their own mosques, and regard Islam as a personal and not a social religion—that is, they are non-political and do not try to establish an Islamic state.

Dervishes. (from 'darwish', the 'sill of the door'). These are Sufis who practice particular methods of attaining trance conditions and a special feeling of closeness to God. The most famous Orders are the 'whirling' dervishes (who practice sacred dance), and 'wandering' dervishes (who do not live in a fixed home). See Sufism.

Despair. Despair is not a characteristic of a Muslim who believes in God and Hereafter(3:139, 146). No matter what a person has done, no-one should ever despair of their circumstances, or of the mercy of Allah (39:53). Allah said to the Prophet: 'If a person draws near Me to a hand's span, I draw near by an arm's length; if a person comes to Me walking, I come at the run.' Also: 'A man said of another — 'By Allah, Allah will never forgive him!' At this Allah the Almighty said — 'Who is this who swears by Me that I will never forgive a certain person? Truly, I have forgiven him already.'

Destiny. See al-Qadr.

Determinism. See al-Qadr.

Devil. See Shaytan.

Dhabiha. See Slaughter.

Dhat. The Essence, meaning the Essence of Allah.

Dhalim. See Zalim.

adh-Dhariyat. The Dust-Scattering Winds; the title of surah 51, a Makkan surah of 60 verses. It includes reference to the Ad and Thamud tribes, Lut, Ibrahim and Musa.

Dhat-un-Ni-taqayn. Meaning 'two-belted woman'. Asma', daughter of Abu Bakr was so named by the Prophet. During the Prophet's migration from Makkah, he hid for three days in a cave with Abu Bakr. Asma and her brother Abdullah came with camels and supplies, but forgot the rope, so she tore her girdle in two so that the supplies could be tied to the camel.

Dhawq (pl. adhwaq); lit. 'taste.' Used in a technical sense in Sufism to indicate the experience of Divine Truth.

Dhikr. (from 'dharaka', to remember, think, relate). The deliberate remembrance of Allah stimulated by such things as the repetition of His Divine Names, certain chanted phrases, and so forth. In general sense all ibadah is dhikr. In common usage it has come to refer to invocation.

Dhimma. Obligation or contract, in particular a treaty of protection for non-Muslims living in Muslim territory.

Dhimmi. A non-Muslim citizen living in an Islamic State, for whose services, care and protection they are expected to pay taxes.

Dhu'l Hijjah. The twelfth month of the Islamic calendar year, in which the Hajj takes place. One of the four sacred months in which fighting is prohibited.

Dhu'l-Hulayfa. The miqat of the people of Madinah now called Bayar 'Ali.

Dhu'l-Kifl. Mentioned in 21:85, along with the Prophets Isma'il and Idris. This may be the Qur'an name of the Prophet called Ezekiel in the Bible. Dhu'l-Kifl means literally 'him of the pledge', derived from the verb 'kafala' signifying to 'become responsible for something.' Another suggestion is that it means 'one who gives a double portion,' or even 'one who used a cloak of double thickness.'

Kafil in Iraq has the shrine of Ezekiel, and Jews visited it on pilgrimage.

The Ezekiel of the Bible was a prophet carried away to Babylon in c.599 BC by Nebuchadnezzar, after his second attack on Jerusalem.

The Biblical records of his sayings are particularly interesting for three things, several descriptions of an 'Unidentified Flying Object (UFO) in which the Prophet rode at least once (Ezekiel 1, 10, 11); his famous vision of the 'Valley of Dry Bones' in which he saw the remains of long-dead people coming back to life at the Day of Resurrection (Ezekiel 37; Surah 75:1-5); and the important teaching in Ezekiel 18 where God revealed that it was wrong for people to think human beings, including a person's children and descendants, were being punished for the sins of another. This significant chapter directly contradicts the notion of inherited Original Sin originating in Adam and Hawwah and passed down until cancelled by God when He 'incarnated' Himself by becoming a human being (Isa) and dying in order to 'save' or 'redeem' humanity. Islam, of course, accepts Isa as a great Messenger, but not a Saviour or Redeemer in the Christian sense.

Dhu'l-Kifl is also mentioned in 38:48 along with Isma'il and Elisha.

Dhu'l-Qa'da. The eleventh month of the Muslim lunar calendar. One of the four sacred months in which fighting is prohibited.

Dhu'l-Qarnayn. A great ruler of the past who was a true believer. His story is mentioned in 18:83. The name means the 'Two-Horned One' or 'He of the Two Generations'—qarn means generation, age, epoch or century as well as horn. The term qarn (pl. qurun) appears 20 other times in the Qur'an, and each time refers to people of a particular epoch. In surah 18, it does refer to a particular powerful and just ruler. The two horns may mean two sources of power, worldly and spiritual. Many commentators identify Dhu'l-Qarnayn with the Macedonian conquerer, Alexander the Great (18:33f), who was frequently depicted with two horns on his head—but there is no evidence that he was a great spiritual leader. The Prophet Musa (Moses) was also shown with two horns owing to a mistranslation of a passage in the Old Testament.

Diet. Muslim diet is to eat foods that are halal, that is, permitted by God. God has refused all products from the pig, meat of animals that have been offered to idols, died by themselves, been strangled, or are carrion eaters, or have not been drained of blood. All fruit, vegetables, sea-food, and meat that falls in the halal categories are acceptable. Some Muslims insist on halal-slaughter, but this is the ideal. The Prophet stated that if one was not sure of the slaughter of the meat, one should pray over it, and eat. The last revelation he received gave permission for Muslims to marry the women of the Jews and Christians, and eat their meat (5:6). Some Muslims have therefore broadened their outlook on meat from such outlets as butchers shops in Christian countries, but others still reject western slaughterhouse methods in which electrocution (which is intended to stun the animal before slaughter) often actually kills the animal. Many Muslims go to the lengths of checking every list of ingredients on packeted foodstuffs (e.g. biscuits, crisps etc.) to make sure it does not contain animal fat or gelatine—which might come either from pork or from beef which was not halal-slaughtered (2:172-173; 5:4; 6:145).

Dikka (or Dakka). A raised platform in a mosque, often near the minbar, used to give the final call to prayer. It can also be used by prayer-leaders other than the main Imam when a large crowd is present; it enables the ritual gestures and prostrations to be seen by the congregation, so that they might keep in unison.

Din. (from 'dana', to owe, be indebted to). Usually translated as 'religion', din means much more than just a set of beliefs; it is the deliberate transaction between a human and God, the awareness of one's relationship towards Him and the consistent living in a manner befitting this relationship. The life-transaction, literally the debt or exchange situation between two parties, in this usage the Creator and the created, Allah says in the Qur'an *"Surely the din with Allah is Islam."*

Din al-Fitrah. The belief that 'truth stands clear from error' (2:256), and that Islam is the belief based on reason, and the natural way of life for all pious thinking persons. See Converts.

Direction of Prayer. See Mihrab, Qiblah.

Dishonesty. Totally forbidden in Islam. A person who has departed from truth has departed from Islam. One can fool other people, but one can never fool God, our Watcher who never slumbers nor sleeps. Muslims should always speak truthfully and without fear. If this truth involved a small matter that it was not necessary to speak up on, or might be no more than personal opinion, or would hurt the hearer (i.e. 'you look awful in that dress, dear!'), then it is better to keep silent. Muslims should also always *behave* truthfully, and be honest in their duties, chores, responsibilities, tax-returns, business deals, and so forth. One should be able to trust a Muslim *without question.* Truth is such a vital concept; even if a person has been caught lying only once, how can one be sure he or she will not do it again?

Dissimulation. See Taqiyah.

Ditch, battle of. See al-Khandaq.

Divination. A practice forbidden in Islam, because it suggests that humans have the right to know in advance what will befall them, or that various fetishes and objects have the power to alter their fate or fortune. This leads to the false notion that such objects have more power than God Himself, if they could alter His will for us, which is a nonsense. Therefore such things as crystal balls, tarot cards, astrological practices, spiritualism, and any lingering antique forms and divination by runes, stones, bones and so on, are forbidden.

Divorce. Of all the allowed things, this is the one most disapproved by God and His Prophet. Marriages do not always work out, and divorce is allowed in Islam for genuine reasons—but it should never be undertaken lightly. It is allowed when one or both partners deliberately refuse to fulfill some part of the marriage 'bargain'. This may involve cruelty, desertion, mental cruelty, unacceptable behaviour (e.g. drunkenness, violence, criminal activity etc.), refusal to satisfy the partner physically, deliberately turning away from the faith. It should not be on the grounds of childlessness if this was due to the will of Allah and not deliberate action. In all these cases, a partner has the right to divorce, if they cannot cope or live with the unacceptable conditions. However, before divorce takes place, every effort should be made to put the problem right. Once divorce becomes inevitable, it should be done humanely and fairly, without unpleasant pressures or recriminations, and great care should be taken over the care of any children involved. Custody would normally be with the mother, unless circumstances were much more favourable with the father. In Shariat Law, divorce involves three statements of intent, with a period of a month between each, during which time the couple should still live together and attempt to reconcile. If marital relations take place, the divorce is annulled. If not, it goes ahead. It is a gross abuse and quite incorrect for a Muslim man to make the statement three times on the same occasion, and imagine that he is divorced—although this abuse does still take place in some circumstances of ignorance and un-Islamic male domination (2:228-241; 65:1-7; 4:35, 128). See also Talaq, Lian, Khul.

Diwan. A collection of qasidas primarily concerned with the declaration of inner truth, descriptions of the shari'ah (or way to find it). The desired effect is to achieve a profound change in the awareness of the reader, a spiritual breakthrough.

Diyyah. This is financial compensation (or blood-money)

for injuries or death. The relatives of a victim of murder, manslaughter, or fatal accident can opt to accept diyyah rather than have the killer condemned to death. The more compassionate the injured parties, the more they are commended and blessed by Allah. See Capital Punishment.

Dogs. Muslims do not generally keep dogs except as guard dogs outside the house, or as shepherd or hunting dogs. The combination of the natural affection and salivation of dogs means that it would be very difficult to keep in wudu for prayer, and so the keeping of them in the house becomes impractical for Muslims. This does not mean that they dislike dogs—on the contrary, many Muslims love them dearly.

Dome of the Rock. See Bayt al-Maqdis.

Doubt. See Waswas.

Dowry. The dowry (or 'mahr') is the payment of an agreed sum of money to the intended wife. It is often paid (at least partly) in advance, and should be completed at the wedding. This money belongs exclusively to the bride, and is hers to keep should her husband later divorce her. The larger the mahr, the less likely he is to divorce; but seeking a large mahr is not in keeping with the principles of Islam. Neither is the paying of it to the bride's father or family leader, or not agreeing to pay it at all. The question of dowry should never be used as an opportunity to insult a woman, or keep her 'prisoner', or force her to remain unmarried (2:229, 236-7; 4:4, 19-21, 25). The bride's family should certainly not pay dowry to the husband or his family—practices abolished by the Prophet.

Drugs. ('khamr'—intoxicating substances). Medicine is allowed in Islam, although it is preferable if the base for the drug does not contain alcohol. Drugs used for 'pleasure', or 'getting high', the cause of so much of today's social ills, are totally forbidden (5:93). Such drugs include hallucinogens and 'pep' pills, hashish, marihiuana, cocaine, heroin, 'smack', and 'crack'. Some argue that mild narcotics are natural substances and gifts of Allah; but the principle is always that which does harm (both to oneself and to others!) is haram, and only that which promotes good and well-being is halal.

Drunkenness. (Ar. sukara). See alcohol. Drunkenness leads to all sorts of antisocial, abusive and dangerous behaviour, and is not condoned in Islam. Sukara does not apply exclusively to alcoholic intoxication. The term sukr signifies any state of mental disequilibrium which prevents people making full use of their intellectual faculties.

Druze. The Druze are a Muslim sect that originated in Cairo, initially developed by Muhammad al-Darazi, a follower and disciple of Caliph Hakim. Its members figured prominently in the wars against the Crusaders. They have secret doctrines on the subjects of Messianism and reincarnation; they permit no conversion or inter-marriage with non-Druzes, and allow the practice of taqiyyah with which they outwardly confirm to any group amongst which they find themselves. The main Druze region today is in the mountains of Lebanon.

Du'a. Private prayers, personal supplication and prayer requests that are not part of the set prayer or salah. Although it is good Islam to accept with patience that which God sends, it is only natural to ask for help, understanding and forgiveness, and the Prophet did this constantly. However, instead of wasting time begging God to let you pass an exam, or not let your sick relative die, it is better Islam to pray for guidance and insight to know what to do in any given situation, and for the ability to keep calm and be of most use and consolation.

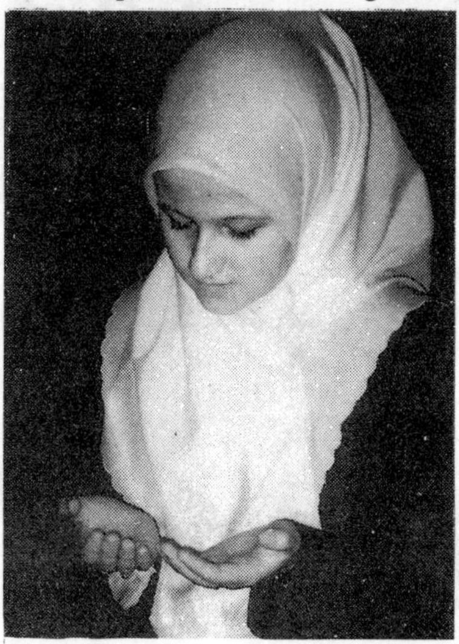

Du'a al-Istiftah. This is personal prayer made before the start of the set rakah.

ad-Duha. The Bright Morning Hours; the title of surah 93 revealed after the Prophet was taunted that God had forsaken him. One of the most moving surahs. a Makkan surah of 11 verses.

ad-Dukhan. Smoke; the title of surah 44 based on the word in v. 10, a Makkan surah of 59 verses. The revelations of the Qur'an is the climax of all divine revelation which has been given since the dawn of consciousness.

Duldul. The name of a grey mule belonging to the Prophet. The name means 'porcupine'! Duldul was part of a gift to the Prophet from the Muqawqis of Egypt. The Prophet rode him to the Battle of Hunayn.

Dunya. The word means 'the world', but in Islam it refers specifically to the attractive and tempting things of this world that entice humans away from right living. Muslims do not regard the world itself as evil, for it is the creation of Allah; but it is obvious that there is plenty of evil around in it, which has to be encountered, resisted, avoided or, hopefully, removed. 'Worldly' things include such things as money, possessions, ambitions and jobs/careers, leisure pursuits, and so on (2:212; 3:14).

Eid. Arabic word for a celebration repeated regularly, as opposed to a party or special festivity for a one-off event such as a wedding or childbirth. All Muslims keep two chief festival days—Eid ul-Adha and Eid ul-Fitr, and many also celebrate the Prophet's birthday, New Year's Day, Ashurah, Laylat ul-Miraj, Laylat ul-Bara'at and Laylat ul-Qadr. The usual greeting is 'Eid Mubarak, meaning 'the blessings of the Eid to you'.

Eid ul-Adha. The 'major festival' of Islam, the feast of sacrifice at the new moon that ends the period of Hajj. The 'id of the (greater) Sacrifice, it starts on the 10th day of Dhu'l-Hijjah (the month of Hajj), the day that the pilgrims are sacrificing their animals. All Muslims celebrate it, whether on Hajj or not. In Muslim countries it is a three or four day holiday. It commemorates the willingness of the Prophet Ibrahim to sacrifice his firstborn son's life for God. Muslims who do not sacrifice an animal (or purchase one sacrificed for them) may pay the equivalent to charity.

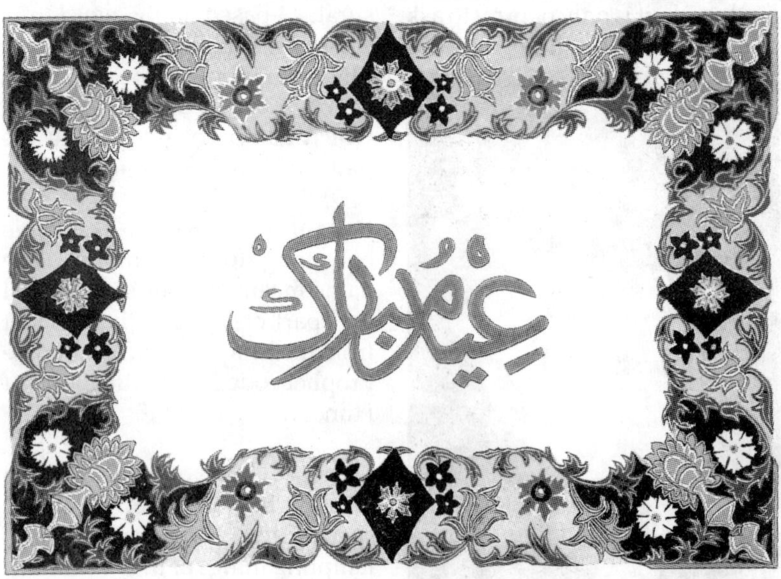

Eid ul-Fitr. This is the 'minor festival' of Islam, although many have far more festive spirit at this time, for it is the feast that marks the new moon at the end of the month-long fast of Ramadan. It is also called 'Bayram'. Both feasts are celebrated with a special prayer in which the whole community tries to join together, including women and children; small mosque communities may link up for this prayer. Large mosque communities sometimes take over open fields or large car-parks, as the numbers run into many thousands.

Elephant, Year of. See Abraha.

Empowerment of women. The Qur'an makes it very clear that all believing men and women are entirely equal in worth, spirituality, responsibility, and so on (Surah 33:35). The religious and moral duties of male and female Muslims are exactly the same. These notions have never been accepted readily by societies where men control power in government, at work and in the home through their wages, and this is still just as obvious in cultures nominally Muslim where Islam has been misunderstood as it is in other male-dominated societies. However, Allah ordained equality and fairness for women in education, opportunity, and in fair property law and divorce settlements.

End of the World. The existence of the earth, solar system, universe and cosmos is entirely dependent upon the will of its Creator, God. It may seem eternal, but it could collapse in a twinkling of an eye. The only element which is eternal is God, Who alone knows the time the world will end.

Envy. Since Allah grants our circumstances as tests, Muslims should not be envious of the fortunes of others (Surah 4:32). Wealth, success, health, good fortune—these could change in a flash. The Prophet recommended that people who were tempted to envy others should 'look down, not up', meaning they should be grateful for what they had and consider the lot of those less fortunate than themselves.

Equal rights for women. One aspect of fairness to women is to take into consideration their physical well-being and to be genuinely considerate to women who are menstruating or involved in childbirth or childbearing. Men are expected to protect and maintain women (Surah 4:34) without denying their rights. The Qur'an statement that women have equal rights 'but men are a degree above them' (Surah 2:228) is often taken out of context—it refers to divorce-law. The word 'but' is better translated as 'for'; it reminds a man leaving his wife and children that he has an obligation from Allah to continue to take care of them, since he is usually in the better financial position. See Empowerment.

Ethiopia (Ar. al-Habash). Also called Abyssinia. Mainly a Christian country, but some of the Companions migrated there in AD 615 and were protected by the ruler, known as the Negus. See Negus.

Euthanasia. The practice of giving a 'good death' or more merciful death. It might involve 'putting to sleep' by injection, or quickly finishing off a creature badly wounded who would otherwise die slowly. In Islam the practice is illegal as regards humans. Attempts should always be made to heal and relieve pain, but no human has the right to end another's life outside the process of law. Many people who go through suffering discover some of life's most important lessons at this hard time—there may be reasons for the suffering that we do not know. See Suffering.

Moreover, the pains of our suffering, if God wills, are taken into consideration by Allah when He is forgiving our sins.

Evil. The deliberate desire to act in a way contrary to the will of God. The inevitable result in a world in which God has allowed freewill.

The Qur'an implies that evil is not an independent factor of life, but the result of human beings giving in to the templations that arise from their own moral weakness, which denies the truth or prevents good (4:76). The supposed power of the negative principle which is symbolized by Shaytan has no intrinsic reality—his guile is weak indeed. It only becomes real through human beings endowed with freewill choosing the wrong course of action.

Most people, of course, do not realise that the evil happening may possibly be a consequence of their own actions or their own wrong choice of option. They usually blame it on the failings or actions of others (4:79).

Everything is from God, the ultimate source of all. In this sense all that is good and all that is evil does flow, in the end resort, from God's will. However, not everything that people regard as evil or bad fortune, is evil. As Allah said: it may well be that you hate a thing whereas it is good for you, and it may well be that you love something that is bad for you; God knows, whereas you do not know (2:216). What seems at the time to be evil may in fact be a test, or Allah's deliberate plan to bring about a person's spiritual growth through suffering. See Suffering, Taghut.

Evolution. The theory that human beings have descended from animals, probably apes. Islam regards all animal life as having been created by Allah, but keeps an open mind as to the process. There is no 'mythology' in the Qur'an about the creation of Adam (Surah 2:30-34). Muslims feel it is still far from being proved.

Exclusiveness. Some leading Islamic schoalrs, particularly Shi'ite ones, claim that only fully qualified scholars who are intellectual equals have the talents and abilities necessary to determine the abilities and interpretations of others.

Should *ijtihad* only be exercised by qualified jurists, or should the consensus of saintly lay-people also be allowed, and if not, why not? See Mujtahid.

Exegesis. See Tafsir.

Expected Imam. See Mahdi.

Extended families. Families which include grandparents, perhaps unmarried or bereaved uncles and aunts, perhaps more than one wife—as opposed to the 'norm' or mother and father and a couple of children.

Extremism. This implies fanaticism, tyranny and competitiveness, none of which are Islamic qualities. Some people are naturally more pious and more enthusiastic about religious practices than others, just as some are more intelligent. This does not necessarily imply greater merit. Allah appreciates our devotion, but He does not place burdens on us (5:90). Muslims who wish to be thought better than others are suffering from pride and misplaced confidence (31:19); sometimes those who seem to be the most devout are the most harsh and unforgiving. Those whose hearts are 'wrong' can spend all day fasting and all night praying, but gain only thin bodies and sleepless nights. Extremists, perhaps from misplaced enthusiasm, often try to impose religious burdens on others that are not necessary. Gentleness and tolerance and consideration for others are the correct Islamic attitude. The main characteristics of extremists are *ghuluw* (excessiveness) *tashdid* (bigotry), *tafkir* (branding others as unbelievers), and 'hair-splitting'. Islam is for all, not just for those with special endurance or who wish to create limits. Extremism generally is too much for normal human nature to condone or tolerate, and it is very often at someone else's expense—someone else is likely to suffer neglect or inconvenience as the result of the extremist's pre-occupation with doing more than others.

Eyedrops and eardrops. These do not invalidate fasting, since the liquids will not reach the stomach. What invalidates the fast is eating, drinking and sex.

Ezekiel. See Dhu'l Kifl.

Fada'il (sing. *fadila*). Excellence, merits, virtues. It is a genre of Arabic literature that praises the excellent qualities in things, people, places and so on.

Fadl. The grace and bountiful blessings of Allah. Allah is Lord of Overflowing Grace, (2:243; 3:74,174; 8:29; 10:60; 27:73; 40:61; 57:21,29; 62:4). He is full of bounty to all the worlds (2:251). Grace is 'in His hand'; He grants it to whom He pleases, (3:73; 57:29; 9:28; 10:107; 62:4). Whoever does good spontaneously, then Allah is aware of it, and bountiful in rewarding,, (2:158). 'Those who give a beautiful loan to Allah, He doubles it and multiplies it.' (2:245; 57:11,86; 64:17).

Faith. See Shahadah, Din, Iman.

Faith Movement. An Indian reformist or renewal movement based on Sufi principles, founded by Maulana Muhammad Ilyas, in Mewat south of Delhi in 1345/ 1927. He taught that Muslims should genuinely and personally feel that they are Muslims. The need for simplicity of life is also stressed. See Tablighi Jamat.

Fajr. The first compulsory prayer of the day, between first light of dawn and sunrise.

al-Fajr. Title of *surah* 89, 'the Dawn'; a Makkan *surah* of 30 verses. The Dawning may symbolise spiritual awakening. The surah reminds humanity of divine punishment.

al-Falaq. Title of *surah* 113, 'the Daybreak'; a Makkan surah of 5 verses. It is a plea for Allah's protection from all sorts of evil.

Falsafa. Philosophy. Islamic philosophy has been influenced by Aristotelianism and Neoplatonism, but is a system of thought in its own right. Many Islamic philosophers are accused of heterodoxy and heresy, usually by those who take a very narrow view of Islam and try to reduce it to a series of correct rituals. Philosophers promote the use of reason, wide knowledge, and understanding of the sciences of the universe. Allah is the Lord of the entire cosmic system, and much greater than the scope of our limited and human minds. However, it is our duty to do our best to understand—blind obedience may be pious, but it has very obvious limitations.

Fakih. See Faqih.

Fakir. See Faqir.

Falah. Success. One of the phrases in the adhan is *'Hayya 'al-al-Falah'*; 'Come to Success.' A person who is successful is known as Muflih. Such a person's deeds and way of life gain the pleasure of Allah.

Family of Islam. See Ummah.

Fana'. 'Annihilation' in Allah, one of the highest stations in Sufism. It is arrived at by withdrawal from the world of senses by means of dhikr, until even that last contact with awareness disappears.

Fanaticism. See Extremism.

Fantasies. Allah forgives us what we may contemplate of offenses and crimes. He takes us to account only for what we actually commit. However, people troubled by fantasies and daydreams should try to discourage them—there may come a day when they fall victim to their active imagination and commit the offences in question.

Faqih (pl. *fuqaha*). One who possesses knowledge or understand-ing, a theologian. A Muslim expert in law, a scholar of fiqh who by virtue of his knowledge can give a fatwa, an authoritative legal opinion or judgement.

Faqir (pl. *fuqara*). The poor; but not just those who are poor—it is those who are content with their poverty, through confidence in Allah. One who is in need, spiritual or physical (see 35:15); a Muslim holy person who has taken the vow of poverty. (The term is also applied to Hindu ascetics). The Prophet said: 'Look for me among the poor'; 'Poverty is all my glory'; and 'Allah loves the poor'.

Fara'id. Rules of inheritance; the portions allootted to heirs. The relatives of a deceased. Such shares are prescribed in the Qur'an 4:11, 112, 176. See Inheritance.

Fard. Compulsory. Certain aspects of Islam are regarded as compulsory, and others are left as voluntary matters. The five pillars of Islam are all fard, for example. There is a basic minimum of necessary beliefs and practices which are always compulsory for a Muslim. In matters of everyday Muslim life, however, the general principles are fard but the details of working them out are voluntary. For example, it is fard to be modest, but we are left to interpret ourselves how we will dress or behave modestly. A woman completely covered in a black chador has not kept the fard principle of modesty if she entices a man with her eyes, feet or hands. It is fard to be honest and truthful and courageous, but it is left to us to work out details in practical situations. See Shahadah, Salah, Sawm, Zakah, Hajj, Rakah, Wudu.

Fard Kifaya. The duty of Muslims to organise, provide or employ the services and facilities needed for the welfare of any community; for example, doctors, teachers, suppliers of water, clothing, food, housing, electricity, etc. It also refers to duties such as making the salat al-janaza and burial of a deceased if there is no relative to do it.

Farewell Pilgrimage. See Sermon, the Last; Pilgrimage, the Final.

Fasik. A sinner, guilty not only of great sins but also of everyday trifling offences against the law.

Fasting. This is the practice of subjecting the human body to discipline, for the sake of spiritual benefit (2:183-184). The purity and self-control is more important than the going without food. Many Muslims fast frequently, but the only compulsory fast is that of the month of Ramadan, either 29 or 30 days, according to the sighting of the moon. During this month, no food or drink must pass the lips from first light of dawn to sunset, a length of time that varies according to the country one is in, and the season of the year. One must also refrain from cigarettes and cigars, and from all sexual activity during the same times. All the forbidden things are allowed during the hours of darkness (2:187). Women are excused fasting during their menstruation, or if they are pregnant or have just given birth (2:185); they may make up the time later. All children, old and sick people are excused. See Ashurah.

Fatalism. See al-Qadr.

Fate. See al-Qadr.

al-Fath. Title of *surah* 48, 'the Victory'; a Madinan surah of 29 verses, revealed at the time of the Treaty of Hudaybiyyah. The surah was revealed after the Prophet made a lesser pilgrimage to Makkah, and the Makkans decided to oppose their entry by a force led by Khalid ibn al-Walid. The Prophet camped at Hudaybiyyah, where a ten-year truce was drawn up.

al-Fatihah. Lit. 'The Opener.' The opening surah of the Qur'an is used in every compulsory prayer, a Makkan surah of 7 verses.

It is a hymn of praise to Allah, and a prayer for guidance on the right path. The surah is also called Fatihat al-Kitab (The Opening of the Divine Book); Umm al-Kitab (The Essence of the Divine Book); Surat al-Hamd (The Surah of Praise); Asas al-Qur'an (The Foundation of the Qur'an). Elsewhere in the Qur'an it is referred to as as-Sab al-Mathani (The Seven Oft-Repeated Verses). According to Bukhari, the title Umm al-Kitab was given to it by the Prophet himself. Ali claimed it was the first revelation, but it is unmistakably shown that 96:1-5 were the beginning verses of the revelation. Ali may have meant it was the first surah to be revealed to the Prophet entire, and not in sections of verses.

'In the name of Allah, the Compassionate, the Merciful. All praise be to Allah, the Lord or the worlds, the Most Merciful, the Most Kind, Master of the Day of Judgement. You alone do we

Surah al-Fatihah

worship, from You alone do we seek help. Show us the (next step along) the straight path of those earning Your favour. Keep us from the path of those earning Your anger, those who are going astray. (1:1-7)

Fatihah recitations after death. Some Muslims hold gatherings on the third, seventh, tenth, fifteenth or fortieth days after the death of a person, in which passages of the Qur'an are recited and meals served. However, these practices are not compulsory and were not done by the Prophet. They are simply expressions of respect towards the memory of the dead person, and condolence towards the bereaved left behind, and are really matters of culture and not of Islam. It is quite incorrect to imagine that the soul of the departed one will benefit from these gatherings and practices, or that the soul would suffer in some way or be punished if these things were not done. We can always cherish the memory of our deceased, and pray for them—but the intensity or number of our prayers are not the basis on which Allah will judge the soul, and will not affect the extent of His mercy. If a person believes he or she is *more* compassionate or just than Allah and therefore can beg, bribe or influence Him to change His will towards any particular soul, this is really a form of shirk. It is certainly misguided. There is nothing special that happens to the soul of the deceased on these days. See Rawdah, Urs, Qul.

Fatimah. The fourth daughter of the Prophet and Khadijah, and the only one of his children to survive him albeit only for a short while. She married her cousin Ali, and they had four children, the sons Hasan and Husayn, and the daughters Zaynab and Umm Kulthum. She was very like her father in looks and temperament, and much loved. For her sake, the Prophet requested Ali not to take a second wife while she lived, which would have hurt her. After Abu Bakr was elected Caliph her relationship with him was cool—either because of a feud with Aishah, or because Ali had been passed over. Also, he refused to allow her claim to inherit the oasis of Fadak, regarding it as part of the spoils and not the private property of the Prophet's family.

In Shi'ite tradition she represents, the embodiment of all that is perfect in womanhood—'the noblest ideal of human conception.' (Syed Ameer Ali). She died shortly after the Prophet, aged 29, only surviving him by a few months.

Fatimids. A dynasty of rulers in Egypt, claiming descent from the Prophet through Fatimah.

al-Fatir. Title of surah 35, 'the Creator'; a Makkan surah of 45 verses. It calls on believers to remember Allah's generosity, and deals with God's power to create and resurrect.

Fatrat al-wahy. The period between the first and later revelations granted to the Prophet. (See Surahs 96:1-5 and 48:3) The second revelation was probably surah 74, al-Muddaththir, the Enfolded One. The length of this break in the revelation is not known for sure, but was something between 6 months and 3 years. It was a time of distress and doubt for the Prophet; it tempted him to believe his earlier revelation was an illusion. Khadijah's undaunted faith in him gave him strength and hope.

Fatwa (pl. fatawa). The legal guidance of a pious and knowledgable scholar on any matter of Islamic law, based on Qur'an, sunnah and Islamic shari'ah.

Fawz al-Azim. The supreme victory, achievement, attainment of happiness, paradise. All other gains and victories count for nothing.

Feasts. Celebrations in thanksgiving for such things as childbirth, personal triumphs and successes, marriages, and so forth. Two special feasts are celebrated in Islam. See Eid entries.

Female Circumcision. See Khafd.

Fida'i. One who offers up his or her life; a name given to Isma'ilis, particularly to those known as Assassins. The word implies being courageous, brave and undaunted; it can also mean the narrator of heroic deeds or a song about the heroic deeds.

Fidya. Ransom. 2:184, 196 demands a fidya for the omission of certain religious duties (i.e. fasting, pilgrimage). A ransom, compensation paid for rites or prayers missed or wrongly practised in ignorance or through ill health. In some areas of Syria and Jordan it means a sacrifice to protect from misfortune; in Morocco it is a ceremony when a person makes preparations for his or her own burial in advance in order to be freed from punishment in the Afterlife. Both un-Islamic ideas.

al-Fil. Title of surah 105, 'the Elephant'; a Makkan surah of 5 verses referring to the attack on Makkah by the Christian king of Yemen in the year of the Prophet's birth. See Abraha.

Final Sermon. See Sermon, the Last.

Fiqh. Intelligence, knowledge. The study of Islamic law and jurisprudence. Experts in Islamic law are known as Fuqahah.

Firawn. Arabic for Pharaoh of Egypt (69:26). Pharaoh is a title and not a name. It means 'the Great House.' The Pharaoh mentioned in the story of Yusuf (Joseph) (12:43) was apparently one of the six Hyksos rulers who dominated Egypt from c.1700-1580 BC, having invaded Egypt from the Sinai peninsula. The historian Manetho called them the 'Shepherd Kings.' The name Hyksos is derived from 'hiq shasu' or 'heku shoswet' meaning 'rulers of nomad lands.'

The Pharaoh at the time of Musa (Moses) belonged to the 14th Dynasty and was probably Mereneptah, a son of Sethos.

First Cause. Nothing exists at all unless it has been caused. A thing which does exist but might not have done is called 'contingent'. Everything that exists now falls into this category—it is quite possible that the sun, for example, might never have existed. The fact that it does means that it must have been *caused* by something. To say the universe was caused by the Big Bang does not answer the questions—what was it that 'banged', where did it come from, why did it 'bang', and so on. All causes either go on to infinity, which defies the logic of our minds, or there was a First Cause at some time, which lies beyond human understanding. This First Cause religious people, including Muslims, generally recognise to be God (3:47).

Fi Sabili'llah. 'In the way of Allah.'

Fitan. The various crises, cosmic and human, expected as the end of the world approaches.

Fitna. Lit. 'burning,' trial, mischief, temptaton, persecution (7:27; 8:28; 29:2; 51:14). Commonly used in the sense of sedition or political upheaval.

Fitra. The first nature; the natural condition of humanity in harmony with nature.

Five Pillars of Islam. These are the five compulsory duties—Shahadah, Salah, Sawm, Zakah and Hajj.

Flood. See Deluge.

Food laws. See Diet.

Forgiveness. One of the key attributes of Allah. In every surah except one He reveals Himself as the Compassionate, the Merciful. No matter what a person has done, if he or she is genuinely sorry, and truly wishes God to forgive, then God will certainly do so, 'even if'—said the Prophet—'your sins are as great as the earth itself'. What matters is genuine repentance, and making a real effort not to repeat the offence or mistake. God is not fooled by false repentance; and a person should not think they can 'buy off' God's justice with sacrifices and so on (22:37). See Ghadab (Condemnation), Com-passion.

Fostering. See Yatim (orphans).

Fountain. See Kawthar.

Freewill. The fundamental ingredient of human activity, and the most difficult of God's gifts to understand or appreciate. Freewill makes sense of human morality; without it, there is no such thing as good or evil conduct or action, for we would simply be automatons. In Islam, the whole fate of our future life after death is based on the decisions we make with our freewill, and how we respond to conscience, faith and so on. See al-Qadr.

Friend by your side. (Ar. *as-Sahib bi'l janb*, 4:36). According to Ali and many companions this phrase referred to one's wife or husband.

Friendship. All Muslims should be firm, constant and trustworthy, caring for their friends and neighbours and never letting them down. Muslims are advised to choose their friends carefully, for it is all too human to be influenced by the people closest to you, and an ignoble friend might lead you into bad ways (3:28).

Fundamentalism. A word much used and misused by Western media. A fundamentalist is basically a believer who wishes to get back to the fundamentals of the faith. In the case of Islam, it means a Muslim who does not rely on the influence and teaching of others—who may be wrong, or corrupt, or ignorant—but who goes back to the fundamental source, the Qur'an. Every hadith of the Prophet should be measured against the Qur'an; if it does not agree with its principles, it is a false hadith. In Christianity, a fundamentalist has a different sort of meaning, for it describes a believer who goes back to their Holy Book (in their case, the Bible), and believes every word to be literally true, even though modern scientifically-minded people no longer accept the mythology, or the morality of some of the text. Muslims are not required to believe any mythology which is not compatible with science, or logic-defying theology, or morality which does not fit happily with a noble conscience—so their 'fundamentalism' does not imply wilful blindness or simplicity. It really indicates the desire to return to an 'ideal' Islam, of the age of the Rashidun. Many Muslims believe that the Islam of the modern era has been corrupted, and they wish to remove any secularisation. This sometimes engenders hostility towards the West in general. See Falsafa.

Fuqahah. The experts in Islamic law (from 'fiqh').

Fuqara. See Faqir.

Furqan. The Criterion, the distinction between right and wrong (2:53; 3:4; 8:29; 25:1). The faculty of being able to discriminate between what is valuable and what is worthless, between what is fruitful and what is unfruitful, between what is good and what is bad for your self and others. To embody the sunnah and follow the shari'ah. One of the names of the Qur'an is 'Al-Furqan.'

al-Furqan. Title of surah 25, 'the Distinguisher between Good and Evil' or 'the Proof'; a Makkan surah of 77 verses. It is the intention to give humanity a stable criterion to judge between right and wrong, the binding moral values. The major theme is the foolishness of those who do not believe.

Fussilat. Title of surah 41, 'They have been made clear', referring to those verses in the Qur'an which are unambiguous; a Makkan surah of 54 verses, the title based on the words of v. 3. Humanity's reasoned acceptance or wilful rejection of divine revelations.

Gabriel. See Jibril.

Gambling. Some things contain both harm and benefit. If their harm outweighs their benefit, they are haram, or forbidden in Islam.

Gambling may seem harmless fun at first, but it is like a drug leading the gambler into wasting more and more money. (2:219; 5:93). Therefore, such addictive things as casino gambling, card games for money, fruit machines, bingo, and National Lotteries are all *haram*.

Generosity. One of the key qualities in Islam (76:7-10). Muslims should always give, expecting nothing in return except that Allah will be pleased with them (2:264).

Ghadab. The Wrath, or condemnation of God. The evil consequence which people bring on themselves by deliberately acting in a way known to be wrong. (See surah 1:67). They have come to be fully aware of God's message, have understood it, and then rejected it. The Justice of Allah requires that wrongs are put right in some way—and there are many ways of doing this from simple apologies to physical or monetary restriction, and so on. People who sin, or make mistakes, or act weakly, or give in to temptations, will face some consequence for what they have done or not done, but Allah loves everyone of His created beings more than the human parent or teacher loves an erring child or pupil. The evil is hated, not the person. If you put your hand on a red-hot metal bar, it will burn until you remove your hand. If you wilfully refuse to move your hand, the burning consequence will continue.

Ghadir al-Khumm. The name of an oasis between Makkah and Madinah, meaning 'the Pool of al-Khumm.' It was here, after the Final Pilgrimage, that the Prophet raised the hands of Ali and declared that whoever held himself as his master should view Ali in similar fashion. The situation arose because some of the Muslim soldiers had begun to complain about Ali's leadership, finding his puritanical streak somewhat excessive. The Prophet wished to show his support of Ali, and to help less 'extreme' Muslims to tolerate Ali's fastidiousness. (The actual incident involved battle and travel-weary soldiers putting on fresh clothes for their arrival in Makkah; but they borrowed breastokates from spoils they had been ordered not to touch, and Ali made them change back into their original clothes.) Shi'ites interpreted these words as meaning that Ali should have been the Prophet's successor, and he is therefore regarded as their first Imam.

Ghafir. Title of *surah* 40, 'the Forgiver'; a Makkan surah of 85 verses, stressing Allah's unity and power. The surah talks of the false pride of those who are smugly self-satisfied and self-important.

Ghafur. 'All Forgiving.' One of the epithets of Allah in the Qur'an.

Ghani. One who is independent, rich. See 35:15.

Gharaniq. 'The exalted birds,' the title given to the three chief pre-Islamic goddesses of Makkah. Gharaniq were probably literally the Numidian cranes that were believed to fly higher than any other bird—hovering, as it were, between heaven and earth, symbolic of interecessors between God and humanity. In Islam, there are no intercessors between God and His human servants. There were angels and jinn, but the goddess-daughters of Allah were figments of the imagination. (See Satanic Verses, Goddesses). The desire for mediators lingers on as wishful thinking amongst those who venerate saints. Not even angels can intercede (53:26). See Saint.

Gharib. 'Unusual'. It is applied sometimes to the text of a hadith and sometimes to its chain of transmission. Thus it may refer to the only tradition known by a certain line of transmission, although the same tradition may be known by other lines; it may refer to a tradition whose text has only one transmitter. It may also refer to a tradition which comes only from a person who is considered reliable.

Gharur. Self deception, anything that deludes. For example, the self-deluding expectation that God will forgive a sin deliberately and knowingly committed. Anything that deludes could include Shaytan, another human being, an abstract concept (e.g. superior or chosen race) or mere wishful thinking. See Ghadab.

Ghasaq al-Layl. The gathering of night, the dusk between maghrib and 'isha.

al-Ghashiyah. The Overshadowing Event; the title of surah 88, referring to the Day of Resurrection.

Ghawth. A qutb who heals. A granter of requests, usually characterised by vast generosity. See Qutb.

al-Ghayb. The Unknown, aspects of Reality which are beyond human perception. Muslims admit that the known part of God's creation is only a tiny fraction; most of it (whole universes, orders of created beings, and so forth) lies beyond human sensory capacity or awareness or imagination. Included in al-Ghayb are such things as the exact nature of angels and jinn, and personal matters such as knowledge of the time of our individual death, and our future fate (6:59; 7:187; 16:77).

Ghaybah. Occulation, absence, concealment, invisibility. The best known occultation is that of the twelfth Shi'ite Imam, Muhammad al-Qa'im. Twelver Shi'ites say he had two periods of occulation—the first lasting 67 years from 260/874, and the second from 329/941 which will only end with this Imam's re-appearance before the end of the world. See Mahdi, Seveners, Twelvers, Shi'ite, Imam.

Ghayr muwakkada. (or Ghair rawatib)—voluntary prayers not stressed by the Prophet.

Ghayra. This word covers a wide meaning: jealousy as regards women, and also it is a feeling of great fury and anger when one's honour and prestige is injured or challenged.

Ghaznavids. An Islamic dynasty which flourished between 366/977-582/1186. They ruled an area stretching from Khurasan through Afghanistan to Northern India, reaching their peak in the reign of Mahmud (388/998-421/1030). They were overthrown by the Afghan Ghurids in 582/1186. They played an important part in Islamic art and architecture.

Ghazwa, pl. ghazawat. A military expedition.

al-Ghazzali. A famous Muslim scholar (1058-1111), professor of Islamic theology in Baghdad, and Sufi mystic. At first persecuted by Muslim clerics, he eventually convinced them of the soundness of his theology and was one of the leading scholars bringing the two extremes of Sunni orthodoxy and ritualism and mystical awareness and devotion together. Al-Ghazzali tried to reconcile Ash'ari thinking with that of the Mu'tazili. He held that reason and argument should be used to defend right belief derived from Qur'an and hadith against those who denied it. His chief work concerned the intimate relationship between observing Islamic law and theology, and their higher meanings. He criticized the philosophers, accusing them that their God was not the God of the Qur'an This challenge was later met by Ibn rush (Averroes), an Andalusian philosopher.

Ghuluw. Excessiveness, and putting pressure on others to follow excessive acts of piety. Examples include making difficulties for new converts by expecting them to follow all aspects of the Sunnah immediately instead of changing their lives gently; and insisting on such details as correct dress, sitting on the floor, eating with the hands and so on, and feeling superior to those who do not do so. Ironically people of this type are frequently neglectful of fard (compulsory) duties to parents, wives or husbands, children, neighbours etc.

Ghurids. A minor Islamic dynasty which flourished between c390/1000-612/1215. They ruled in

Afghanistan. They were overthrown by the Khawarazm-Shahs.

Ghusl. A full bath or shower to make one ritually clean. Necessary after sexual intercourse, menstruation, childbirth, or contact with dead body (5:7).

al-Gilani (d. 1166). One of the great teachers, a descendant of the Prophet. He came from Gilan in north Persia, but lived and died in Baghdad. He founded the Qadiri Order of Sufis and his followers are spread throughout the Middle East, the Asian subcontinent, Syria, Turkey, the Cameroun, the Congo, Mauritania, Tanzania, and in the Causacus, Chechen and Ferghana in what was the Soviet Union.

Goddesses. Islam denies the existence of any power other than Allah. The pre-Islamic Arabs worshipped many goddesses, including Al-Lat, Al-Uzza and Manat. They had sanctuaries at Makkah, Taif, Petra, etc. Some people considered them to be consorts (wives) or daughters of the Great God, Il-Lah, the Powerful One (6:100; 19:92; 61:57; 53:19-20).

God-trinities were common in the ancient world and were connected with the cycle of fertility of the earth and its seasons. In these trinities there was usually a Father-God (generally symbolized by the Sun), a Mother-God (either the Moon or Venus the Evening Star) and a dying and rising Son of God, who was frequently virgin-born. The Old Testament of the Jews knew these systems by the name 'Baalism'—Baal being the 'master,' the dying and rising one.

Comparisons with Christian theology of a Holy Trinity are obvious, although in Christian theology the Virgin Mother is a human being (see Maryam, Mary), and the second person in the Trinity is called the Holy Spirit. See Satanic Verses, Gharaniq.

Gospel. See Injil.

Gratitude. In the religious sense, this refers to the feeling of thankfulness for being alive, being a living and conscious soul, enjoying God's blessings. This feeling often leads people to the realisation that the gift of life and consciousness is not accidental, and they arive at the 'moment of truth' when they become aware of Divine Presence and Purpose (4:147).

Graves. These should be very simple in Islam, and not luxurious or trying to be impressive or to claim glory for the deceased. On the other hand, they should be obvious so that people do not walk on them. The Prophet recommended a small raised mound with a simple marker at the head. See Burial.

Greed. Disapproved in Islam, in any aspect. One should be moderate in all things—moderate in eating food, and also in one's desire to possess anything.

Green Islam. Humans are expected to be Allah's vicegerents (*khulafah*) in looking after the earth He created. They should not spoil or abuse their environment, but keep it healthy and productive and pleasant. Any spoiling activity (such as pollution, destruction of trees, poisoning of rivers, etc.) or unnatural and unpleasant ways of production (e.g. factory farming) is *haram* (forbidden) in Islam (6:165, 45:12-13).

Greetings. The usual Muslim greeting is 'Salaam alaykum', meaning 'Peace be with you'. The reply is 'Wa-alaykum as-salaam', 'and to you also be peace'.

Guardian angels. Every person has two special angels allotted to be with them throughout life. In the Qur'an, they are called our 'protecting friends' (41:30-32). Their purpose is not so much to guard as to record, but it is a positive record as far as possible. When someone is sorry for wrongdoing, the bad record is wiped out, but the record of good deeds is kept for the Judgement Day. When people feel their conscience being stirred, or have some intuition stopping them doing something, it may well be they are picking up the desire of their guardians to keep them on the right track (41:46; 45:15; 17:13-14).

Ha Mim. Another name for Ha Mim Sajda or al-Fussillat. Surah 41 of the Holy Qur'an.

Hadath. This consists of two parts: (1) Minor—passing wind, stool or urine. Impurity. Requires *Istanja* and *Wudu*. (2) Major—sexual discharge, menstruation and childbirth. Requires Ghusl.

Hadd. Singular of *Hudood*. Boundary limit between the *Halal* (lawful) and *Haram* (unlawful), set by Allah. See Hudood.

Hader. Fast recitation of the Holy Qur'an.

al-Hadi. A cow, sheep or a goat that is offered as a sacrifice by a pilgrim during the Hajj.

al-Hadid. Title of *surah* 57, 'the Iron;' a very late Madinan surah of 29 verses, the title taken from the word in v. 25. It stresses Allah's omnipotence, and the transience of this world. Believe in the Almighty and Eternal God, and live in such a way as will benefit you in the life to come.

Hadith. (pl. ahadith) (news, report) The sayings and teachings of the Prophet, the second source of information for Muslims concerning the right way to live. Everything the Prophet said or did was carefully noted and remembered. Needless to say, in a very short time these reports ran into thousands. Unfortunately, not all are reliable—some were remembered wrongly, misquoted, or even deliberately invented. Pious inventions have caused much confusion for Muslims. The best guideline to 'test' a hadith is to compare it with Quranic teaching. Any hadith which does not agree in principle with the Qur'an cannot be genuine (e.g. 'if you do not grow a beard you cannot go to Paradise'). The Prophet was very concerned about people trying to use his words as an example if not a law, but getting things wrong. He asked them to take great care that nothing should be attributed to him falsely. His best early companions checked meticulously, but others made mistakes. Aishah is known to have corrected several reported early hadith, including those of Abu Hurayrah and Ibn Umar. The practice of desiring to learn lots of them and regarding this as merit was greatly disapproved of by the first Caliphs. If a person *did* record a hadith, he or she had to record also the *isnad* or chain of information—i.e. from whom did that saying come? Collections of sayings of the Prophet written down by his companions during his lifetime or by their immediate successors are called *sahifas.* The earliest surviving work on hadith is the Muwatta of Imam Malik (d. 795). Two collections are regarded as fully authentic—those of Imam Muhammad al-Bukhari (which lists 2762) and Imam Muslim ibn al-Hajjaj (which lists 4000); other reliable collections are those of Abu Dawud, Tirmidhi, ibn Majah, an-Nas'i, Darimi, Darqutni, Ibn Hanbal, ibn Sa'd. Later scholars were eager to compile longer lists, but the early collectors were scrupulous in selecting hadiths and deliberately left out thousands when making their choices. See Mustadrak, Mustakhraj.

Hadith Nabawi. A report transmitted directly from the Prophet.

Hadith Qudsi. (From 'qudus' meaning holy). These are not the sayings of the Prophet, but messages from Allah Himself that were not part of the Qur'an. The Prophet did not *recite* them, but when telling them used his own words and expressions.

Hadra. From 'hudur' (presence); meaning 'being in the presence of Allah'. A term used by mystics. Also used by Ibn Arabi to represent stages of Being. Dervishes call their regular meetings hadra. In this context, the invocation of Allah, usually done standing in dhikr, a practice to increase awareness of the Presence of Allah.

Hadrat. A title of respect for saints, prophets etc.

Hafada. (i) Obedient service or work. (ii) Descendant—son, daughter, grandchild, great-grandchild, etc.

Hafiz. (pl. Huffaz) a person who has learned the entire Qur'an by heart.

Hafsah. The fourth wife of the Prophet. She was the daughter of Umar, and was known to have inherited his fiery temper as well as his intelligence and piety. Her husband died when she was only 18, and the chance to marry her was not seized by either Abu Bakr or Uthman, who claimed that they knew the Prophet wished to marry her himself. It is recorded that she sometimes argued with the Prophet, but he was not offended. She had a keen intellect and learned the Qur'an by heart; when it was written down, it was given into her safe keeping. She lived to be 63.

Hafsids. An Islamic dynasty which flourished between 625/1228-982/1574 in Tunis. Their name came from a companion of the Almohad Ibn Tumart called Abu Hafs Umar. The ruler al-Mustansir (647/1249-675/1277) made a treaty with the Crusaders led by St. Louis, who died in Carthage. On al-Mustansir's death the Hafsid period of tranquillity ended.

Hajar. The Egyptian wife of the Prophet Ibrahim (Genesis 16), the mother of his firstborn son Isma'il (Ishmael). It was she who ran back and forth between the hills Safa and Marwah, in a search for a caravan bearing water. This is now ritualised during the Hajj as the Sa'i.

Hajar al-Aswad (al). The 'Black Stone," a stone which some say fell from heave, set into one corner of the Ka'bah in Makkah by the Prophet Ibrahim (Abraham), peace be upon him, which the pilgrims, in imitation of the Prophet Muhammad, may Allah bless him and grant him peace, kiss, so unifying all the Muslims throughout the ages in one place. See Black Stone.

Hajj. The pilgrimage to the Ka'bah mosque in Makkah and the nearby Mount Arafat, during the 8th to the 13th of the month of Dhu'l Hijjah, the twelfth month of the Islamic calendar. All Muslims are required to try to perform this duty once in their lifetime, provided they have the means to do so, and are physically and mentally fit. Their funds must be honestly acquired, they should not be in debt, and their dependents should be cared for in their absence (2:158, 196-203; 3:97; 5:3; 22:26-33). These moral principles are important. A Muslim who behaved unscrupulously, dishonestly, or ruthlessly in order to claim for himself or herself the benefit of Hajj would actually invalidate his or her Hajj. There are three types of Hajj: (1) Hajjat-Tamata'a (interrupted). Umra followed by Hajj, but taking off the Ihram in between these two stages. (2) Hajj al-Qiran (combined). Umrah and the Hajj without taking off the Ihram. (3) Hajjal-Ifrad (single). Hajj without Umrah. A pilgrimage to Makkah in the twelfth month of the Islamic calendar. See Ihram, Ka'bah, Tawaf, Sa'i, Arafat, Wuquf, Mina, Muzdalifah, Eid ul-Adha.

al-Hajj. The title of surah 22, derived from the references to the pilgrimage and its rituals.

Hajj al-Akbar. The Day of Nahr (i.e. 10th of Dhu'l-Hijjah)

Hajj al-Asghar. Umrah, the smaller or lesser form of Hajj. A pilgrimage done at a time other than the Hajj dates.

Hajj al-Ifrad. 'Hajj by itself,' the simplest way to do the Hajj, in which it is not necessary to do an umrah as well, or to sacrifice an animal or fast instead.

Hajj Mabrur. Hajj accepted by Allah for being perfectly performed according to the Prophet's tradition.

Hajj al-Qiran. The 'joined' Hajj, where the pilgrim does an umrah and then does the Hajj, without changing out of ihram between the two. A person doing the Hajj al-qiran must either sacrifice an animal or fast instead, three days during the time of Hajj, and a further seven days after returning home.

Hajj at-Tamata'a. The 'interrupted' Hajj, where the pilgrim does an umrah and then changes out of ihram until it is time to change back into ihram in order to do the Hajj proper. A person doing the Hajj at-tamata'a must either sacrifice an animal or fast instead, three days during the time of Hajj and a further seven days after returning home.

Hajjat al-Wada'. The final Hajj of the Prophet Muhammad, may Allah bless him and grant him peace. See Pilgrimate, the last.

Hajj by intention. If a Muslim has grown old without being able to perform Hajj for some genuine reason, although they had every intention of doing so, they may pay for another person to go, or make a donation of the equivalent amount to some form of charity. This then counts as their own Hajj. However, this is not to be used as an excuse for someone who *could* do Hajj, but simply cannot be bothered.

Pause for contemplation

The Cave on Mt. Hira where the Prophet Muhammad received his first revelation.

Aerial view of Ka'bah taken before 1980.

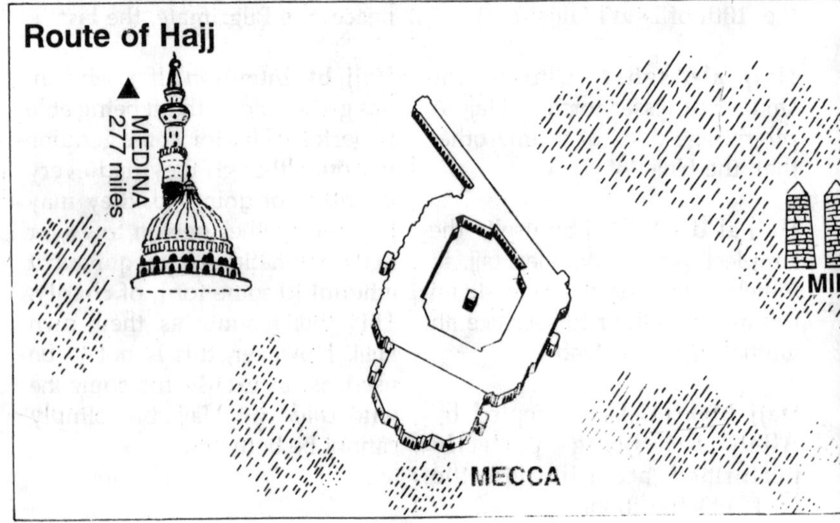

Praying towards the Ka'bah

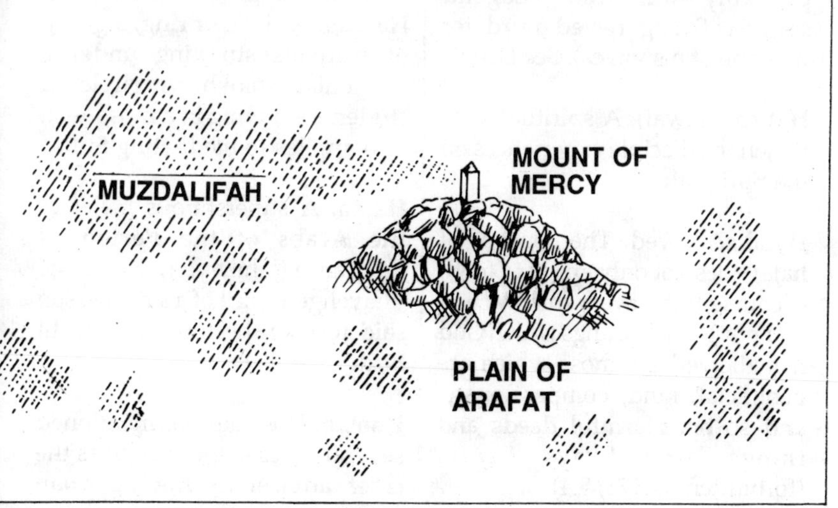

Hajji, Hajjah. The title of a pilgrim who has performed the Hajj.

Hakim. 'All-Wise,' one of the many epithets for Allah in the Qur'an. Also means a wise person, particularly a doctor.

al-Hakim (375/985-411/1021). The 6th Fatimid caliph in Egypt, who succeeded his father at the age of 11. He gained a reputation for madness, which some scholars claim was undeserved. He issued edicts against the Jews and Christians, banned the popular Egyptian food mulukhiyya, killed all the dogs in Cairo, and banned ladies shoes—to prevent women from leaving their homes. On one occasion he ordered his troops to burn al-Fustat. Towards the end of his life he was led to believe that he was divine, and disappeared in the hills of Muqattam, where he was probably murdered. (Legend suggests the aggrieved murderer was one of his wives). See Druze.

Hal (pl. ahwal). A spiritual state which the disciple experiences on the Sufi path.

Halal. Allowed. The concept of halal does not only apply to food, of course, but to every sort of action and matter. The things which God has allowed are those which are beneficial, kind, compassionate, and so on. Harmful deeds and things are always haram (forbidden) (2:173; 5:4).

Halimah bint Abu Dhu'ayb. The foster mother and wet nurse of the Prophet for the first two years of his life. She belonged to the Banu Sa'd ibn Bakr, a branch of the Hawazin tribe.

al-Hallaj, al-Husayib ibn Mansur (244/857-309/922). A famous Persian mystic accused of heresy and executed by the establishment because of his frequent shocking outbursts expressing his inner intoxication and union with God. His utterances, actual and alleged, provoked much controversy. The best known was the phrase 'Ana'l Haqq—'I am the (Divine) Truth.' He was crucified in Baghdad. He believed the highest rank of piety was such humility and love of God that all thoughts of self ceased to exist; the greatest achievement was a mystical union or oneness with God. His critics regarded this as blasphemy and arrogance.

Halqah. A circle or ring; a group of students studying under a particular shaikh. A circle of students studying in a mosque. It also applies to meditating Sufis.

Hama. A superstitious belief of the Arabs of the Period of Ignorance (Jahiliyyah). It was the unavenged spirit of a slain person said to take the form of a night bird.

Haman. This man was mentioned several times in the Qur'an as the chief adviser of the Egyptian

Pharaoh. Critics of Islam have used this as a 'proof' of the 'ignorance' of the Prophet and his 'garbled knowledge' of Judaism, Christianity and the Bible in general—for in the Old Testament (Esther 3ff) Haman is a Persian official from another place and another time. However, the Haman of the Qur'an is not a proper name, but the Arabicized version of Ha-Amen, the title of the high priest of the Egyptian god Amon. The Pharaoh asked Haman in 28:38 and 40:36-37 to build him a lofty tower—this may be a reference to the great pyramids and the function of the high priest as their architect.

Hamanids. An Islamic dynasty ruling in Aleppo and elsewhere in the 4th/10th century. It reached its peak with Sayf al-Dawla (r. 333/944-356/967), whose court was famous for its poets, scholars and writers, including the great philosopher al-Farabi and the poet al-Mutanabbi.

Hamd. Lit. 'praised', glory, glorification. The word is included in the name Muhammad, meaning 'the praised one,' and the phrase 'al-hamdu lillah' meaning 'praise be to Allah'—the response polite Muslims usually use when something good happens.

al-Hamdu lillah. 'All thanks be to Allah,' an expression of gratitude and awareness of Allah's blessings. It is also used to express modesty, as a Muslim would say this when complimented for something (see Hamd).

Hamzah ibn Abd al-Muttalib (d. 3/625). Famous uncle of the Prophet and brother of Safiyyah. He was younger than the Prophet, one of the sons of Abd al-Muttalib born in his old age, and he was a companion of the Prophet from the cradle. He grew up to be a warrior famous for his strength and courage. When the Prophet first commenced his ministry, Hamzah was not convinced—but one day he was told how Abu Jahl had sneered at the Prophet and spoken badly about him. He leapt to the Prophet's defence, and declared he had become Muslim too. He became known as the 'Lion of God.' The Battle of Badr commenced with single combat, and the champion Hamzah killed Utbah ibn Rabi'ah, the father of Abu Sufyan's wife Hind. He also killed two of her sons in the ensuing battle, and she swore that one day she would eat his liver. Hamzah was killed in the next battle (Uhud), and the savage Hind not only chewed a morsel of his liver but also mutilated his corpse.

Hanif. A devout person, who believed in One True God at a time before the revelation of the Qur'an, when it was normal to worship many gods and idols. Derived from the verb, hanafa 'to incline' and it means those who turned away from sin and worldliness. There were four famous hanifs—Waraqah ibn Nawfal, who became a Christian; Ubaydallah ibn Jahsh, who became a Christian; Zayd ibn Amr, the half-brother of Umar's father Khattab; and Uthman ibn al-Huwayrith, who also became a Christian. See Tahannuf.

Haqiqah. Inner reality, truth, science of the 'inward'. From haqqa, to be true, right, just, authentic, valid, and haqaqa, to make something come true.

Haqiqat. The realities, the inward illuminations of knowledge which flood the heart of the seeker. The realm of meanings, the science of the 'inward.'

Haqiqi. The practice of combining two of the compulsory prayers together at the same time; permissible when circumstances are very difficult, as when one is on a journey.

Haqq. Truth, rightness, justice, the state of being just, proper, right, correct or valid.

al-Haqqah. Title of surah 69, 'the Inevitable' or 'the Calamity'; a Makkan surah of 52 verses, whose major theme is the Day of Judgement.

Haram. (i) A thing or matter or action which is forbidden (2:173; 5:4) by the shariah. (ii) a protected area, an inviolable place or object. (iii) a protected area in which certain behaviour is forbidden and other behaviour necessary; for example, the areas around the Ka'bah in Makkah and the Prophet's tomb in Madinah.

Haram Sherif. The Noble Sanctuary—the Grand Mosque in Makkah which encompasses the Ka'bah, the hills of Safa and Marwah, and the well of Zam-Zam.

Haramayn. The two Harams, of Makkah and Madinah.

Harun. The Prophet Aaron, brother of Moses (Musa) (19:53). His grave is on a mountain-top at Petra in Jordan (Mt. Hor in Numbers 20:22-29 and Jabal Harun in local parlance). The Qur'an presents him as a sincere prophet who did not encourage his people to worship an idol of a golden calf (7:150; 20:94).

Harut and Marut. Two angels who saw human sinners and were contemptuous to them. Allah proved to them that if they were put in the same position, they would do no better (2:102). They got sent to earth as an experiment, and were ordered to abstain from idolatry, whoredom, murder and drinking wine. They fell for the latter, thinking it no very great sin, and then promptly committed the other three sins.

Harun al-Rashid (149/766-193/809). The 5th and most famous Abbasid caliph, around whom much legend accumulated as the result of such works as 'The Thousand and One Nights'. He spent most of his rule fighting, away from his capital Baghdad.

Hasad. Jealousy. This is not a suitable feeling for a Muslim, except perhaps to be jealous of one who can memorise the Qur'an, or be able to do good for the sake of Allah.

Hasan. 'Approved'. A hasan tradition is like a *Sahih* tradition except for the fact that some of its narrators are found to have a defective memory in comparison to the narrators of *Sahih* hadith.

Hasan. Grandson of the Prophet, the eldest son of Fatimah and Ali. The Shi'at Ali (Shi'ites, or supporters of Ali's claim to be the successor to the Prophet) hoped that Hasan would become Caliph after his father, instead of Abu Sufyan's son Mu'awiyah—but he died suddenly. It is claimed that he was poisoned. Mu'awiyah's son Yazid became the heir.

Hasan. An adjective describing a married person, from the noun hisn, a fortress. A person who has been made hasan by marriage (muhsan) incurs the full hadd punishment for illicit sexual relations.

Hasan al-Askari (230/844-260/874). The 11th Shi'ite Imam. Born in Madinah, he lived a restricted life in the army camp (askar) of Samarra, imprisoned by the Caliph al-Mu'tamid, who is believed to have poisoned him. He married a slave-girl Narjis (or Saqil), who was the mother of the 12th Imam.

Hasba. A place outside Makkah where pilgrims go after finishing all the ceremonies of Hajj.

al-Hashr. Title of surah 59, 'the Gathering' or 'the Exile'; a Madinan surah of 24 verses; it mainly concerns to the conflict between the Muslims and the Jewish tribe of Banu Nadir Jewish/Muslim relations.

al-Hashr. A name of the Prophet, may Allah bless him and grant him peace, meaning the Gatherer, before whom people are gathered on the Day of Gathering (Yawm al-Hashr).

Hawari. Apostle, a word derived from Ethiopic. Zubayr ibn al-Awwam was known as al-Hawari. The collective name al-Hawariyun was used for 12 people oppointed as naqibs of the Madinese at the 'Second Aqabah' gathering. The tradition maybe referred to 3:52 and 41:14.

Hauz. The Indian word for the ablutions tank in the courtyard of a mosque.

Hawala. The transference of a debt from one person to another. It is an agreement whereby a debtor is released from a debt by another becoming responsible for it.

al-Hawiya. The Abyss, Chasm, or bottomless pit, one of the layers in Hell. Tradition later consigned the hypocrites to this layer.

Haya. Modesty in clothing, manners and way of life.

Hayd. Hayd, or menstruation, is the natural process Allah created for women in order for them to produce an egg that could be fertilized by male sperm to become a new human being. The process is called ovulation, and the normal period is to ovulate once a month. If the woman's egg is not fertilized, it leaves her womb and is ejected, along with the lining of the womb and a variable amount of blood. A woman in this condition is called Hayz. While menstruating (bleeding) women are excused from performing salah and from fasting—although they should make up the fast-days later on. When the flow stops, ghusl should be performed. While Hayz, a woman should not touch the Qur'an, or have full sexual intercourse with her husband. Husbands, however, are encouraged to be kind and considerate, and may enjoy all caresses of their wives that do not make them unclean by contact with the blood.

Heaven. Paradise, Jannah. The place of reward in the Afterlife for those accepted and forgiven by Allah. Descriptions are given in detail in the Qur'an (e.g. Surahs 37:43-48; 38:52; 43:70; 48:5; 56:17-26 etc.), but most scholars take the point of view that these are to be interpreted symbolically, since the Qur'an states clearly that the true nature of the Afterlife lies beyond human knowledge and understanding (Surah 32:17; 56:60-61).

Hegira. See Hijrah.

Hell. The place of punishment in the Afterlife, described as a terrible, scorching, place of torment, sorrow and remorse (e.g. Surahs 5:72-73; 14:16-17; 38:55-58; 43:74-76; 56:42-44; 80:33-42; 84:1-19). The descriptions are detailed, but most scholars interpret them symbolically (Surah 32:17; 56:60-61). The idea of harsh punishment seems hard to reconcile with God's mercy, but it is clear that no-one will be condemned to Hell unless absolutely determined to ruin himself or herself (Surahs 16:61; 92:14-16).

Henna and hair-dye. There is nothing specific about prohibiting or discouraging the use of henna as a red or black dye. Katam is a similar substance which may be used. There is no harm in using such stuffs to enhance personal appearance, but it should never be used in order to give a false and misleading impression. In the days of Caliph Umar a girl was married to a man who had dyed his hair to make himself appear much younger than he really was. Umar ruled the marriage null and void.

Hidayat. The guidance of Allah. Allah knows all and sees all, and is witness to all our tests and strugglings. He guides whom He pleases to the right path (2:142,213; 4:175; 5:18; 6:39; 10:25; 22:54; 24:46), and leaves to stray whom He wills (7:155; 13:27; 14:4; 16:93; 35:8; 74:31). He does not guide unjust people (qaum az-zalimin —2:258; 3:86; 5:54; 6:144; 9:19,109; 28:50; 46:10; 61:7; 62:5) or unbelieving people (qaum al-kafirun—2:264; 5:70; 9:37; 16:107), or people who insist on committing sins (qaum al-fasiqin —5:111; 9:24,80; 61:5; 63:6). His is the only true guidance, and whoever accepts His guidance is not led astray. If it had been His will, He could have forced His guidance on all people, but He does not force, He allows us the use of our free will (6:35,149; 13:31; 16:9; 32:139).

Hidden Imam. The Shi'ites divided into two major branches, according to whether they believed in seven or twelve Imams. In each group, it is claimed that the last Imam mysteriously disappeared without dying, and lives on in a mystical way, guiding the faithful in their times of need. He will reappear one day to establish righteous rule at the era which will see the end of the world. See Ghaybah, Mahdi.

Hifazat. This is the power of Allah to guard and protect. Allah is the Best Guardian, and Most Merciful of the Merciful (12:64). He sets angels over every individual to warn, guard and protect, according to His will (6:61; 13:11; 42:6; 82:10; 86:4).

Hijab. (literally: barrier, cover, veil). The original hijab was a curtain which the Prophet put up to separate an area in his wives' houses where they could be in private (33:53). The hijab of women's clothing is not to put on a kind of 'uniform,' but to dress modestly, in such a way as the outline of the female body is not visible. This is intended to reduce potential attraction between men and women who are not intending to be marriage partners. Inner hijab refers to the attitude of modesty, the intent not to arouse (Surah 24:30-31; 33:59). Both outer and inner aspects are characteristic of Muslim women; one aspect is meaningless without the other. The word is often used these days to refer to a head-scarf, but this is not its real meaning.

A famous hadith refers to the Prophet stating that after puberty a woman should only show 'this and this' in public. He pointed to his face and his hands. However, the Qur'an passage 24:31 does not mention covering the *head* but 'veiling one's gaze,' and referred to both men and women. Women were required to cover their bodies modestly. When the Prophet pointed to his face, one could argue equally he was pointing his *head* and not just his face.

Head-veils were normal dress for women of the Prophet's time, but they were often worn decoratively and not modestly. The verse in 24:31 asked Muslim women to use them to cover their bosoms which were often carelessly revealed by women involved in suckling children. Face veils were worn by high-ranking ladies in several cultures as a point of pride and superiority—the very opposite modesty.

The real hijab was for women to be modest, and to dress modestly, and make sure their bodies were decently covered.

The recommendation for a head-veil is like the recommendation for a beard. They are recommended, but not compulsory. What is compulsory is for women not to wear skin-tight or transparent clothing, or to breast-feed their babies in front of strangers.

Hijaz. The region along the western seaboard of Arabia, in which Makkah, Medinah, Jeddah and Ta'if are situated.

Hijr. The semi-circular unroofed enclosure at one side of the Ka'bah, whose low wall outlines the shape of the original Ka'bah built by the Prophet Ibrahim, peace be on him. It marks the burial place of Hajar and Isma'il, the wife and son of the Prophet Ibrahim. It was the place where the Prophet's grandfather, Abd al-Muttalib, the guardian of the Ka'bah, used to have a special couch to sleep on. The Prophet himself was asleep here when he experienced the Laylat al-Miraj.

al-Hijr. The name of a region in Arabia mentioned in surah 15:80, and used as the title of this surah, which belongs to the Makkan period and has 99 verses. It is a place name, and not ust a 'rocky tract.' The town of Hegra was mentioned by Ptolemy, and by Pliny as Egra. The surah describes, among other things, the disobedience of Iblis, who is described as 'stoned' or 'cursed' ('rajim').

Hijrah. (Lit. exodus or going out). Derived from hajara (to migrate). It is used in two sense in the Qur'an. Firstly, it refers to the historical emigration of the Prophet and his Companions from Makkah to Madinah. The year, 622, is regarded as Year 1 in the Muslim calendar.

Secondly, it has a moral meaning—that of the migration of a human being from evil towards God. This obviously does not imply leaving one's homeland in the physical sense—although this is suggested as a good idea if one was living in evil circumstances or surroundings (4:97). Personal hijrah involves both physical and moral effort, maybe even the sacrifice of one's possessions or even one's life.

The hijrah from Makkah to Madinah was strongly advised for all believing Muslims up to the year 8 AH (630 AD), when Makkah was conquered and re-created as a Muslim city. The spiritual exodus from evil to righteousness is still demanded from Muslims. (See Ansar, Muhajirun). Those who do not attempt to migrate from evil unto God are not taking their beliefs seriously.

Hilal. The crescent, new or half moon. A symbol frequently found on domes and minarets. It was of significance because it signalled the start and finish of Ramadan, and other months.

Hilf al-Fudl. An order or chivalry founded while the Prophet was a youth, whose object was to protect the weak and oppressed, and bring about justice. The chief of Taym (Abdallah ibn Ju'dan) gave his house as headquarters, and the Prophet's uncle Zubayr was a founder member. The members made a pact at the Black Stone. Muhammad went to join along with Abu Quhafah of Taym and his son Abu Bakr. He said later: 'I was present at so excellent a pact that I could not exchange my part in it for a herd of red camels; and if now, in Islam, I were summoned unto it, I would gladly respond.'

Hilm. The forbearance and clemency of Allah. If Allah were to punish us as we deserve, not a single living creature would be left alive. (16:61; 18:58; 35:45)

Hikmah. Wisdom and tact.

Himma. Yearning. It is the heart's yearning that urges the seeker to find the goal, Allah.

Hima. A pre-Islamic institution by means of which the chief of a tribe took a pasture for his animals, preventing others from grazing their animals in it while he himself could graze his animals in the others' pasture. Islam cancelled such an institution and allowed it for Zakat animals only.

Hind. The wife of Abu Sufyan. For her story, see the entry on Hamzah. She finally accepted Islam, but never lost her fiery temperament or bold outspokenness.

Hisham (72/691-125/743). The 10th Umayyad caliph, their last able ruler before the Abbasid Revolution. During his rule the Arabs reached the end of their advance into Europe, being stopped by Charles Martel at the battle of Poitiers in 114/732.

Hiyal (sing. hila). Devices, tricks, ruses, subterfuges. In law, the term means legal stratagems which often frustrated the intention and spirit of the law. The term became particularly associated with the Hanafi schools, but was condemned by the Malikis and Hanbalis.

Hizb. A word with several meanings, the most important being a prayer of particular efficacy. An example is the Hizb al-Bahr ('Prayer of the Sea') of al-Shadhili, often sung in Sufi hadras. This prayer is much favoured by sailors, and was used by Ibn Battuta at the start of his 'Rihla.' (ii) It is also used to mean a 60th part of the Qur'an.

Hizb Allah (Hezbollah). The Party of God, the name of a major fundamentalist Shi'ite organisation, founded after the 1979 revolution in Iran.

Holy War. See Jihad.

Homosexuality. Sexual intercourse between members of the same sex. This is forbidden in Islam (26:165-166; 4:16-18) as is all sex outside marriage.

Many societies of the past practised homosexuality openly, notably the Greeks and Romans. However, it is worth stressing that love of people for members of the same sex is not the same thing as physical, homosexual relationships. Men who made love to boys were generally despised as being debauched and corrupt.

In this century, research is now in progress as to the causes of homosexuality. People may have hormonal or genetic reasons for being homosexual; cases arise of people feeling they are men trapped in a female body or vice versa. Where there is some factor in the creation of a homosexual that is not at all the fault of the person involved, they cannot be blamed for their characteristics and inclinations, and should be treated with compassion.

However, in Islam these matters are regarded as something to be cured if possible, and not just accepted as normal. Where men and women prefer members of their own sex physically as a result of distaste for, fear of, or disappointment with the other sex, this is a matter which should be looked into to discover the causes, and find solutions.

Honesty. To always tell the truth, and act openly and according to a reliable code of conduct. One of the key virtues in Islam. One should be able to trust a Muslim to be absolutely honest in all dealings.

Horse-riding. This is permissible for women, as for men, so long as their clothing is acceptable from an Islamic point of view. It is not forbidden for a woman to ride astride a horse.

Hospital. It is always preferable in Islam for invalids to be treated by doctors of the same sex. Muslims face several practical problems in western hospitals; they may not have a choice of doctor, they may not be offered halal food, they may not have the privacy they are used to; and if death occurs they may be surrounded by regulations that break Muslim traditions—such as allowing relatives to wash the body as quickly as possible in a particular manner, and for the burial to take place speedily.

Hospitality. Being generous to guests and visitors. One of the key Muslim virtues. Muslims should be generous to all people, no matter whether Muslim or non-Muslim. If a guest arrives, it is considered courteous to offer full hospitality for a period of up to three days. After that, a guest should not put a host into difficulties as regards being paid for (2:254, 261, 274).

Houri. See Huri.

Howliya. A very large gathering of dhikr attended by several shaykhs.

Hubal. An idol worshipped in the Ka'bah at Makkah before the Prophet cleansed it. One of the major idols of Arabia.

Hud. (i) Said to have been the first Arabian Prophet (see 7:65). He may be identical with the Biblical Eber, the ancestor of the Hebrews (Ibrim), who probably originated in South Arabia. (See Genesis 10:24-25 and 11:14). The ancient Arabic name is reflected in that of Jacob's son Judah (Yahudah). The name Eber (Ar. Abir) signifies 'one who crosses over' and may echo the fact that this tribe crossed from Arabia to Mesopotamia. (ii) Title of surah 11, the proper name of a prophet sent to the 'Ad tribe; it is a Makkan surah of 123 verses, on the theme of Allah's revelation through Prophets and gives the story of Hud.

Hudaybiyyah. A plain outside Makkah where the Prophet made camp and offered sacrifice when a force led by Khalid ibn al-Walid refused him entry to Makkah for pilgrimage. They expected to have to fight to the death, but took a pledge of allegiance. The Makkan truce was the first peaceful contact between Makkah and Madinah after the Hijrah.

Hudood. Plural of 'hadd'; it means the limits imposed by God, and is usually used to refer to the punishments laid down in the Qur'an for specific crimes such as theft and adultery (5:41; 17:32; 24:2-5)

Hadd punishment is meant to be a deterrent so that people may not become complacent and commit crimes simply because they find the punishment so trivial (a situation common in the west). However, the judge must make sure that the crime was definitely

Al-Hudaybiyah, where a historic peace treaty was signed which was called by the Qur'an an "obvious victory".

committed—if there is the slightest doubt, he should refrain from giving the hadd punishment. The Prophet said: 'As far as possible, refrain from awarding hadd punishments to a Muslim. If there is found slight excuse (or doubt), leave him/her alone—because it is better for the judge to err in acquitting the accused rather than erring in awarding punishment' (Tirmidhi; Mishkat, Kitab al-Hudud).

Hujjah. 'Proof' from Allah; a designation for the Shi'ite Imams; also used by Sunnis to refer to certain great scholars.

al-Hujr al-Aswad. Arabic name for the Black Stone set in the Ka'bah shrine. See Black Stone.

Hujurah. The place where Prophet was buried beneath the floor of Aishah's room.

al-Hujurat. Title of surah 49, 'the Rooms' or 'Private Apartments'; a Madinan surah of 18 verses. The title comes from a reference in v. 4 to the Prophet's rooms adjacent to the Mosque in Madinah. It deals with social ethics, the principle of the single family of all believers, and all humanity.

Hullah. A shroud made of a single sheet of cloth.

Human rights. Human rights in Islam include such things as the right to life, equality, freedom, freedom of speech, political freedom, justice, social welfare and the basic necessities of life, education.

al-Humazah. The Slanderer; the title of surah 104, referring to those who try to find real or imaginary faults in others. It is a Makkan surah of 9 verses.

Hums. The tribe of Quraysh, their offspring and their allies were called "Hums". This word implies enthusiasm and strictness. The Hums used to say, "We are the people of Allah". They thought themselves superior to the other people.

Hunayn. Site of an important battle which took place at this oasis on the route from Makkah to Taif, between the tribes of Huwazin and Thaqif against the Prophet in 8/630. It was the first battle when the Prophet's troops were led by Khalid ibn al-Walid.

Hunting. In Islam, hunting should not be done merely for sport. If one takes the life of an animal, one must intend to eat it, or take some other benefit from it. Anything killed without just cause will have to be accounted for on the Day of Judgement. Hunting is totally forbidden while in the state of ihram (5:2, 98). Weapons used for hunting should be those that pierce or are sharp, such as arrows, knives, spears and bullets, and not blunt instruments such as clubs or stones.

All hunting is prohibited in the vicinity of the Ka'bah—that is, within the precincts of Makkah and its surrounding districts, because it is a sanctuary for all living beings (2:125; 5:97).

Hunut. A kind of scent for embalming the dead.

Huri. Surahs 37:48, 38:52 and 55:56 describe the new 'mates' or spouses of the people of Paradise, as being of modest gaze, most beautiful of eyes, as if they were hidden eggs. The expression *qasirat at-tarf* (such as restrain their gaze) appears chronologically for the first time in the revelation of 38:52. According to Zamakshari, the 'hidden eggs' refers to an ancient Arabian figure of speech derived from the habit of the female ostrich, which buries its eggs for protection.

In 56:34 it is made clear that all righteous women, no matter what their age and condition at the time of their deaths, will be resurrected 'made new,' in beautiful and youthful heavenly bodies.

In 38:52, the 'well-matched mates' applies not just to females but to the righteous of either sex, who in the life to come will be reunited with those they loved on earth (see 9:72; 4:124; 16:97 and 40:40). In surah 36:56 we are told that in Paradise they and their spouses will recline on couches, in peace and fulfilment with one another.

This idea is also suggested in 56:34 where 'bed' or 'couch' is often used in classical Arabic idom to refer to one's wife or husband. The 'spouses raised high' are identical to the hur mentioned in v. 22 as well as 44:54; 52:20 and 55:72.

The term huri appears in 56:22—pure companions. It is a plural of both ahwar (masc) and hawra (fem), either of which means 'a person distinguished by hawar'—white eyeballs and intensely black irises of the eye. Sometimes 'hawar' just means 'whiteness' or 'purity.' See also 52:20; 44:54.

Most of the earliest commentators took it to mean the righteous Muslim women whom God would resurrect as new beings (e.g. Al-Hasan al-Basri, Tabari). In 44:54 the noun 'zawj' (lit. a pair) applies to either of the sexes, as does the transitive verb 'zawaja'—'he paired' or 'joined' one person with another.

Sadly for those misguided Muslim men who think otherwise, it does not mean that after a saintly life-time of sexual control and denial of rampant passions, men who arrive in Paradise will be suddenly endowed with enormous sexual prowess and appetites, which they will be allowed to satiate on beautiful untouched heavenly virgins created just for that purpose! What, do they imagine, would happen to all such virgins once used (abused) in this manner? And what about their poor wives and loved ones of the female sex who made it to Paradise?

Husayn. The second son of the Prophet's daughter Fatimah and Ali. He refuse to acknowledge Yazid the son of Mu'awiyah as Caliph. He left Makkah and took the road to Kufa but Yazid's appointed governor of Iraq—Ubaydallah ibn Ziyad—had cavalry patrolling the roads. Husayn's supporters were surrounded at Karbala, where access to the Euphrates was cut off, to make them surrender through thirst. On 10th Muharram, 61 AH (10th October 680) he was defeated and killed. The celebrations of the 10th Muharram are held in his honour in Shi'ite societies. See Ashurah.

Husayniyyat. Places of Shi'ah worship or halls for the performance of religious dramas commemmorating the death of Husayn.

Husayn Taha (1306/1889-1393/1973). An Egyptian literary critic, novelist and scholar, one of the most prominent literary figures of the 20th century in the Arab world. Although he went blind at the age of two, he obtained doctorates from both Cairo and the Sorbonne in Paris.

Husband's rights. In Islam, a husband has the right to sexual fulfilment (so long as his wife is not ill or otherwise unavailable through no fault of her own); if she is 'not in the mood' a polite man will wait, or try to put her in the mood, and not attempt force! However, if a wife refuses her husband, she must remember that the agreement to satisfy each other is an important part of the contract that denies sex outside marriage to either partner. A husband also has the right to discretion, faithfulness, and obedience so long as his requests are in accordance with God's will.

Husn. Beauty; this includes not only physical beauty—for the interpretation of this is always 'in the eye of the beholder'—but also the rightness and proper development of any thing or person in the fitness of what they are supposed to be, in God's design. For example, we may think a wrinkled, smelly wart-hog to be an ugly thing—but if it is mature and healthy and fulfilling the role in nature it is intended to fulfil, it is full of husn.

al-Hutamah. That which shatters, wrecks or smashes. One of the seven layers of Hell, the word occurring only twice in the Qur'an.

Hypocrisy. Pretence, claiming to be what one is not. This is quite pointless in Islam, as it may be possible to fool human observers, but it is never possible to fool God (2:9-20, 44: 9:64-65). See Munafiq.

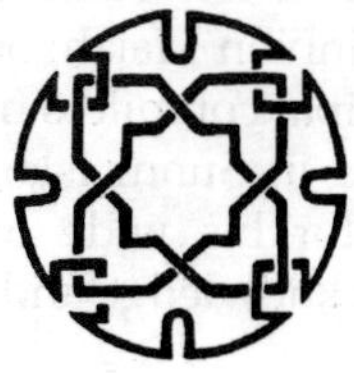

Ibadah. From 'Abd a servant, meaning the concept of worship, servanthood, being a servant of God. It does not just mean prayer, but any permissible action with the intention of serving Allah.

Ibadis. Members of a branch of the Kharijites, named after their founder Abdullah ibn Ibad, a Kharijite leader. They are a moderate wing of the Kharijites. Today there are Ibadis in Oman, East Africa and North Africa.

Iblis. Iblis is the name given to the jinn in 7:11 who refused to prostrate himself before Adam at God's command when the angels did. The passage is taken by some scholars to indicate that Iblis was one of the angels, but this is contradicted by all other references that call him a jinn and also by the next verse (7:12) where he is stated to have been created from fire (a feature of jinn and not angels). (38:76)

Western scholars often assume that the name Iblis is a corruption of the Greek word 'diabolos,' from which the English 'devil' is derived. However, it is more likely that the Greeks derived their concept from the much earlier South-Arabian civilisation.

'Iblis' is derived from the verb 'ablasa', 'he despaired' or 'gave up hope' or 'became broken in spirit.' See Shaytan.

Ibn Abbas (619-686 AD) a much revered recorder of hadiths. He was Abdullah, the third son of Abbas.

Ibn Anas. See Malik.

Ibn Arabi (d. 1240). A great philosopher of Andalus, known as the Shaykh al-Akbar. He was possibly the greatest exponent of Islamic metaphysics, and his works include the monumental 'Makkan Revelations' and 'the Seals of Wisdom', still used by many serious students of Islam. His teachings were later transmitted by such as Al-Jili, Imam Shadhili, Jalal ud-Din Rumi and Mulla Sadra. He formulated a detailed vision of the universe as an endless flow of existence from and returning to the Divine Creator. He explained the unity of being, that all created beings were manifestations of the particular attributes of God through the mediation of images, while human beings were capable of manifesting these realities. He put forward the idea of the perfect, complete, human. This all drew considerable criticism from the ulama, especially from Ibn Taymiyah.

Ibn Battuta (d. 1378). A Muslim famous for his extensive travels, from Tangier to Sumatra. He wrote copious travelogues, and is nicknamed the Arab Marco Polo.

Ibn Gabirol (c.411/1021-c.45/1058). A Jewish Spanish philosopher who is known in the West as Avicebron. He was a major exponent of Neoplatonism from the Hispano-Arab philosophy school and wrote in both Hebrew and Arabic.

Ibn Hazm (384/994-456/1064). A Mediaeval Spanish theologian, jurisprudent and moralist, one of the foremost of the Zahiri or 'Literalist' school of Law.

Ibn Ishaq (c.85/704-c.150/767). He collected materials for a 'Life' of the Prophet, which were then edited into their most popular form by Ibn Hisham (d. 218/833). The 'Kitab Sirat Rasul Ullah' is regarded as one of the earliest and therefore most important of all sources for the life of the Prophet.

Ibn Khaldun (732/1332-808/1406). One of the best-known Arabo-Islamic figures in the West, a great sociologist and historian born in Tunis. He was the qadi of Cairo and had a famous meeting with Tamburlaine. His best known work is his 'Muqaddima' or 'Introduction' to history; his theory was cyclical—a nomad tribe comes to power, becomes corrupt and luxurious and is overthrown.

Ibn Majah (c.209/824-c.273/887). Full name Abu Abdullah Muhammad ibn Yazid al-Raba'i al-Qazwini ibn Majah; one of the six principal compilers of Islamic traditions in Sunni Islam. He is famous for his wide travels in search of knowledge and genuine hadith.

Ibn Rushd (c.520/1126-c.595/1198). Known in the West as Averroes, he was Spain's greatest Hispano-Arab philosopher, and most notable commentator or Aristotle. He held the post of qadi in Seville and Cordoba, but was sometimes accused of being false in theology. See Falsafa.

Ibn Sina (c.369/979-c.428/1037). Known in the West as Avicenna, he was a great Spanish Islamic Neoplatonist philosopher, an eminent Muslim thinker, poet, doctor, scientist and philosopher. He was born in Afghanistan, and was said to have been the most knowledgeable and gifted person of his age. He explained the digestive system, and was an expert in bacteriology. He wrote major works on medicine and metaphysics, and his most famous work was the 'Book of the Cure' (Kitab al-Shifa'). He died in Hamadan.

He articulated the truth of Islam according to Aristotelian logic and Greek metaphysics. Central to his thought was the assumption that human reason could ultimately lead to the attainment of truth. He referred to the Divine Light by which a person was able to attain higher understanding.

Ibn Taymiyah (c.661/1263-c.728/1328). Distinguished Hanbali jurist and theologian, whose literalist interpretations form the bedrock of Wahhabi doctrine. He argued along the line that humans could only draw near to God by simple and literal obedience of His commands. (See Wahhabism). He was born in Harran and taught and died in Damascus. He was important for maintaining that the gate of ijtihad should remain open.

Ibn Tufayl, Abu Bakr (d. 581/1185). He was a Hispano-Arab philosopher, known in the West as Abu Bacer. His epistle 'Hayy ibn Yaqzan' provided the model for Defoe's novel 'Robinson Crusoe.'

Ibn Tulun (c.220/835-c.270/884). Founder of an important dynasty in Egypt, the Tulunids. Egypt prospered under his rule. He came to Egypt as a deputy for the Abbasids, but carved out his own power base. The Tulunids were eventually overthrown by the Abbasid caliph's general in 292/905. Ahmad Ibn Tulun was famous for building the great mosque in Cairo which bears his name, and has a unique spiral minaret, allegedly modelled on that of the great mosque of Samarra.

Ibrahim. Title of surah 14, named after the Prophet; it is a Makkan surah of 52 verses, and makes considerable reference to the Prophet Ibrahim.

Ibrahim. Known in the Bible as Abraham. A tribal shaykh from Ur in Mesopotamia, who became known as 'al-Khalil'—the Friend of God. Called by Allah to reject the Sun and Moon idol worship of his family and tribe, he smashed their statues and proved they were powerless (21:51-71). Under Allah's guidance, he then left his homeland for a lifetime of wandering. He prayed for the gift of a righteous son, and his Egyptian wife Hajar gave birth to Isma'il (37:100-101). His other wife, Sarah was childless. Idol-worshippers had offered animal and human sacrifices as attempts to please or 'bribe' their gods, and Ibrahim dreamed that Allah wanted him to sacrifice Isma'il, to prove his obedience. He told Isma'il, and they both agreed to do what they thought was Allah's will. However, Ibrahim was mistaken, and just as he was about to kill Isma'il Allah stayed his hand and told him he had already proved long ago his intention to be obedient! (37:102-107). A ram was slaughtered instead for a happy feast, and this event was the origin of the 'tremendous sacrifice' of Eid-ul-Adha at the end of the Hajj. Allah then granted a son, Ishaq (Isaac) to Ibrahim's barren wife Sarah (32:112).

'Id. See Eid

Iddah. The period of time for which a woman must wait before remarrying after divorce (3 months) or mourning for the death of her husband (four months and ten days), to ensure that there is no confusion about the paternity of children born after these events. A pregnant woman's iddah finishes as soon as her child is born (2:228-235; 33:49; 65:4-7).

Idols. (Ar. Awthan, Inath). Statues or cultic objects either representing 'gods' or powers of nature, or being regarded as 'homes' or 'focus points' where those powers might dwell or be concentrated. 360 such objects were said to have been placed in and around the Ka'bah shrine before the Prophet cleansed it and restored it to the worship of the One True God.

The term inath, which is the plural of untha—a 'female being'—seems to have been applied by pre-Islamic Arabs to their idols probably because most of them were considered to be female. However, idols were really lifeless, inanimate things (4:116).

Iftar. Breakfast; usually used literally to refer not to the first meal of the day but the meal that ends the day's fasting during Ramadan. (The western use of 'breakfast' refers to breaking the fast after one's sleep at night).

Ihram. The state of purity entered by Muslims on Hajj, symbolised by the putting off of normal clothing and the wearing of two simple white cloths (for men), or clothing covering all the body except face and hands (for women). Clothing often indicates a person's status, wealth or occupation—all these are set aside in this reminder that all people are equal before Allah, whether they be royalty or roadsweepers. The cloths, like shrouds, also remind people of the mortality of their bodies, and the life after death of the soul.

Ihram rules. Pilgrims must not be dishonest or arrogant or impatient; marry, get engaged, or indulge in sexual activity; use perfume; carry weapons; kill or harm living things; break or uproot plants; wear shoes that cover the ankles; cut hair or clip nails; men must not cover their heads; women must not cover their faces.

Ihram rules (the meanings). The ihram rules encourage the pilgrim to set aside the cares and pleasures of this world in order to concentrate on Allah, but at the same time to feel love for God's creation and unity with it, in acknowledgement that everything belongs to Allah. They also express purity, modesty, trust, simplicity, humility, non-aggression and gentleness (5:3).

Ihsan. Awareness of God, realisation. When a person believes and acts in the knowledge that although they do not see God. He sees and knows everything they do and every intention in their minds and hearts.

Ihtilam. A wet-dream; ejaculation of seminal fluid while asleep. It could happen at any time, and you are not responsible for it, and it is not a sin. One should take a full bath (ghusl) and change the bed-sheets. A muhtalim (in this state, before ghusl) should not touch the Qur'an or perform salah until purified.

Ihya Ulum ad-Din. The major work of the famous Sufi teacher Imam Abu Hamid al-Ghazzali (d. 1111).

Ijaz. The doctrine that the Qur'an cannot be imitated. The sacred text challenges those who oppose it to produce its like.

Ijazah. A document given by a teacher to a student certifying that he or she is capable of teaching or transmitting a particular work of his or her master.

Ijma. The consensus of religious scholars whose competence and piety are beyond question to provide legal opinion on a subject not directly ruled upon in the Qur'an.

Ijtihad. (literally 'utmost effort')—the exercise of reason in order to try to find an appropriate ruling on a matter not directly ruled upon in the Qur'an. To make use of principles, similarities and comparisons.

Ikhlas. Sincerity. A person consciously doing everything possible in life for the sake of Allah only (98:5).

al-Ikhlas. The Declaration of

God's Perfection. Title of surah 112, meaning 'loyalty' or 'sincerity'; a Makkan surah of 4 verses stressing the Oneness of God, and that He has neither father nor son nor equal.

Ikhtilaf. The 'difference,' technically, the difference between the four schools of Law on points of fiqh.

Ikhwan. Brotherhood, brethren. The noun actually includes men and women alike and does not mean just males. (As in 49:10) It usually denotes groups of people who are actually related, or those who share the same views, or the same environment. See 50:13; 7:83; 11:77-83, and Muslim Brotherhood.

Ila. The refusal of a husband to have sexual intimacy with his wife. If this continues longer than four months, it is considered as grounds for divorce.

Ilhad. Atheism. Deviation. Refusal to believe in God.

'Ilm. knowledge, learning, science—especially theoretical knowledge of the religious sciences, truths derived from the Qur'an and prophetic traditions. The knowledge that makes people aware of Allah.

Images. There is a notion that the Qur'an forbids the representation of the human form; this is actually not the case. It was certain hadith literature open to debate which instituted such a prohibition, and advised that artists would be punished on the Day of Judgement. What the Qur'an specifically forbade was the worship of idols (ansab); it reveals Sulayman causing the jinn to build him statues (tamathil). The courts of the caliphs usually ignored the hadith prohibition, depicting humans, angels and sometimes even showing the Prophet, but with his face blanked out. See Art in Islam.

Imam. Not a priest, but a respected person who leads the prayers. (See Shi'ite and Madhhab). To be an Imam has sometimes become a paid job because of circumstances and convenience, but this is not the ideal. Any respected person who has good knowledge of Islam and is of good character can act as Imam, and anyone who knows the prayer can lead it. Ladies do not lead if there is a man available, but they may lead other women and children. They lead the prayer from the centre of the line, and not from a position in front. It would not be courteous for a woman in authority to insist on leading the prayer for her household if a suitable man was available. The hadiths mention one lady, Umm Waraqah bint Abdallah, whom the Prophet appointed as an Imam for her household.

In Shi'ite Islam, there is another concept of Imam—a supreme leader, a descendant of the Prophet, who is considered to have special supernatural guidance so that his words are infallible. See also Ayatollah, Madhhab.

Imamah. Political and/or religious leadership; the office of the Imam.

Imambara. The tomb of a Shi'ite Muslim holy man.

Iman. Faith (from 'amana'—to believe and 'amina' to be tranquil at heart and mind, to be safe or secure, to trust, to have a serene confidence). In Islam 'faith' means the conscious application of Islamic principles in a person's life so that faith and trust in Allah govern every action and intention.

Iman-i-Mufassal. See Seven Beliefs.

Imran. See Al Imran.

Infallibility. See Isma'.

al-Infitar. Title of surah 82, 'the Cleaving' or 'Splitting'; a Makkan surah of 19 verses referring to the signs of the Day of Judgement.

Inheritance. The leaving of property and money after death is subject to various rules in Islam, which ensure that people are provided for justly. Relatives receive inheritance in set proportions, so that personal preferences or hostilities do not come into it. One may only leave a small proportion of one's property to individually chosen causes (2:180-182, 240; 4:7-9, 11-12, 19, 33, 176; 5:109-111).

Injil. Meaning 'Gospel', but not the same thing as the present Gospels included in the New Testament. It means the pure, unadulterated message from God that was revealed to the Prophet Isa (Jesus)—not the human attempts to 'write up' about him.

Innovation. See Bid'a.

Insan. A masculine noun usually translated, as 'man' but really meaning 'human being' as it refers to both sexes alike (46:18).

al-Insan. Title of surah 76, meaning 'Humanity'; also called ad-Dahr (Time), it is a Madinan surah of 31 verses, dividing mankind into the grateful and ungrateful with their various fates.

Insha Allah. Lit. 'If God wills.' A phrase used by Muslims after stating a future course of action or intention e.g. 'I'll go tomorrow—if God wills.' The point is, you do not know if it is God's will for you to be alive tomorrow (18:23).

al-Inshiqaq. Title of surah 84, 'the Splitting Apart'; a Makkan surah of 25 verses, referring to the coming of the Last Hour and the new reality.

Inshirah. Solace (94:5), comfort from distress.

Insurance. This is permissible in Islam, because it safeguards the interests of people and reduces the burden of a catastrophe. Also, it presents an agreement to share the burden among so many people who are liable to have the same sort of disaster. It is in effect a pledge of cooperation between a large number of people to reduce the effects of disaster which may befall a small number of them. Therefore, it is perfectly legitimate to claim costs under an insurance policy.

Intention. See Niyyah.

Intercession. Many people, out of pious humility, feel they cannot approach God direct, but must use intercessors or mediators to plead their case for them. This is in opposition to the spirit of Islam, and a form of shirk. Islam teaches that no person or entity has any ultimate power, save Allah Alone. The notion of praying to an influential saint, or angel, or anything else, smacks of the idea of being able to 'bribe' or 'corrupt' a judge in order to alter his decision—the judge in this case being Allah! Angels, the Prophet himself, and anyone else, can only intercede 'as God wills' (53:26). Prayers should never be addressed by Muslims to dead saints, pirs, angels, or even dead family members, who are believed to have 'closer access' to Allah because they have 'gone in advance.' Obviously, the Christian notion of prayers to Jesus, the Virgin Mary and other saints, are all regarded as blasphemy.

The issue of intercessors lay behind the question of the Satanic Verses. See Satanic Verses, Gharaniq, Goddesses.

We are all judged for our own deeds and misdeeds and nobody can bear our burden, or atone for us, or 'buy us off.' On Judgement Day, we stand alone as individuals and are responsible for ourselves. See Crucifixion, Isa.

Interest on money. See Riba.

Iqamah. The second call to prayer, performed not from the minaret but inside the mosque, when the Imam is ready to gather up the people in their rows ready to start the prayer.

Iqbal, Muhammad (1290/1873-1357/1938). A famous poet, born in Sialkot, studied in Lahore, Cambridge and Munich. An Asharite theologian who practised a speculative exegesis of the Qur'an, championing the right of ijtihad. His most famous book was 'The Reconstruction of Religious Thought in Islam,' an attempt to synthesize Eastern and Western thought.

His main medium of expressing his thoughts was poetry. He believed that western civilisation would kill itself by its own dagger, for it had no future without faith. He was also critical of Muslims who no longer really practised the Islam of the heart. He sought to create an ideal Islamic man, the Mard-e-Mu'min. He proposed the creation of a separate homeland for Muslims at the All India Muslim League's meeting in 1930, which ultimately led to the creation of Pakistan in 1947.

'Iqra! 'Recite!' The first word of the revelation given to the Prophet. The first revealed words are believed to be Surah 96:1-5, followed by Surah 48:3 and following verses.

Iqrar (also called 'Iqrar bi'l lisan'). The confession of belief in Allah and His messenger, given in actual spoken words.

Irtidad. Lit. 'to turn back.' The sin of apostasy. Leaving the faith. This is not punished by death (as some extremists have suggested), but the fate of the apostate is left to Allah's mercy in the Hereafter (16:106; 2:217; 3:86-91; 5:54).

Isa. Arabic name for the Prophet Jesus. The Qur'an tells of his miraculous birth from the Virgin Mary, but do not deduce that this made him a 'Son of God' in the Christian interpretation. God can do whatever miracles He pleases. He only says 'be!' and it is so (3:47). Muslims also do not believe that Isa was sacrificed for us, or died to save us from our sins as a Redeemer or Saviour; each person is responsible for their own sins, and no-one can 'buy you off' (35:18). Muslims also believe that Isa was miraculously saved from death on the cross, and that he ascended into Heaven and will come again before the end of the world. Important Quranic passages referring to Isa are 2:87; 5:46; 43:63; and 57:26). See Crucifixion.

Isaac. The son of the Prophet Ibrahim, granted to his childless wife Sarah as a reward for their obedience to God's will in the matter of the sacrifice of Isma'il.

'Isha. Evening, and in particular 'isha prayer, the evening obligatory prayer, performed at some time during the hours of darkness.

Ishaq. See Isaac.

Isharat al-Sa'a. The Signs of the Hour (i.e. of the Last Day). A large number of such signs are given both in the Qur'an and the hadith literature—a darkening sun, boiling seas, moving mountains, a general breakdown in morals and the arrival of the Dajjal, Isa and/ or the Mahdi. There is also the interesting suggestion that the peoples of the West would awaken to true spirituality and flood a high place in Islam.

Islah. Reform. To make better, to put right. For example, the reformism proposed by Muhammad Abduh in the C19.

Islam. The true peace gained by willing submission to Allah's divine guidance. See 3:85 Iman, Amal, Taqwa, Ihsan, Din.

Islamic banking. A system which incorporates adherence to the prohibition of riba. It is an important Islamic principle that there should be equality of risk. From a banking point of view this means that the risks and rewards should be shared between borrower, bank and depositor. Muslim banks should not finance goods or schemes which are themselves forbidden in Islam.

One of the chief dangers of banks is that those who wish to borrow money for whatever reason usually end up paying enormous sums of interest as well as repaying the loan. Banks are a business, not a charity. They make their income from the money they loan out. Hence many people become enticed into borrowing money which is going to entrap them in debts, sometimes for many years or even a lifetime. If the money was borrowed for a business venture that went wrong, the borrower is still saddled with the debt to the bank until all is paid off. See Mudaraba.

Islamic Relief. A Muslim charitable association aiming to raise money for poverty, catastrophe or war stricken Muslim communities or individuals.

Isma'. Infallibility. The doctrine which states that the prophets, especially Muhammad (pbuh), were protected from sin (ma'sum) during their lifetimes. It is a quality attributed by Shi'ites to their Imams.

Isma'il. The eldest son of the Prophet Ibrahim. His mother was Hajar, an Egyptian lady, possibly from the Royal House. Ibrahim had dreamed that God wanted him to sacrifice his son—but a stranger appeared who tried to make him think again. Was the command no more than a dream? Had he gone crazy? Should the lad run away? Isma'il became famous for his calm acceptance for what he believed was God's will, and the Devil was driven off. He lay down on the altar without bonds, and begged his father not to look at his face, or to hesitate. At the last moment, God stayed Ibrahim's hand and the boy was spared.

Isma'ilis. A Shi'ite sect that came into being after the death of the sixth Imam Ja'far as-Sadiq in 765. Ja'far's son Isma'il had died while his father still lived, but a group of followers still held that he was successor. Isma'ili doctrine stresses the dual nature of Qur'an interpretation, the literal and the hidden meaning. The first Isma'ili caliph was Ubaydụllah, who conquered Tunis and then Egypt and founded the Fatimid dynasty. When al-Mustansir died in 1094 his son al-Musta'li was recognised in Egypt and his elder son Nizar in Syria and Iran. Isma'ili rule ended in Egypt in 1171, but survived in Yemen and Gujarat in India, where they are now called Bohras. The Nizaris split into two groups, and that headed by the Agha Khan moved from Iran to India in 1841. The last Agha Khan is buried near Aswan in Egypt. The present Agha Khan is an ardent worker for charitable causes, and a high official in the UN.

Isnad. The chain of transmission of a hadith, carefully examined to check if it is reliable or not. Hadiths that are not in keeping with the principles of the Qur'an are most likely well-meaning but misleading pious inventions.

al-Isra'. (i) The night journey made by Muhammad from Makkah to Jerusalem. (See Laylat ul-Miraj). (ii) Title of surah 17, 'the Night Journey'; a Makkan surah of 111 verses, which refers to the Prophet's ascent through the heavens. (See Laylat al-Miraj). The surah used to be called Banu Israil. According to Aishah, the Prophet used to recite this surah every night (Tirmidhi, Nasa'i, and Ibn Hanbal).

Israfil. The angel who takes souls to Judgement.

Istanja. Washing the private parts after toilet.

Istawa. Lit. 'to be straight,' 'to stand erect,' 'to sit down,' 'to mount,' and even 'to be cooked.' It refers to the debate about giving anthropomorphic attributes to Allah; e.g. 'He sat down,' 'in His hands' etc. Can God sit? Does He have hands?

Isti'adha. Seeking refuge from Shaytan (16:98; 23:97). Prayer before commencing the salah.

Istibsar. The ability of conscious human beings to perceive the truth. It is this which makes us morally responsible for our own doings, and hence for our failure to resist our own evil impulses (29:38).

Istihsan. Legal discretion, preference. A discretionary decision of approval on a point of law given by a judge where the public interest may be concerned.

Istikhara. The practice of asking guidance from Allah when faced with two conflicting decisions. A special form of trust; a prayer of turning to Allah for guidance and direction over a particular problem, and leaving the outcome with Him, trusting that it will be made clear what is the right thing to do. It does not imply receiving special signs or dreams (although these might occur, if Allah wills), but submitting one's will entirely to Him and leaving it in His 'hands'. If Allah means it to happen, the way forward will become clear and easy; if it is not meant to happen, obstacles will prevent it and make it difficult, or your conscience will trouble you, which you should accept as a message. Either way, you must be prepared to accept that 'His will be done.' See Trust.

Istiqamah. See Steadfastness.

Istishab. Lit. 'seeking a companion or link.' A technical term for maintaining the status quo; Islamic law presumes a past situation or state to continue until the opposite is shown.

Istislah. Taking into consideration the public good, a supplementary principle of Islamic law particularly liked by the Malikis. It seeks to discover the maslaha—the public welfare.

Istislam. 'Greeting' the black stone at the Yemeni corner of the Ka'bah during tawaf by kissing, touching, or saluting with outstretched hand.

Ithm. One of the Quranic terms to denote crime or transgression of God's Law. In this case, it means people conducting themselves in such a way that makes them weak, depressed and listless, unable to keep in step with the required standards. Every action which weakens human personality.

I'tikaf. Seclusion from the world in order to concentrate on prayer; usually, but not necessarily, performed during the last ten days of Ramadan. Men may perform i'tikaf at the mosque, and women where they normally pray, in their homes—where helpers should take over from them all their household duties.

Ittaqo Allah. Usually translated as 'Fear God.' This is an inadequate translation. We should do our good deeds and worship God out of love for Him, and not from fear. The root word is 'taqwa,' meaning to 'ward off' or 'be on one's guard.' We should always fear displeasing God and doing what incurs His displeasure; what we should guard against is doing what God has forbidden. God has only forbidden that which is harmful and evil. See 2:4-5.

Iwan. A large arched recess, especially one containing the entrance of a major mosque. A rectangular arched facade of a vaulted open hall in a mosque.

Izar. A piece of cloth used as a waist-wrapper both by men and women.

Izzat. The honour of Allah, the Lord of Honour and Power (4:139; 10:65; 35:10; 37:180). Allah grants honour to whom He pleases, and abases whom He pleases (3:26; 6:83; 12:76; 22:18).

Ja'far. He was the brother of Ali, his senior by 10 years. He was one of the earliest Muslims and was the leader of the emigrants to Abyssinia. He returned to the Prophet after the Victory of Khaybar in 7 AH. He was sent to the battle of Mu'tah in 8 AH where he was killed. He had lost both arms in the fight. The prophet commented that he would have wings in Paradise and was therefore given the post-mortem title of at-Tayyar (the Flyer). His wife was Asma, and they had three sons, Abdallah, Muhammad and Awn. After his death, Asma married Abu Bakr.

Ja'far al-Sadiq (80/669-148/765). A descendant of the Prophet and a renowned scholar of religious and natural sciences. The sixth Shi'ite Imam, and the last to be commonly recognised and revered by both Isma'ilis and Ithna Asharis. He was born, lived and taught in Madinah, and was buried there. A notable scholar of hadith, with a reputation for his saintliness. He was offered the caliphate by the Abbasids, but refused it. Malik ibn Anas and Abu Hanifa (see Madhhab) were among his students, which were estimated at over 4,000. The Shi'ites consider him to be the founder of their School of Law, called Ja'fari Fiqh.

Jahannam (lit. 'depth'). See Hell.

Jahri. The three compulsory prayers said at evening, night and pre-sunrise.

Jahiliyyah. The 'time of ignorance' before the coming of Islam (5:50; 33:33). The word jahiliyyah also refers to the state of affairs characterized by a lack of moral perception. People without a high moral sense of duty and conscience will usually act just in ways which are expedient for them, whether a particular thing will be useful to them or will harm them. They are not submitting their lives to the search for a higher good, which may involve some personal sacrifice. They are not aware of God's standards and demands.

al-Jahim. One of the seven ranks of Hell; the word appears 25 times in the Qur'an, and is the region to which tradition consigns idolaters.

Jalal ud-Din Rumi. See Rumi.

Jali. A perforated stone screen, a frequent decorative feature in mosques.

Jalsa. The sitting position during and after prayer. It usually involves the right foot being upright, with the toes pointing to qiblah, but this is not compulsory.

Jama'ah. A gathering of people, a congregation. The Salat ul-Jama'ah is the gathering of as many Muslims as possible for the prayer at mid-day on Fridays.

Jamaat-i-Islami. A group founded by Maulana Abul Ala Mawdudi (1903-1979). His political party was founded in the 1920s and opposed the creation of Pakistan on the basis that nationalism was alien to Islam. They propagate their message through publishing books, magazines, youth movements and mission organisations.

Jamarat. Lit. a small walled place, but in this usage a stone-built pillar. The three stone pillars at a bowshot distance from each other in the valley of Mina near Makkah represent the three times the Prophet Ibrahim and his son resisted the temptations of Shaytan (see Isma'il). One of the rites of Hajj is to stone them. Stoning the jamras is sometimes referred to as stoning the shaytans. (See also Hajj, Mina, Shaytan). Pilgrims on Hajj gather small stones at Muzdalifah, and hurl

One of the Jamarat being stoned by pilgrims on Hajj.

them at the jamarat, while rededicating their lives to God and promising to try to obey His will throughout their own lives.

Jamara. Lit. 'a pebble.'

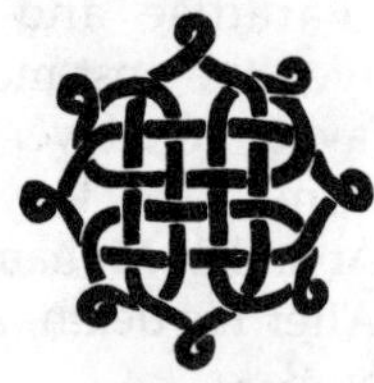

Jamrat al-'Aqaba. One of the three jamras at Mina. It is situated at the entrance of Mina from the direction of Makkah.

Jami'. Hadith collections which contain all the eight topics listed under Risala—for example, the Sahih of al-Bukhari. The Sahih of Muslim is not Jami' because it does not contain traditions relating to all the chapters of the Qur'an.

Janaba. The state of being ritually unclean, from which a person requires full ghusl. To be junub is to be in the state of janaba—for example, after sexual intercourse. The verb 'janaba' signifies remoteness—in this case to be remote from prayer because of sexual passion.

Jannah. See Heaven.

Jarrahi Order. This order of Sufis was found by Shaikh Nur ad-Din Muhammad al-Jarrah of Istanbul (d. 1720). It is limited mostly to Turkey, with some followers in West and North America.

al-Jathiyyah. Title of surah 45, 'the Kneeling'; a Makkan surah of 37 verses, based on the word in v. 28. It refers to the nations kneeling before Allah the Sovereign Lord. Human beings will face their final judgement in complete humility.

Jaza'. Recompense paid by Allah (i) in the Hereafter (40:17; 45:28; 53:41; 77:41-44); (ii) in this world (12:22; 16:30; 28:14; 46:25; 68:17-20); (iii) not paid in proportion but according to His generosity (6:160; 40:40) (iv) not transferable to another (4:123; 31:33).

Jerusalem. The third most important site of Islam after Makkah and Madinah. From around 1000 BC it was the capital city of the Jewish people, captured from the Jebusites by the Prophet-king David (Dawud, Daud). His son Sulayman built the Jewish Temple to the One True God there. Captured by the Romans in 66 AD because of a Jewish Revolt, it was largely demolished by them and Jews were banished from the site. Places there which were associated with Jesus became prominent after the conversion of the Roman Emperor Constantine to Christianity in C4. It was from Jerusalem that the Prophet ascended through the heavens on Laylat al-Miraj. The Christian patriarch Sophronius handed the city peacefully to Caliph Umar. Captured by the Crusaders in 1095 with a great massacre of the populace, but recaptured by the Muslims under Saladin in 1187, and has never again been in Christian hands. The city was split into Jewish and Muslim territory in the arrangements of 1948, and has been in Israeli hands since the 6-Day War in 1967. Muslims are concerned that the Jewish ambition to rebuild the Temple in Jerusalem will mean the destruction of the Dome of the Rock and the al-Aqsa mosque.

Jesus. See Isa.

Jews. The original 'People of the Book' (Ahl al-Kitab) to whom God granted a series of special revelations through His special chosen messengers, the Prophets. Muslims do not accept the Jewish theory that they are a 'chosen race', however, merely that the prophets were chosen. In Islam, all races are equal (see Surah 5:20). In fact, the Jewish race in general became notorious for their hard-heartedness and consistent rejection of God's prophets (see Surah 4:153-161). The stream of prophetic revelation is generally directly opposed to the priesthood and sacrificial cult-system. Those Jews who kept the pure faith and might be regarded as the 'righteous remnant' referred to in their own scriptures are accepted and recommended by Allah in the Qur'an (Surahs 2:62; 4:162; 5:132; 6:197; 28:53; 29:47). At the time of the Prophet, he hoped to convince the Jews of Madinah and bring them back to the truths of God's message, but they often acted treacherously and jealously for political reasons. Two of the Prophet's wives were Jewesses, Safiyah and Rayhanah, both widows of enemies defeated in battle. Some Muslims misguidedly feel the need to be hostile towards Jews in general, and interpret Quranic passages which referred specifically to particular Jews involved in treachery in and around Madinah as applying to all Jews, including those of today. This ignores all the teachings of love and tolerance towards the People of the Book, and the fact that individuals are always judged by Allah as *individuals*, and not as members of a particular race. No one person bears the sins of another.

It is important to remember that Jews, Christians and Muslims all worship the same One True God, the Creator, the Source of Revelation—even if human brains interpret things differently and adopt different practices in their worship.

Jibril. (Gabriel) the chief angel of God; sometimes functions as the means by which God sends His messages and revelations; seen by Ibrahim and the Virgin Mary as well as the Prophet Muhammad (Surah 69:38). Jibril is frequently referred to in the Qur'an as Rouh al-Qudus (the Holy Spirit) or Rouh al-Amin (the Trustworthy Spirit). Muslim scholars wonder whether the action of Jibril as 'spirit' of God and extension and activator of God's will is the origin of the Christian doctrine of the Holy Spirit as the third part of a Holy Trinity.

Jibt. 'Something which is worthless in itself' or 'something in which there is no good. It also means enchantment or anything that is worshipped instead of God, and consequently applies to idol worship. It is used in 4:51 to denote belief in baseless mysteries, confusing ideas (dijl), fanciful surmises (awham), fictitious stories (khurafat), superstitious beliefs and practices, like soothsaying, foretelling the future, relying on good or bad omens, ouija etc.—all condemned by Allah (see Magic). It could also be used to refer to various theological statements of an arbitrary nature—such as an assertion that one is a 'chosen person' and therefore immune from God's condemnation, or the assertion that Isa (Jesus) is part of a Trinity, or that his death can in any way pay for the sins of another.

Jihad. (from 'jahada', to strive, struggle, exert oneself); being willing to strive and fight in the way of good against evil. It denotes striving in the cause of God in the widest sense, including moral effort. The Great Jihad or jihad an-nafs is against one's own lower tendencies (such things as lust, greed, pride, dishonesty etc.). It means self-purification of one's own passions and weaknesses (29:6). There is also the jihad in relation to the outer world which involves helping others, teaching, improving social conditions and so forth (49:15). Finally, there is the military sense of the word, which is the one most misused. For a war to be justified as a 'Holy War' it must be in defence of the cause of Allah, and not for conquest; be to restore peace or freedom of worship or freedom from tyranny; be led by a spiritual leader; be fought only until the enemy lays down arms and sues for peace. It does *not* include wars of aggression or ambition, border disputes, national rivalries, the intent to conquer, suppress, colonise or exploit, or to force people to accept a faith they do not believe (2:190-193; 22:40; 41:34; 49:9, 15). Ordinary warfare in the physical sense is better referred to as qital.

al-Jilani (Abd al-Qadir) (470/1077-561/1166). A notable Hanbali preacher and ascetic after whom the tariqa of the Qadiriyya was later named. He spent most of his life in Baghdad, where he is buried, and his tomb much visited.

Jinn. Elemental spirits, non-human beings created from 'fire' (in the same way that humans are 'from humus' or 'earth'). The plural noun jinn is taken from the verb 'janna' implying veiled or concealed from sight. It signifies beings that are hidden from human senses. They are neither exclusively good nor evil, and can be either; they were created before humanity as were the angels, but they appear to be a lesser order of beings than humans, although they have freewill like humans. They inhabit the same universe, but on a different 'plane', so they are not normally visible to humans, although humans are sometimes aware of them, and frequently frightened by the atmosphere of unseen and perhaps malevolent entities in the vicinity. The Prophet said that they were attracted to places like deserts, ruins, and places where humans and animals fulfilled their basic natural functions. Occasionally they attempt to possess human bodies, and have to be exorcized. They are not always malevolent, however, and surah 72 mentions jinn that were converted to Islam. Many people who are aware of them treat them gently and find them helpful, although they can be mischievous. The chief jinn is Shaytan or Iblis, who is always malevolent towards humanity (through his original jealousy), and tries to lure humans away from obedience to Allah. See Surah 114:4-6, also mentioned in surahs 6:100; 15:27; 34:41; 46:29-32; 55:15.

al-Jinn. The Unseen Beings; the title of surah 72, a Makkan surah of 28 verses in which the jinn are described as listening to the Qur'an, and some of them accepting its message.

Jizya. The protection tax imposed on non-Muslims living under Muslim rule. See Dhimmi.

Job. See Ayyub.

John the Baptist. See Yahya.

Jonah. See Yunus.

Joseph. See Yusuf.

Jubn. Cowardice. Islam places emphasis on personal courage and bravery in the face of tyranny, persecution and evil. One should never try to desert the field of battle. A martyr's death is an honour although Allah does not force people to choose this. When people believe that Allah already knows the time of their death from their moment of conception (if not before), it makes cowardice a pointless nonsense.

Judge. It is not for us to judge others. Allah is our only real Judge, who has full knowledge of all our circumstances, conscious and unconscious. Sometimes we think people to be great saints, whereas there are many things in their lives and characters—unknown to us—that show them really to be sinners, proud, self-righteous, etc. Sometimes we think people to be great sinners, whereas there are many things in their lives and characters—unknown to us—that show them to be struggling hard, generous, compassionate, and so on. God represents perfect Justice, a fairness always tempered by His mercy. Human judges should act as far as possible according to His principles, and be beyond corruption. The Prophet was well aware of the differing standards of different judges. A Muslim judge would rather mistakenly excuse a guilty person than mistakenly condemn an innocent one.

Judgement Day. The Day of Resurrection when all humans will discover their eternal fates. Humans do not necessarily get what they expect, or what they have deserved; for Allah has full knowledge of all our circumstances and intentions, conscious and unconscious (16:61;

34:45). His perfect justice is always tempered by His mercy, and those who showed repentance during their lifetimes are forgiven, if it is His will. According to many hadiths, it is *always* His will, alhamdu lillah! However, those who have wronged others do not escape the justice of having this put right—there is no overlooking of sins and hurts caued. (See Accountability). Allah knows everything. Our books recorded by our angels are shown to us, so that we can be in no doubt of what we have done. This is not to inform God, or help Him judge us—He already knows everything; it is to make it clear to us. Some people who have believed themselves to have lived wonderful lives will discover occasions when they unwittingly (or even uncaringly) hurt others; the hurt ones will be recompensed for this.

al-Juhfa. The miqat of the people of Sham (Greater Syria).

Jumada al-Akhir. The sixth month of the Muslim calendar.

Jumada al-Awwal. The fifth month of the Muslim calendar.

Jumu'ah. Arabic name for Friday, the day when Muslims try to meet for salat al-Jum'ah (62:9). If they do not attend, they may still perform salat al-Zuhr. Although shops close during the time people are in the mosque in Muslim countries, Friday is not regarded as a 'holy day' or a 'day of rest'. The Qur'an teaches that Allah never rests, and there is no tradition of a 'rest' after He created the universe.

al-Jumu'ah. The Congregation; the title of surah 62, a Madinan surah of 11 verses which counsels believers to hurry to the remembrance of Allah when they hear the call to prayer on Friday.

Junub. The state of ritual impurity after sexual intercourse and before a full bath or shower.

Juwayriyyah. (also called Barrah) a wife of the Prophet, daughter of al-Harith the chief of the Banu Mustaliq. She was taken captive after a battle against this tribe, and was afraid that once it was discovered who she was, an exorbitant ransom would be demanded. She asked to be taken to the Prophet, and when their marriage was arranged all the booty from her tribe was released and the captives set free. She married the Prophet when she was 20, and he was 58. She lived 33 years after his death and died at the age of 65.

Juz. (i) A collection of hadiths reported by one single individual, whether a Companion of the Prophet or a member of the succeeding generation. The term is also applied to collections of hadiths compiled on specific subjects, such as Intention, the Vision of God, etc.

(ii) The Qur'an is 'divided' into thirty sections for the purposes of study and reading during the tarawih prayers in Ramadan. Each section is called a juz.

Ka'bah. The cube-shaped shrine in the Great Mosque at Makkah, the place towards which all Muslims turn when saying their salah prayers. The word Ka'bah means 'Cube'. In Muslim tradition, this was the site of the first shrine on earth built for God, by the first human, Adam. It has been repaired many times, and all later shrines have been rebuilt on the same foundations. At the time of the Prophet it had become a 'collection-point' for some 360 idols and cultic objects. When the Prophet became ruler of Makkah he cleansed it and destroyed the idols, and re-established the worship of the One True God.

There was another Ka'bah in Najran on the Sa'udi-Yaman border (discovered by D. Philby in 1936) and one at San'a.

The Ka'bah at Makkah is built of layers of grey stones from the surrounding hills. It stands on a marble base 10" high. The corners roughly indicate the four points of the compass. The North-east (front) and opposite wall (back) are 40' long and 50' high. The other two walls are 35' × 50'.

The Ka'bah shrine in Makkah.

The four walls are covered by a black curtain which reaches to the ground and is fastened by copper rings. Gaps are left only for the water spout and the door. The old covering is taken down before Hajj and covered with a white cloth—it is said to have put on the ihram. At the end of Hajj it receives a new cloth. The door is covered by a separate cloth, called al-burqa (the veil).

Kaffarah. A 'covering' action made by someone who has made a mistake or committed a sin. It could be a gift of money or food to the poor, or fasting, or extra prayers. Where the offence has been committed against a fellow being, an apology should be part of that 'covering' action.

al-Kafi. The title of the book of hadiths compiled by Muhammad ibn Yaqub Koḷeini, a Shiah scholar.

Kafir. (pl. kuffar or kafirun) An unbeliever, a person who does not believe in the One True God, and feels no sense of gratitude to or trust in a Divine Creator. A person who commits kufr.

al-Kafirun. 'Those who Deny the Truth'; the title of surah 109, a Makkan surah of 6 verses stressing that faith should be freely chosen and held. Those who refuse to believe will worship as they choose, while those who choose Allah will abide by that choice.

al-Kahf. Title of surah 18, 'the Cave'; a Makkan surah of 110 verses which refers to the story of the Companions of the Cave, (Ashab al-Kahf), given in vv. 13-20. It is denoted to a series of parables or allegories on the theme of faith in God as opposed to too much attachment to the life of this world. Life here is a test.

Kalam. (Lit. 'speech'). The 'science' of dialectical discourse on the matters and social ramifications of faith. Questions regarding such matters as freewill and predestination, the nature of the Quranic text (whether it was a creation of God in essence only or in sound and letters), reincarnation and the Hereafter. Dialectical theology originated during the first century of Islam with the study of the tenets of the faith, from which developed the Mu'tazili teaching of applying reason and dialectical speculation to all religious and philosophical matters. In the 11th century Mu'tazili teaching was suppressed under the Abbasid and Seljuk rulers, but it remained an important part of Shi'ite theology. In the Sunni world, it was overtaken by Ash'ari thought. See Mu'tazilis, Al-Ash'ari.

Kalimah. The 'word' or declaration of faith. See Shahadah.

Kanz. Wealth concealed to avoid zakat.

Kanun. Administrative law.

Karamah (pl. karamat). A miracle attributed to the Prophet, or other saintly person. See Miracle.

Karbala. The site of the battle between the Prophet's grandson Husayn and his rival Yazid; place of Husayn's burial. One of the holiest shrines of Shi'ite Islam. The battle, in 661 CE, marked an important turning point in the history of Islam. It reminded people of the need to follow spiritual leadership, and not merely the worldly rule of greedy kings, and to honour the sovereignty of Allah by following in the Prophet's footsteps. This became the key issue for the emerging Shi'ite sect—that whoever was chosen as a temporal ruler should also be the most qualified person spiritually—and not a ruler who, while living in affluence and luxury himself, terrified them.

Kawthar. This term is an intensive form of the noun kathrah, denoting 'abundance,' 'multitude', 'copiousness', 'plenty'. 108:1 gives the only instance of the use of this word in the Qur'an, where it relates to the abundant bestowal on the Prophet of all that is good in the spiritual sense—like revelation, knowledge, wisdom, the doing of good works, and blessing here and in the Hereafter.

The verses are addressed to the Prophet, and through him, to every believer.

Abdullah Yusuf Ali's translation renders 'Kawthar' as Fountain of Abundance, or Fountain of unbounded grace and knowledge, mercy and goodness, truth and wisdom, spiritual power and insight. That Fountain quenches the spiritual thirst of humanity and confers overflowing blessings of all kinds. Before he died, the Prophet promised his followers that he was going ahead of them, he would wait for them and meet them by to pool of the waters of Kawthar.

al-Kawthar. Title of Surah 108, 'the Abundant'; a Makkan surah of 3 verses urging humanity to pray to God.

Kazimayn. Lit. 'the two Kazims'. A site in Baghdad containing a splendid shrine over the tombs of Musa al-Kazi and Muhammad al-Taqi. The shrine, which was built by the Buyids was given its present form by the Safavids and redecorated by the Qajars, amongst others.

Khabar. Allah's characteristic of being aware of everything. See Omniscience, Witness.

Khadijah. The first wife of the Prophet, and his only wife for 25 years until she died. He never remarried while she lived, and so we have two 'sunnahs'—that of monogamy, and that of multiple marriage in different circumstances. Neither monogamy nor polygamy are compulsory or recommended to Muslims. Khadijah was the daughter of Khuwaylid, and had been married and widowed twice before, and already had four children before her marriage to the Prophet. She was a wealthy, beautiful and noble lady, who traded with the money she had inherited as a merchant. She employed the youthful Muhammad to take her caravans to Syria. When he was 25, and she in her early forties, she proposed marriage to him, and despite their age difference, it was a famous love-match. Although polygamy was normal amongst the wealthy Quraysh, the Prophet never considered another woman while she lived. They had six children, two boys (Qasim and Tayyib—who both died in infancy) and four girls (Zaynab, Ruqaiyyah, Umm Kulthum and Fatimah). She was the Prophet's first convert and his staunch supporter during all his times of persecution. She became ill during the three years when Muslims were boycotted by the clans, and died in 620 at the age of 64. The Prophet never ceased to remember or miss her, until he died 12 years later. He once said to Aishah: 'She believed in me when no-one else did; she accepted Islam when people rejected me; and she helped and comforted me when there was no-one else to lend me a helping hand.'

Khafd. Female circumcision. This is a cruel and barbaric pre-Islamic practice. When the revelations of Islam began, it was commonplace for men to be circumcised, and also for some girls. Although it caused only temporary hurt for the male and was thereafter beneficial to him, it was a totally different matter for the female. The practices of female circumcision varied, and the most severe of them were the equivalent of the removal of the penis for the male. Although female circumcision is no part of Islam, and is now almost universally banned, some Muslims still regard it as a part of Islam on the grounds that some of the women in the Prophet's household had been circumcised. In fact, the only hadith of the Prophet forbade full female circumcision, which removed the clitoris (the female equivalent of the penis).

The practice possibly originated along with the habit of a Pharaoh taking large numbers of women as concubines for political reasons, not from sexual desire. Removal of a woman's clitoris would wipe out most of her sexual feelings and make her, in theory, content to live without sex. Certainly, even today, some misguided people regard such mutilating circumcision as a method of keeping their girls chaste.

Female circumcision has caused horrendous distress and trauma, and should be considered haram on the general principle that it is a very harmful practice with no benefits.

Apparently, around 97% of Egyptian women are still circumcised, despite the appalling conditions in which some of these 'operations' are performed. The not-surprising results are infection, trauma, sterility, sexual disfunction and even death, and many Egyptian men use aphrodisiacs (including forbidden drugs) because their unfortunate wives are sexually unresponsive. Egypt has one of the highest divorce rates in the world.

There is no call for this practice in the Qur'an, and the few hadiths quoted to support the practice are unreliable. Needless to say, millions of Muslim women are not circumcised, and their eternal reward is not compromised in any way by this.

For those who advise circumcision of a cosmetic nature (which reduces protruding labia but does not touch the clitoris), this should be a matter of free choice for the adult woman concerned, and not imposed by anyone else on female children. The same Islamic principles should apply to this as to any other form of cosmetic surgery.

Khalayf al-Ard. Inheritors of the Earth (6:165; 27:62; 35:39). This implies great responsibilities rather than privileges. No human being is invulnerable. Many generations have been and will be wiped out (10:13-14). Humans are entrusted with their lives as a kind of trial.

Khalid. Son of Walid of Makhzum, originally an enemy of Islam, and a leading officer in the battles of Uhud and the Trench against the Muslims, he was converted to Islam after the conquest of Makkah. He had been responsible for the deaths of many Muslims, and naturally feared vendettas, but the Prophet assured him that his conversion wiped out all the past. This essential principle on entering Islam signified spiritual birth and was the way to bring peace. Khalid was sent by the Prophet to destroy the shrine of al-Uzza at Nakhlah, which proved his new allegiance for previously he had regarded al-Uzza as a goddess and worshipped her idol. However, when wars broke out after the death of the Prophet, Khalid put down the revolts with too much bloodshed, and despite Umar's disapproval, took the enemy chief's daughter in marriage while he lay dead on the battlefield. Abu Bakr who was Caliph at the time, refused to dismiss the man now called 'the Sword of God', and he went on to capture Damascus (peacefully). He amassed vast amounts of riches and spoils of war, once again betraying true Islamic principles. When Abu Bakr died and Umar became Caliph, he recalled Khalid and dismissed him. He died a pauper two years later.

Khalif, pl. khulafa. Lit. 'one who stands in for someone else,' in this case, the leader of the Muslim community. See also Caliph, Imam, Amir al-Mu'minin.

Khalil. This means one who is superior to friend or beloved, and is the one whose love is mixed with one's soul. The Prophet Muhammad had only one Khalil i.e. Allah, but had many friends. Al-Khalil was a title given to Ibrahim also.

Khalq. A scent made from saffron, disliked by the Prophet.

Khalwah. The Sufi practice of retreat combined with spiritual practices, prescribed for 40 days—considered to be the optimum duration. The purpose is to leave all external thoughts behind and concentrate solely upon Allah. The intake of food has to be carefully regulated, and the mental, emotional and physical states of the seekers are monitored by the retreat-master. One form is called a *chilla*, which means forty.

Khamr. An intoxicating substance. See Drugs.

Khan. A title, originally the ruler of a state.

Khanaqah. A Sufi dwelling for board and instruction, often containing a mausoleum. During the Mameluke era there was a considerable proliferation of such buildings, especially in Egypt.

al-Khandaq. 'The ditch.' In 5 A.H. the Makkan idol-worshippers assisted by the Jewish tribes of Banu Nadir, Banu Ghatafan and Banu Asad, marched on Madinah with an army of ten thousand soldiers. The Persian Christian convert, Salman, suggested that a ditch be dug on the unprotected side of Madinah and manned constantly. The enemy were halted and were forced to lay a dispirited siege. See Salman.

Kharaj. Lit. 'yield' or 'produce'. In Islamic terms, it has the specific meaning of 'land tax.'

Kharijites. An early sect of extremist Muslims, that had its origins in the disputes between Ali and Mu'awiyah. Small groups still remain within the Arab world.

Khatm. From khatama, 'to end, conclude.' The technical term for a complete recital of the Qur'an from beginning to end.

Khatam al-Nabiyyin. The 'Seal of the Prophets', the title given to the Prophet Muhammad in 33:40 (al-Azhab). What it recognises is the fact that the prophet Muhammad did not bring or invent a new teaching, but was the culmination and seal of approval of all the teachings of earlier messengers from God.

Khawarij. The people who dissented from the religion and disagreed with the rest of the Muslims. Also called Kharijites.

Khaybar. A wealthy Jewish oasis in the northern Hijaz, successfully captured by the Prophet in 7/628. Some of the Jews of Khaybar had been exiled from Madinah for their disloyalty, and stirred up continual discord against Islam.

Khayr. That which is good; when people use their faculties and power in accordance with the laws of Allah, and bring improvement to their own personalities as well as to the general welfare of the planet.

al-Khazraj. The major Arab tribe in Madinah, possibly originating in the Yemen. Son of the Arab heiress Qaylah, a founder of one of the tribes of Yathrib/Madinah.

Khidma. The service of Allah.

Khidr. In ancient tradition said to have been not only a prophet but also a person who never died, and that he appears to people disguised as a person in need, in order to test their generosity. Most likely connected with legends of the 'Green One,' Adonis, who has shrines all over the Middle East.

Khilafah. The concept of taking responsibility or ruling in God's name. It refers to many aspects of life—care of the Muslim community, care of the planet, of one's family and dependents, and improving and protecting all sorts of conditions of life. See Caliph.

Khimar (pl. khumur). This was a head-covering customarily used by Arabian women before and after the advent of Islam. According to most classical commentators, it was worn more or less as an ornament in pre-Islamic times, and trailed loosely and gracefully down the wearer's back. In the prevailing fashion, the upper part of a woman's tunic was open at the front and her breats left bare. When Allah told believing women to cover their breasts with a khimar it was to make it clear that a woman's breasts should not be displayed to those other than her husband (24:38).

Although traditional exponents of Islamic law have restricted the definition of 'what may be (decently) apparent' to a woman's face, hands and feet (and sometimes less than that) the meaning of *illa ma zahara minha* is actually wider and probably allowed for many interpretations of modest fashion. See Hijab.

Khirqah. The patched garment of a Sufi.

Khitan. See Circumcision.

Khiyar. Right of withdrawal in a business transaction.

Khomeini. See Ayatollah Khomeini.

Khojas. The majority of Khojas in India and Pakistan are Nizaris, and most of them acclaim the leadership of the Agha Khan. They supported the claims of Nizar as Fatimid caliph of Egypt on the death of al-Mustansir in 487/1094. The word Khoja derives from the Persian 'khwaja' meaning 'lord' or 'master'. Originally it indicated an Indian Islamic caste which had converted from Hinduism to Ismailism in the 9th/15th century. There are large numbers in East Africa, Bombay and Gujerat.

Khuffs. Leather socks or slippers. If they are completely clean, it is not compulsory to remove them for prayer. Also, one may perform wudu over the khuffs without removing them, if one's feet are already in wudu when putting them on.

Khul'. The divorce of a husband by a wife. She applies to a judge, giving her reasons, and generally gives up some (or all, or occasionally more) of the dowry she received from her husband when he married her. This is the only form of Islamic divorce where it is considered reasonable to repay this money.

al-Khulafa ar-Rashidun. The rightly guided Caliphs, the first four successors to the Prophet (see Abu Bakr, Umar, Uthman, Ali).

Khuld. Eternity, endless time. Paradise is sometimes called Dar al-Khuld, meaning 'the House of Eternity.'

Khuluq. Way of life, a person's character, disposition, nature, habitual behaviour. Aishah repeatedly stressed of the Prophet that his way of life (khuluq) was the Qur'an.

Khulwah. Privacy, a man and woman being alone together in a situation where there is no fear of intrusion by anyone else, so that an opportunity exists for sexual intimacy. In Islam, only the members of one's immediate family are allowed to be in privacy with the ladies of that family. For other males, there should be a chaperon present. This does not indicate lack of trust, but is intended as a protection (24:31; 33:35). In circumstances where incest is feared, some females would be wise not to be left alone even with family members.

Khumra. A small prayer mat, just large enough for hands and forehead.

Khums. The contribution (additional to zakah) of a fifth of surplus income, paid by Shi'ah Muslims. Sunni Muslims only apply it to the fifth of the booty set aside for the cause of Allah.

Khutbah. Lit. 'a speech.' A sermon, usually referring to the sermon (now usually preached in Arabic and in the normal language of the community) given by the Imam before the Friday Prayer and at the two 'Ids. The two Khutbahs are separated by a short sitting pause.

Killing. See Qatl.

al-Kindi (d. after 252/866). The first important philosopher in Islam, and a master of calligraphy, mathematics, chemistry, astronomy and medicine. His philosophical approach was based on harmony between reason and revelation, and he advocated the allegorical rather than the literal interpretation of the Qur'an. Called the 'father of Islamic philosophy,' who paved the way for such successors as al-Farabi and Ibn Sina. In his lifetime his library was confiscated and he was beaten, as a result of the Mutazilite strands in his thought and his association with Mutazilite rulers. His major contribution was to set up a metaphysical terminology upon which others could build. One of his greatest works was 'Fi'l Falsafa al 'Ula'—'Epistle on First Philosophy.' See Falsafa.

Kiraman Katibin. Our recording angels (82:11-12).

al-Kiswah. Arabic name for the black cloth draped over the Ka'bah shrine, like a lady's veil. It is lifted during the Hajj to show the building beneath. It is traditionally made new each year, because at the end of Hajj it is cut up and distributed to the pilgrims as souvenirs. Special pieces are sent as gifts to various mosques and celebrities. The gold thread embroidery round the edge consists of verses from the Qur'an.

Kitab. The Book, the Qur'an.

Kitaba. A contract by which a slave acquires his freedom against a future payment or installment payments to his owner.

Kohl. Antimony powder used both as a decoration and a medicine for the eyes.

Kufa. A place in Iraq, near to Najf, that was the chief military garrison and administrative centre of the Muslims when they conquered Iraq.

Kufic. Script used for many early Qur'ans and monumental inscriptions. Named after the Islamic centre of learning at Kufa, Iraq.

Kufr. To cover up, to reject Allah. The act of declaring disbelief. An unbeliever is a kafir. In the Qur'an the word refers to idol-worshippers and atheists. Basically, the word means 'to cover or conceal.' Kufr is the denial of the truth, or the prevention of or defiance to the laws of God. Kufr means open denial and not hypocrisy; the hypocrite professes to believe in something that he/she does not accept in the heart. The kafir, on the other hand, at least has the forthrightness to proclaim that lack of belief. One of the worst attributes of extremists is 'takfir,' the tendency to brand others as kafir. For example, some extremist Sunni Muslims regard Shi'ites as kafirs; some Muslims have considered Jews or Christians to be kafirs. This is nonsense—all Jews, Christians and Muslims of any description believe in the One True God, the Life to Come and the Judgement of each individual. See Takfir.

Kunya. A respectful way of calling people as the Father of so-and-so or the Mother of so-and-so, the parent taking the name of a child; for example when Ahmad and Layla have a child, Husayn, the father becomes Abu Husayn and the mother Umm Husayn.

Kursi. (i) A throne or chair, usually the name of the carved wooden stand on which Qur'ans are placed. (ii) The name of a famous verse of the Qur'an, the verse of the Throne or ayat al-Kursi (2:255).

Kutubullah. Belief in the Books of Allah—that is, the Tawrat (Torah of the Prophet Musa/Moses); Zabur (the Psalms of the Prophet Dawud/David); Injil (the Gospel of the Prophet Isa/Jesus); and Qur'an (the revelation to the Prophet Muhammad).

Labbayka Prayer. 'At your service,' it is part of the call (talbiyah) that the pilgrims make to their Lord on Hajj. The pilgrim's personal answer to the Divine Call to come to Makkah. The words are 'Labbayka, Allahumma labbayka; labbayka, la sharika laka labbayka; innal-hamdawan-ni'mata laka wal-mulk, la sharika laka'; which mean—'At Your command, here I am, O God, here I am! At Your command I am here, O Thou without equal, here I am! Thine is the kingdom and the praise and the glory, O Thou without equal, God Alone.'

Lahd. A qiblah niche made in the side of a grave, to indicate the direction of Makkah.

Lanat. The curse of Allah on those who persist in doing evil, even though they know it to be evil.

Last Prophet. Muslims do not

think that the Prophet Muhammad was the founder of Islam or that Allah was/is a different God from the One worshipped by Jews and Christians. Allah has always revealed His will through special chosen people; the Prophet Muhammad was the last in a very long line of Messengers (see 3:84, 5:86 etc.). Muhammad, however, was given his message in a particular and unique way—a series of revelations which were remembered, collected up, and written down word for word over a period of 23 years. That message was complete, and intended for every generation in every place. Hence, the Prophet Muhammad was the SEAL of all previous prophets, and it was revealed that he would be the last prophet. This does not mean that other people would not be inspired by God; God always inspires people, and devout people always gain fresh insights. There will always be new reformers and teachers. It does not mean that God does not have the right to change His mind, should He so wish. However, since the time of the Prophet 1400 years ago, there has been no other Prophet offering revelation of God's will in the way that the bringing of the Qur'an did—so the claim that Muhammad was the last Prophet does stand to this day. See Khatam al-Nabiyyin.

al-Lat, al-Uzza. Well-known idols in Hijaz which used to be worshipped during the Pre-Islamic period of ignorance. See Uzza, Gharaniq, Goddesses.

Latif. This term denotes something that is extremely subtle in quality, and therefore intangible. Whenever the term occurs in the Qur'an with reference to Allah, it is invariably used to express the idea of His being inaccessible to human perception, imagination or comprehension.

al-Lawh al-Mahfuz. The Preserved Tablet. This is a tablet in Heaven on which is to be found the original text of the Qur'an, It is referred to in the 2nd and last verses of surah al-Buruj. See Tablet.

Laxity. Carelessness, negligency, failure to follow the basic teachings of Islam. Laxity may be due to ignorance, weakness, social pressure, culture, upbringing, lack of understanding or laziness. A lax Muslim is not making full use of God's guidance—but this does not mean that he or she has left Islam.

al-Layl. Title of surah 92, 'the Night'; a Makkan surah of 21 verses about the guidance of Allah, promising a happy end to generous and pious believers, but the opposite to the misers.

Laylat ul-Bara'at. The 'Night of Blessing' or 'Night of the Decree'; celebrated on 14th Shabaan, the night of the full moon in the month before Ramadan, when the Prophet used to begin his preparations for Ramadan by passing whole nights in prayer. Many Muslims celebrate this night by staying up and reading the Qur'an all night. On the 15th they may visit the graves of departed loved ones, to pray for their souls. The 'Decree' refers to the belief that on this night Allah decrees the fates of certain people—He makes known to the angels which persons will live and who will die, and whose sins will be forgiven and who condemned.

Laylat ul-Qadr. The 'Night of Power' when the Prophet received the first revelation of the Qur'an in the cave of Mt. Hira (97:1-5), and therefore the most important night in Islam. The date is not certain; it can be observed on any of the 'odd' dates during the last ten days of Ramadan. It is frequently held on the 27th. Many Muslims stay up all night reading the Qur'an, or spend the entire night at the mosque. Some Muslims, in order not to miss the night, (and if it does not deprive or inconvenience others) spend the entire last ten days at the mosque (see I'tikaf).

Laylat ul-Miraj. The 'Night of Ascent', usually celebrated on 27th Rajab. The Prophet was a guest in the house of Abu Talib's daughter Umm Hani. He slippped away to pray at the Ka'bah, and dozed off to sleep in the Hijr. Suddenly, he was summoned from his sleep and taken to Jerusalem, from whence he ascended through the heavens to the Throne of God (surah 17:1). It is so unlike other records of the Prophet's life that Muslim scholars are divided in opinion as to whether it was a miraculous event that really happened, or should be thought of as taking place while the Prophet was in a trance, or was a vision. One tradition suggests that as he left his bed he tipped over a cup of water, and when he returned from the heavens, the liquid was still emptying. Another tradition tells of how one incident on his journey involved his taking liquid from a water-bag carried by an animal on a caravan journey without the owner knowing—when the owner later arrived in Makkah with the caravan, it was seen to be so. The tradition also states he was awoken by angel Jibril, and carried to Jerusalem on a winged creature called al-Buraq (the Lightning), a strange horse with a human head. As he and Jibril rose through the heavens they saw other prophets, including Musa, Ibrahim, Yahya and Isa, and prayed with them. Discussion with Musa involved how many times per day Muslims should pray, and it was as the result of this that the number was fixed for all time as five. Neither the Prophet nor the angel could approach close to the Throne of God, which was surrounded by brilliant light. This experience, be it miraculous journey or vision, occurred shortly after the Prophet's loss of both his dear wife and his closest friend, Khadijah, and his uncle Abu Talib, in the Prophet's 'year of sorrow'. Like the first 'Night', it changed his life again and brought him fresh hope and vigour.

Umm Hani actually begged the Prophet not to tell anyone, as she feared he would simply be ridiculed—as was indeed the case. However, Abu Bakr earned his title as-Siddiq, witness to the Truth, when he insisted that no matter how out unlikely it sounded, if the Prophet said a thing was so, then it was so.

Laza. Lit. 'flame'; one of the seven ranks of Hell, described in verse 5 of surah al-Ma'arij as a great furnace.

Left-handedness. Most Muslims will not eat or write with their left hand, because in some societies it is used for very basic toilet purposes. Since it is washed, this does not mean the hand is unclean, however. It is not sinful to be left-handed, and to eat or write with the left hand or to use it for any other purpose, is not a sin. A left-handed person has not chosen to be so, and it is Allah Who created in this way. Using one's right hand for certain purposes is not compulsory, it is only a sunnah; therefore a person will not be punished for omitting it.

Lian. If a husband accuses his wife of zinah without witnesses, they each have to swear four times that what they say is true, and the fifth oath brings a curse on themselves if they are lying. If the wife swears a fifth time that she is innocent, she is not condemned, but the couple are irrevocably divorced, and can never remarry (24:6-10).

Life after Death. See Akhirah.

Liwan. The prayer hall, or covered part of a mosque.

Loyalty. A characteristic virtue of the Arabs has always been, and still is, an unflinching loyalty to members of their family, clan, or tribe. This is shown by their readiness to protect them against their enemies with their own lives, if necessary.

On conversion to Islam, the Prophet, in Allah's name, asked them to sacrifice this loyalty for the sake of Allah. Their new family was the Ummah of Islam, and their loyalty to the Ummah had to over-ride all other previous loyalties.

This did often result in members of the same family taking arms on the field of battle against each other in the early days of Islam.

Love. Arabic Mahabba. One of the chief qualities of a Muslim towards all fellow humans, and towards the whole of Allah's creation (2:190, 222; 3:31, 76, 146, 159; 5:42; 30:21; 61:4).

Luh. A writing board, often used by those who are learning the Qur'an by heart.

Luqman. A wise man after whom surah 31 was named. A legendary figure from the time of Arabian paganism; a sage, a teacher of proverbs, famous for his wisdom. (31:19-27). Very little is known of his life. He is usually associated with long life, and was through to be the ideal of perfect wisdom. Some people identify him with the Greek wise man who wrote the famous 'Fables'—Aesop—but there is no historical evidence for this.

Lutf (pl. lata'if). Subtlety, the all-pervading texture of the universe that cannot be grasped or defined. Its opposite is kathif or thickness.

al-Ma'ad. The Hereafter. The place or state to which one returns; one's ultimate destination in the life to come.

al-Ma'arij. Title of surah 70, 'The Ascents' or 'Stairs'; a Makkan surah of 44 verses. It examines the challenge which unbelief and unwillingness to believe offers to faith.

Madhhab. A 'school' of religious law, or a system of fiqh. Four madhhabs (correct plural 'madhahib') have been accepted as authoritative by Sunni Muslims. The Hanafi (from Abu Hanifa 669-767), the Maliki (from Malik ibn Anas 717-795), the Shafi'i (from al-Shafi'i 767-820), and Hanbali (from Ahmad ibn Hanbal d. 855). Shi'ite Muslim groups developed their own system of law and moral precepts from their sixth Imam, Jafar al-Sadiq (d. 765). Abu Hanifa placed his emphasis on broad interpretations based on individual reasoning and analogy; Imam Malik taught that the ways of the elders of Madinah should be uncorrupted by new converts or 'modern' influences; al-Shafi'i brought greater clarity to the bases of making legal decisions, using general principles as well as specific Quranic commands—the Prophet's practice as recorded in hadiths was more important than the practices of various communities; ibn Hanbal developed al-Shafi'is thought, and emphasised methods of choosing hadiths carefully—but preferred even weak hadiths to strong analogies. Jafar as-Sadiq regarded concensus as valid only if the opinion of the Imam was included, because of the belief that Imams were infallible, and did not need to resort to analogy. In this century, most Muslims follow one or other of these schools, but although these eminent teachers are so highly venerated, it is not to be assumed that no further thought can be added to theirs.

A simple Mosque made of mud in Saudi Arabia

al-Madinah. Lit. 'the City', more properly al-Madinah al-Munawwarah, the Enlightened City. The town of Yathrib that invited the Prophet to leave Makkah and come to be their ruler. The year he migrated to Yathrib is known as the Hijrah (622). The Muslims who left Makkah were known as Muhajirun, and the people of Yathrib who rushed to invite them to share their homes became known as Ansars ('helpers'). The town took the name Madinat-al-Nabi (the town of the Prophet), or Madinah for short. Muslims look back with nostalgia to that time when the Prophet ruled his city-state and Islamic Law was developed.

Madrassah. The mosque school, for training Muslims in Islamic subjects, how to recite and understand the Qur'an, how to carry out Muslim practices, and the general principles of Islam. Many youngsters attend madrassah schools for around two hours every day, after their normal schooling.

Mad'u. Non-Muslims exposed to the teachings of Islam (i.e. recipients of da'wah).

Maghazi (sing. maghzat). Raids, military campaigns, expeditions, especially those undertaken by the Prophet.

Maghfirah. Forgiveness. This does not really mean to be 'let off' the consequences of some wrong action, but to be protected and fortified in some way. (A Mighfar means the helmet or piece of mail with which a soldier protects his skull and neck). In Allah's Law, every human action has a natural and logical outcome for which there can be no 'forgiveness'. Maghfirah is like an antidote or a medicine; when a person is in good health, they can generally resist the attacks of germs; if the germs are too strong, and the person falls ill, his or her resistance needs strengthening to halt the disease and bring about a cure. This preventive and curative process is maghfirah. If people infringe God's laws, their personalities become weakened. Whatever halts that deterioration and restores them to strength and tranquility is maghfirah.

Maghreb. Arabic name for the West. Usually taken to mean the Muslim countries of North Africa—Morocco, Algeria, Libya and Tunisia. However, it worth noting that Islam is now the fastest growing religion in the UK, USA, and Europe.

Maghrib. Sunset, lit. 'the west.' The compulsory prayer performed just after sunset before the fall of darkness. It is forbidden to make this prayer at the exact moment of sunset, in case of links with sun-worship.

Magians. Zoroastrian fire-worshippers.

Magic. (Ar. Sihr). This does not mean 'doing tricks', but involves trying to predict the future by the use of horoscopes, divination, astrology, omens and so forth. In Islam it is counted as a deadly sin (2:102). At the time of the Prophet numerous mediums, diviners and soothsayers claimed special powers through contact with elemental spirits or jinn, and other secret sources. Those who seek such powers not only commit shirk, but are being tricked by evil entities. The Qur'an states that whatever these sources are revealing, it is based on falsehood and cruel delusion, for no-one knows the future but Allah Himself (5:93-94; 7:188; 27:65; 10:107; 34:14; 35:2). Those who seek out 'magicians' are therefore committing shirk as well as being duped by possibly malevolent entities. See also Charms.

Mahdi. The title of the Hidden Imam, who had disappeared from earth in mysterious circumstances, but who would reappear at the end of the age to defeat the Dajjal and usher in the final years of Earth's existence before the end of the world, and Judgement Day (4:159). The Shi'ite 'Expected One'. Usually believed to be either the seventh or twelfth Imam, some Shi'ites believe the Mahdi may be the Prophet Jesus returned to Earth for his second coming; one famous historical contender for the title was Muhammad-Ahmed of the Sudan, who fought General Gordon of Khartoum in 1884. He admired Gordon and hoped he would convert to Islam, and ordered that he was not to be killed, but his supporters speared him to death. This Mahdi died five months later but he had introduced the idea of freedom to his people (finally granted by Britain in 1956!).

al-Mahi. A name of the Messenger of Allah, meaning the Effacer, by whom Allah effaces kufr.

Mahr. Dowry given by husband to wife on marrying. See Dowry.

Mahram. A person with whom marriage is forbidden. A relationship by marriage or close blood ties that permanently prohibits marriage between two people, and therefore they are allowed to be in private together unchaperoned. For example, those mahrem to a woman are her husband, father, grandfather, son, brother, uncle or nephew. However, some women may find it prudent to take precautions even with their own relatives, in view of the increase of the crimes of incest

al-Ma'idah. 'The Repast;' the title of surah 5, which refers to the disciples of Isa asking if the Lord can send down a table from heaven covered with food taking its title from v. 112. A Madinan surah of 120 verses. One of the last sections of the Qur'an to be revealed. See v. 3.

Majhul. 'Unknown'. A tradition which has been transmitted by someone in an unrecognised manner.

Majlis. An assembly.

Makhzum. Important merchant clan of the Quraysh tribe.

Makkah. The city in Saudi Arabia where the Prophet was born, and where the Ka'bah is located. The place to which all Muslims turn for qiblah when they pray, and the place of pilgrimage on the Hajj. Its original name was Bakkah.

Makruh. An action disapproved of in Islamic law but not forbidden, such as divorce.

Makruh tahrimi. A reprehensible action, utterly discouraged, but where evidence for its total prohibition is uncertain.

Mala'ikah. Allah's forces at work in order to fulfil His purposes; the agencies through which God's word is revealed to the various Messengers. The belief in angels. See Angels.

Malak al-Mawt. The Angel of Death, Azrail (32:11).

Malakut. The dominion and power that Allah has over all things (2:165; 5:123; 11:56; 38:65; 43:85). The regulation and command over everything is 'in His hands' (3:154; 4:47; 7:54;

10:3,31; 11:123; 13:2,31; 30:4; 32:5). See Omnipotence, Omniscience, Qudrat.

Male supremacy. This is a much misunderstood concept. Allah made it crystal clear in the Qur'an that male and female are equal souls and of equal value; however, out of concern for the many extra pains and physical weaknesses women suffer, it was expected that a good Muslim man would take care of, protect and nurture his womenfolk, and therefore men had a position of great responsibility which was not to be abused (4:34). The request for Muslims to seek as much education and knowledge as possible throughout their lives applies equally to men and women. Women usually run the Muslim household, and increasing numbers of Muslim women hold positions of authority in business, trade, politics and so forth.

Malik ibn Anas (d. 795). The founder of the Maliki school of Law; he was born and died in Madinah. His book, al-Muwatta, is the earliest collection of hadith, and the first book of law. Maliki fiqh is dominant in North and West Africa.

Mamelukes. (Lit. 'Owned'). Descendants of Turkish and Circassian slave-soldiers who rose to be military rulers in Egypt. Instead of making the mistake of hereditary leadership (which risked sickly, weak and corrupt rulers) they promoted talented rulers who acted like the chairman of the committee. The most famous was Baybars (d. 1277), who drove the Crusaders out of Syria and halted the Mongol advance. As a result of their success, Cairo became the centre of the Islamic world, and the al-Azhar university the most important seat of orthodox Islamic learning. The Mameluke dynasty lasted from 1250-1517 CE, when they were defeated by the Ottomans.

Mamnu'a. What is prohibited in acts of worship in the shari'ah.

Manaqib. The virtues of various people and places.

Mandub. An action which is recommended in Islam, but not compulsory; this includes any aspect of the Prophet's personal example, for example hospitality.

Maqam. A station; the state arrived at when the servant of Allah has acquired inner certainty.

Maqam Ibrahim. A large rock protected by a shrine upon which the Prophet Ibrahim is said to have stood while directing the rebuilding of the Ka'bah sanctuary (See 2:125). It marks the place of prayer following tawaf of the Ka'bah.

Maqam al-Mahmud. (i) The 'praiseworthy station' of

remembering and worshipping Allah in every waking moment. (ii) The highest place in Paradise which will be granted to the Prophet Muhammad œ and none else.

Marabout. Moroccan term for a holy man, saintly person. Pious people in some Islamic cultures guard their graves with great devotion and veneration, but this is officially disapproved because it runs the risk of tempting the un-Islamic practice of praying to the marabout to grant requests, fertility, etc. The word is a French corruption of Arabic, and means a man 'tied' to God.

Marja' al-Taqlid. 'Source of imitation;' a leading religious figure in Shi'ite Islam.

Ma'rifah. Realisation, (from 'arafa—to know, recognise, differentiate, perceive). The 'arif (the person who knows) is aware of God in everything, and His laws behind everything. In Sufism, this is one of the three prime qualities—the other two being *makhafah* (the awe and respect felt for God), and *mahabbah* (ardent love for God).

Marriage. In Islam marriage is a contract involving rights and responsibilities (see Husband's rights). Successful marriages are not 'made in heaven' but the result of a great deal of tolerance, hard work and goodwill. Many first marriages are arranged by the parents of young people (see Arranged marriages and Nikah). Muslim males may marry Christian or Jewish women, but Muslim women are expected to marry Muslim men. If either spouse breaks the contract terms, or denies the rights of the other, divorce is permitted (4:22-24; 5:6).

Martyr. A martyr is someone who dies for what he or she believes in. In Islam, any loss of life is regretted, but if it is done for the sake of Allah, and is in the true cause of justice, then it has to be accepted. Islamic principles demand that oppression be tackled, and this sometimes involves sacrifice of life. A martyr in the cause of Allah is called shahid. It is important to remember that many people lay down their lives for causes that are dear to them (for example, nationalistic causes), and this makes them martyrs, but not martyrs for Islam. Any Muslims who do sacrifice their lives for Islam earn forgiveness for any wrongs they committed in their lifetimes, and will receive Paradise.

It is a sunnah to bury martyrs without washing their corpses, in the place where they fell.

Marwa. The name of one of the small hills between which the Prophet Ibrahim's wife Hajar ran seeking water for her son. See the Sa'i.

Mary. See Maryam.

Maryam. (i) Title of surah 19; a Makkan surah of 98 verses referring to the mother of the Prophet Isa (Jesus).

The surah which Ja'far recited to the Christian ruler of Abyssinia, the Negus, in order to explain the Muslim beliefs about Jesus (Isa). The title is based on the story of Mary and Jesus, Zachariah (Zakariyah) and John the Baptist (Yahya), which occupies about a third of the surah. (ii) Muslim name for the Virgin Mary, the mother of the Prophet Jesus (Isa). She is mentioned more times in the Qur'an than in the New Testament, and her purity, nobility and innocence is never questioned. Some Christians, knowing her parents' names to be Joachim and Anna, regard the Qur'an as inaccurate when it calls her 'the daughter of Imran'; however, this is acknowledging her Levitical descent from the father of Musa (3:35). See also St. Luke's Gospel 1:5 where Mary's cousin Elisabeth is called 'a daughter of Aaron (Harun)' in similar fashion. When she saw the angel Jibril, she asked how it was possible she could be pregnant, since she had never 'known a man', and received the famous answer that Allah has only to say 'Be', and it is so (3:47). All Muslims accept the virgin birth of Jesus without drawing the conclusion that this made him a 'Son of God' in the Christian sense. God can perform whatever miracle He wishes (3:35-51; 4:156; 19:16-33; 21:98; 66:12).

Maryam Qibtiyyah. Mary the Copt, the last wife of the Prophet. She was a high ranking Egyptian lady, who was sent with her sister Shirin to the Prophet by the Muqawqis, the Coptic ruler of Egypt. Some scholars have maintained that she was only a concubine, but this is disputed. She was much loved by the Prophet, and bore him a son Ibrahim. Sadly, her son died in infancy, like the Prophet's previous sons by Khadijah. Soon after, the Prophet himself died. Maryam became a recluse, only going out to visit their graves. She died five years after the Prophet, in 648.

al-Masad. Title of surah 111, 'the Palm Fibres', 'The Twisted Strands'; a Makkan surah of 5 verses referring to the rope that would be placed round the neck of Abu Lahab. It relates to the bitter hostility of the Prophet's uncle Abu Lahab and his wife Umm Jamil towards Islam.

Mashhad. Lit. 'Judgement.' The time or place where people go or are taken, to give evidence or be judged. It refers both to ordinary courts of law, and the Day of Judgement.

Mashhur. This is a tradition which

is handed down by at least three different reliable authorities, or, according to another view, a tradition which, although widely disseminated later, was originally transmitted by one person in the first generation.

Al-Masih ad-Dajjal. The anti-Messiah. See Dajjal.

Al-Masih ibn Maryam. The Messiah, Jesus, see 'Isa ibnu Maryam.

Masir. The concept of Allah as the Final Goal of all things. There is no God but He, and to Him all things will return, and be accountable.

Masjid. A mosque, (from 'sujud'—prostrate or bow down, meaning literally a 'place of prostration'). The Prophet said that one could pray in any clean place, thus making it a masjid. He said: 'Wherever the hour of prayer overtakes you, you shall perform it. That place is a mosque.' God can be worshipped anywhere, and the most important place of worship is the heart. Some mosques are extremely simple, and others very grand places. Muslims generally prefer not to be ostentatious, and not every Muslim approves the spending of lavish sums on elegant buildings.

al-Masjid al-Haram. The Sacred Mosque; the Great Mosque in Makkah inside which the Ka'bah is located. See Haram, Ka'bah.

Maslahah. Public Welfare.

Mathalib. The defects of various people and places.

Maulanah. See Mevlana.

Maudu'. 'Forged'. This is a hadith which a liar fabricates and then attributes it to the Holy Prophet (may peace be upon him). Presumably this was done for pious reasons, but the confusion this has caused in the faith makes it a strongly condemned practice. In early times, creators of false hadiths could be executed. Unfortunately many modern persons claim to be scholars for their knowledge of hadiths, many of which are patently false.

Maulid an-Nabi. The birthday of the Prophet, not known for certain, but generally thought to be 20th August, 570 CE. In the Muslim calendar it is celebrated on the 12th Rabi al-Awwal. Societies using both calendars may be confused by this. Some celebrate it twice. Some Muslims celebrate it with processions, special prayers and Qur'an readings, parties, etc.

in honour of the Prophet. Other Muslims feel this is a matter not requested by the Prophet, and disapprove of celebrating a festival that is in honour of a human being, not God.

al-Ma'un. 'Assistance,' 'Charity' or 'Alms'; the title of surah 107, considering the fate of those who refuse to give assistance to others. Some verses were revealed in Makkah and some in Madinah.

Mauquf. 'Stopped'. A tradition which stops at one of the Companions and is not traced back to the Prophet.

Mawali (s. mawla). 'Clients' or 'freedmen'; a mawla was any Muslim who was not a full member by descent of an Arab tribe. They claimed economic and social equality with the Arab Muslims, but this was never fully conceded by the Arab aristocracy during the Umayyad period. In the Muslim armies, they generally fought as infantry with a lower rate of pay and booty than the Arab cavalry. They increased rapidly in numbers and soon outnumbered the Arab Muslims. Their mass settlement in garrison towns formed a discontented and dangerous urban population, which found expression in the Shi'ite movement. Shi'ism became essentially the expression in religious terms of opposition to the state and the established order. They brought many ideas from their Christian, Jewish and Persian backgrounds into Shi'ism, notably the concept of the Mahdi, an ideal figure who started as a political leader an ended up as a Messianic religous 'pretender.' Their most famous revolt against the Sunni caliphs was by Mukhtar in 685-7 CE, in the name of Muhammad ibn al-Hanafiya, a son of Ali by the wife he married after the death of Fatimah.

Mawaqit. (pl. of miqat). See Miqat.

Mawdu'at. Forged hadiths; false sayings. Sayings not in keeping with the spirit of the Qur'an. See Maudu'.

Mawdudi. Abul A'la Mawdudi (1903-1979) a prolific writer and thinker concerning Islam, editor of 'Tarjuman al-Qur'an'—a monthly magazine which become the major vehicle for his views. His early writings concentrated on the conflict between Islam and the Western world. He was a chief opponent of Ghulam Ahmad Parvez. He argued strenuously against nationalism as being a foreign invention and anti-Islamic. He felt that nationalism in India would result in the destruction of the Muslim identity there. In 1941 he founded the Jama'at-i-Islami, the 'Islamic Society,' and remained its head until 1972. His goal was to effect a change in the life of Indian society. In 1947 he emigrated to Pakistan and vowed to help establish a truly Islamic state. His method was to involve the Jama'at-i-Islami in Pakistani politics, with constant criticism of the political powers, which led to his imprisonment. His major work 'Tafhim al-Qur'an' is a translation and explanation of the Qur'an in Urdu, presenting it in a clear style for people of today.

Mawla, pl. mawali. A person with whom a tie of wala' has been established by manumission. It usually refers to the freed slave, but it can also mean the former master or a man of religious authority. 'Mawlana' (Mevlana in Turkish) means 'our master', and the plural form is mawali. It is sometimes applied to non-Arab converts to Islam.

Mawlid. See Maulid.

Mawqif (pl. mawaqif). A standing or stopping place. There are two places where those doing the Hajj must 'stop,' Arafah and Muzdalifah.

Maymunah. Wife of the Prophet; the daughter of al-Harith, sister of Abbas's wife Umm Fadl, half-sister of the Prophet's fifth wife Zaynab bint Khuzaymah, and Asma the wife of Ja'far (who married Abu Bakr in his old age), and Salma the wife of Hamzah. Her real name was Barrah. She proposed to the Prophet herself when he was sixty and she was thirty-six, and he accepted her after receiving the revelation of 33:50. Her name Maymunah means 'blessed'. Of her, Aishah said that 'she had the most fear of Allah among us, and did the most to maintain ties of kinship'. She lived forty years after the Prophet died, dying at the age of eighty. The famous recorder of hadiths, Ibn Abbas, was her nephew.

Mazalim (pl. of Mazlamah). The court of complaints where judicial inquiries were conducted, originally by the Caliph in person and later by his officials, into charges brought against government officials.

Medrassah. The mosque school. See Madrassah.

Menstruation. See Hayd.

Mevlana. Title of Jalal ud-Din Rumi.

Mevlavi Order. The Sufi Order of whirling dervishes founded by the Mevlana Jalal ad-Din Rumi of Qonya. Today his followers are found mainly in Anatolia and North America.

Migration from Makkah. See Hijrah.

Mihrab. A Niche in the wall of the mosque that shows the direction of Makkah.

Mika'il. A named angel, whose role is to protect the faithful and holy shrines. One of the chief angels. Named in Qur'an in 2:98.

Milk-brothers. Milk-brothers or sisters are people who have suckled the milk of the same woman, not necessarily their own mother but it could be a wet-nurse. This was a common practice in Arabia at the time of the Prophet, and he was suckled by Halimah bint Abu Dhu'ayb, a Bedouin woman of the Bani Sa'd ibn Bakr, an outlying branch of Hawazin. She also suckled Abu Sufyan the Prophet's cousin, the son of Harith ibn Abd al-Muttalib. Milk brothers and sisters were not allowed to marry each other. There was debate as to how many sucklings qualified a person as a milk-relative; in a domestic 'emergency' a woman might suckle someone else's baby on the odd occasion—which did not count. It had to be a regular practice of more than six sucklings.

Mina. The site of the place on the Hajj route where pilgrims hurl pebbles at three stone pillars which represent the Devil, or Shaytan. Pilgrims arrive there by the morning of 10th Dhu'l-Hijjah. The ritual commemorates the testing of Ibrahim and his family, to see if they would be obedient to Allah and accept the command to sacrifice Isma'il. Shaytan appeared as a stranger, and insinuated thoughts into their heads, but they drove him away with pebbles. Mina is now joined to Makkah by modern walkways. There are some hotels at Mina for pilgrim accommodation, but most camp out in tents.

It is part of Hajj to spend three nights in Mina during the days of tashriq.

Minaret. A tall tower, used for the call to prayer.

Minbar. A pulpit or raised platform from which sermons can be given.

Miqat. (pl. mawaqit) This is 'a place appointed'; that is, the distance from Makkah at which an intending pilgrim must put on ihram. The miqat are between 31 miles (from the east) and 155 miles (from the north) from Makkah. Many pilgrims these days put on their white cloths before boarding their planes.

Miracles. Miracles are regarded as acts of God that somehow break the laws of nature, or intrude upon them in order to bring about some amazing event. Pious people tend to have a strong belief in miracles, on the grounds that Allah can do as He wishes, and may intervene and disturb the laws of nature as He wills. However, the Qur'an gives clues that reality is more in keeping with natural science, and that Allah does not readily break His own created laws on behalf of humans. We are urged, over and over again, to ponder the phenomena of nature, for in them 'are significant signs for those who are wise' (45:5). Humans are never compelled into belief; they are always given the freedom to choose between right and wrong. When certain non-believers tried to get the Prophet to perform certain miracles so as to enable them to believe in his message, the request was refused. 'Say: My Lord is high above these things. I am only a man and His messenger' (17:90-93). Miracles much greater than their foolish whims could devise were already before them. The Qur'an itself was such a great miracle that it would last for all times to come.

'Yet they say: Why are not signs (or miracles) sent down to him from his Sustainer? Say: The signs are indeed with God; and I am indeed a clear warner against the consequences of going the wrong way' (29:50).

The Prophet said: 'I have no control over what may be helpful or hurtful to me, but as Allah wills. Had I the full knowledge of the Unseen, I should increase the good and evil should not touch me. I am only a warner, and an announcer of good tidings to those who believe.' (7:188)

Miraj. See Laylat ul-Miraj.

Miskin (pl. masakin). A desperately poor person, one in a state of misery. The utterly bereft in poverty, the helpless needy.

Miswak. A soft stick of the Arak plant; when the end is bitten off it forms a frayed edge, and this was used as a primitive toothbrush. It was very effective, and is still used by many Muslims.

Moderation. To do one's best to follow Islamic principles and practices without intolerance or extremism.

Mohkam. Quranic verses which are not abrogated.

Monasticism. This is the withdrawal from the world to live a life of renunciation either alone or in a community. It usually involves giving up sex and suppressing the sexual urge. This is disapproved in Islam; as long as a person has the means to marry, he or she is not permitted to abstain from it on the grounds of dedication to the service or worship of Allah. Some of the Prophet's companions wished to relinquish the world, forsake their wives and families, and become like monks, but he ordered them not to do this (see 57:27). See Rahbaniyyah.

Mongols. Savage warriors from Central Asia that swept through the Islamic world in the 13th-14th centuries. The most famous Mongol leaders were Ghenghis Khan (d. 1241), his grandson Hulagu, and Timur the Lame (Tamberlaine). Ghenghis Khan was legendary for his vicious destructive cruelty. He slaughtered unbelievable numbers of Muslims, burning down not only precious libraries and mosques, but entire cities, including Bukhara, Samarkand and Balkh. His grandson Hulagu destroyed Baghdad, the then cultural centre of the world, with three-quarters of its population. He only spared the Christians because he was in league with the Christian king of Armenia, whom hoped he would destroy Islam entirely. The Caliph of Baghdad was killed, and for the first time Islam had lost its Ruler. The Mongols were eventually defeated by Baybars the Mameluke. Eventually the Mongols were converted to Islam, but ironically the name of Islam has suffered by the reputation they earned with their bloodthirsty raids and conquests.

Moon Crescent. New moons serve as time markers indicating such things as when to fast, to put on ihram, calculating iddah etc. Apart from such things, there is no religious significance in new moons (2:189). The crescent moon on many mosque minarets has nothing to do with moon worship. (The five pointed star symbolises the five pillars of Islam).

Moon splitting. Surah 54:1 mentions briefly the moon splitting asunder. Many commentators see in this verse a reference to a phenomenon said to have been witnessed by several of the Prophet's contemporaries, when the moon appeared one night to split into two distinct parts. Whatever the nature of that phenomenon, the Qur'an verse does not seem to refer to that at all, but to a future event, namely, to the approach of the Last Hour. The Qur'an frequently employs the past tense to denote the future, as in this passage.

This verse also seems to link up closely with 53:57, the end of the previous surah, so we may assume that both were revealed at approximately the same time, at the end of the early part of Muhammad's prophethood. See Miracles.

Moors. The Muslims of Spain who originated from Morocco.

Moses. See Musa.

Mosque. See Masjid.

Mother. The most important person in a Muslim family, responsible for running her household, educating her children in the first steps of Islam, and generally seeing that her family has a halal environment of peace, contentment, safety and satisfaction.

Mourning. Grief for a dead loved one is natural and expected; however Muslim grief is tempered by the certainty of the existence of God and a future life to come. Muslims should also accept that life on earth is Allah's gift, and it is part of submission to be willing to return one's soul to God when He wills it. Therefore excessive displays of mourning are frowned on, especially the custom in some societies for women to weep and wail loudly. It is thought proper to mourn a friend or relative for three days, and a spouse for four months and ten days (2:234). Relatives and friends should always support the grieving bereaved person and give practical help whenever they can.

However, the notion put about in some hadith that weeping is wrong, or even that a dead person would be made to suffer if relatives wept, was corrected by Aishah. The Prophet himself wept copiously because of the deaths of many of his loved ones. Weeping was natural and expected, and not a sin. He wept for his mother and for Khadijah many years after their deaths.

Mount Hira. Another name for Mount Nur.

Mount Nur. The 'Hill of Light', a prominent hill just outside Makkah, the place where the Prophet used to climb up to a cave for his private meditations, and where he received his first revelation.

Mozarab. From the Arabic 'mustarib' which means 'one who has become Arabized.' They were Christians living under Muslim rule in Mediaeval Islam i.e. Spain, who adopted the customs of their masters yet maintained their Christian faith.

Mu'abbirun. Experts in the interpretation of dreams. A companion of the Prophet famous for this gift was Abu Bakr. The Prophet Yusuf was particularly renowned for this.

Muadhdhin. See Muezzin.

Mu'allal. 'Defective'. A tradition which may ostensibly be sound but has some weakness not readily apparent. This may consist of pretending that a *mursal* tradition has a full *isnad*; or that a *mawquf* tradition goes back to the Prophet; or two traditions may be jumbled together, or there may be some misconception introduced by a transmitter.

Mu'aqqibat. (sing. mu'aqqib). Our guardian angels. See Angel.

Mu'awiyah. The fifth Caliph, the son of Abu Sufyan and Hind. The first of the Umayyad Caliphs (their dynasty ruled from 661-750 CE).

Muawwidhatan. Name for the last two surahs of the Qur'an, numbers 113-114.

Mubah. An action not ruled on in the Qur'an, but left up to the conscience of the individual. For example, should one smoke cigarettes, wear make-up or tell a white lie to save hurting someone's feelings?

Mubahalah. A prayer for the curse of Allah to fall on those who lie (3:59-63).

Mubarak. Blessed; receiving the blessings of Allah.

Mubashirat. Lit. 'good news', good dreams.

Mudabbar. A slave who has been given a tadbir, a contract to be freed after his master's death.

Mudaraba. Technical term in Islamic business and banking indicating limited or silent partnership. In practical terms, it operates like this—an Islamic bank agrees to lend money to a customer so that he or she can build up a business. They will receive annually a percentage of the profits over a specified time. In this way the loan is repaid and some profit is earned.

al-Muddathir. Title of surah 74, 'the Shrouded One;' a Makkan surah of 56 verses in which the Prophet receives his initial command to preach the Revelation.

The second revealed surah following a period of no revelation at all. (See Fatrat al-Wahy). the surah outlines almost all the fundamental concepts to which the Qur'an is devoted, the oneness of God, resurrection and judgement and the life to come.

Mudhakkirun. Popular preachers.

Muezzin. (Muadhdhin). The person who makes the call to prayer. The first such caller was the Abyssinian ex-slave Bilal.

Mufassal. The surahs of the Qur'an starting from Surah Qaf (surah 50) to the end.

Mufrid. A person who is constantly aware of the love and presence of Allah.

Mufsida. Anything that invalidates an act of worship in the shari'ah.

Mufti. One who delivers, or is qualified to deliver, a fatwa. A specialist in Islamic Law. Usually a private person whose advice is sought by others owing to his scholarly reputation and piety.

Muftir. Things which break the fast. (The meal that breaks the fast is iftar). Muftir are those things which one must abstain from, which if resorted to intentionally, would break the fast. If they were done unintentionally, through forgetfulness, the fast is still valid.

Rinsing the mouth with water, using a miswak, cleansing the nostrils, taking a bath or shower, using perfume and swallowing one's own saliva do not break the fast. Anger, hatred, bitterness and jealousy do.

Mughals. A dynasty of Muslim rulers in India founded by Babar. His grandson Akbar (1556-1605) ruled virtually the whole of India but was disapproved of because he deviated from pure Islam. His grandson Aurangzeb (1658-1707) led persecutions of the Hindus which led to hatreds that later split India. Mughal power was gradually broken by internal strife, the resentment of the poor, the dissatisfaction of displaced royalty, and eventually the growing influence of European powers.

Muhajirun. The 'Emigrants', the Companions of the Messenger of Allah, who accepted Islam in Makkah then left their homes and possessions and went with the Prophet to make their homes in Madinah.

Muhammad. Title of surah 47, a Madinan surah of 38 verses referring to belief and the fates of believers and unbelievers. Perhaps the earliest of the Madinah revelations, it deals mainly with aspect of fighting in God's cause.

Muhammad. Lit. 'The praised one'. The man chosen by Allah to receive the Qur'an. Born 570, the Year of the Elephant, in Makkah. His father Abdallah died before he was born and his mother Aminah when he was only six. Raised then by his grandfather Abd al-Muttalib and his uncle Abu Talib. Became a shepherd and trader, famous for his honesty, kindness and sound judgement. At the age of 25 married his employer, the widow Khadijah, and fathered six children by her. At the age of forty was called by Allah to be His Messenger and received the revelation of the Qur'an over the next 23 years. Persecuted by his own people, he eventually left Makkah and became the ruler of Madinah. Captured Makkah in 630 without bloodshed. Died in 632, in the arms of his wife Aishah. May peace be upon him.

Muhammad al-Baqir (57/676-died between 114/732 and 126/743). The fifth Shi'ite Imam, the grandson of Hasan. In Shi'ite tradition he was martyred, and is buried in Madinah.

Muhammad al-Muntazar (c255/868-ghayba 260/874). The Twelfth Shi'ite Imam of the Ithna Asharis; his return is expected, and for this reason he is also called al-Mahdi. He was the son of Hasan al-Askari; he made a single appearance as Imam, when he attended his father's funeral as a young boy; he then entered the state of ghayba.

Muhammad al-Taqi (195/810-220/835). The ninth Shi'ite Imam, the son of Ali al-Rida. He became Imam when he was only seven years old; he lived in Baghdad and married a daughter of the Abbasid caliph al-Mamun. Shi'ite tradition has it that his wife poisoned him. He is buried in Baghdad.

Muhammad ibn Isma'il. The seventh Shi'ite Imam of the Isma'ilis, a son of Isma'il, a son of Ja'far al-Sadiq. Isma'il should have been the next Imam, but he died before his father. The Ithna Asharis support the claim of Isma'il's brother Musa al-Kazim.

Muharram. The first month of the Muslim year, which is based on the lunar calendar, and one of the four inviolable months during which fighting is prohibited (haram), from which its name is derived.

Muhrim. A person in ihram.

Muhsan. A person who is hasan.

Muhsanat. The feminine of muhsan. As well as meaning a person guarded by marriage, it also refers to a chaste unmarried free woman, who is sexually protected, as opposed to an unmarried slave woman over whom her master had sexual rights before Islam revealed otherwise.

Muhsar. A person detained from Hajj by an enemy or an illness. A Muhrim who intends to perform Hajj or 'Umrah but cannot because of some obstacle.

Muhtasib. Market inspector, charged with the detection of false weights and the punishment of public acts of immorality; his task is defined as 'commending the good and preventing evil.'

al-Mujadalah. The Pleading; title of surah 58—alluding to the wrongs done to women in pre-Islamic times and zihar divorce. A Madinan surah of 22 verses, referring to the case of Allah hearing the plea of Khawlah bint Tha'labah, a woman who cried to Him for help against her husband, Aws ibn al-Samit, an extremely pious man who wronged her by neglecting her sexual needs.

Mujaddid. A renewer of faith, the traditional renewer of religion reported in one hadith to appear in the Muslim community every 100 years, in order to revive the true spirit of Islam through the process of tajdid, renewal.

Mujahideen. Warriors on jihad or 'holy war'. People prepared to sacrifice their lives in the service of Allah. The name frequently given in common parlance to resistance fighters in political struggles in Islamic areas of the world—e.g. Afghanistan, Iran.

Mu'jam. This refers to collections of hadiths on various subjects, arranged in alphabetical order.

Mu'jam al-Sahaba. Musnad collections arranged alphabetically under the name of the Companions.

Mujtahid. A Shi'ite religious scholar.

Mukat-ab. A slave (male or female) who binds himself (or herself) to pay a certain equivalent for his (or her) freedom.

Mukallaf. A person of full legal responsibility.

Mulhid. An atheist, a complete disbeliever in God and all matters pertaining to God.

Mulk. The phenomenal world, the universe, the visible realm, that which is perceived by the senses.

al-Mulk. Title of surah 67, 'the Sovereignty'; a Makkan surah of 30 verses, referring to Allah the Creator and Sovereign. People are ever unable to encompass the mysteries of the universe with their limited and human faculties, hence the other dependence on revealed guidance.

Mulla Sadra (979/1571-1050/1640). A Persian philosopher and mystic, Muhammad ibn Ibrahim Sadr al-Din al-Shirazi. His thought was much influenced by Aristotle as well as Ibn Sina and al-Suhrawardi. His best known work is 'the Four Journeys.'

Mullah. A teacher.

al-Multazam. The area between the Black Stone and the door of the Ka'bah, where it is recommended to make du'a.

Mu'min (pl. Mu'minun). Lit. faithful. One who possesses iman, or deep faith and trust in God, a believer. A believer in One God, Allah, who follows the injunctions of Islam.

al-Mu'minun. Title of surah 23, 'the Believers'; a Makkan surah of 118 verses which proclaims the triumph of those who believe. It stresses the existence of an Almighty Creator, and the stream of unceasing Divine Guidance. All believers, therefore, form one community which has existed through the ages, which is damaged by human selfishness, greed and ambition. One's true reward will be in the life to come. See Ummah, Akhirah.

al-Mumtahana. Title of surah 60, 'the Woman who is tested'; a Madinan surah of 13 verses based on the word in v. 10. It deals with the problems of the relationships of believers and unbelievers, referring to the fact that believing females among new muhajirun should be tested in their belief and not sent back against their will to unbelieving husbands. It was revealed after the treaty of Hudaybiyyah, when the Quraysh demanded the return of Umm Kulthum bint Uqbah, half-sister of Uthman ibn 'Affan. She was allowed to stay in Madinah.

Munafiq. A hypocrite. The term derives from the noun nafaq, which denotes an underground passage having a different outlet from the entrance—like the burrows of a lizard, or field-mouse. The animal can easily escape, or outwit a pursuer. A person who is munafiq is 'two-faced,' always trying to find an easy way out of commitments, either spiritual or social, by adapting to a course of action which will bring him or her an advantage. Such people usually pretend to be better than they really are. The Arabic term does not only mean those who deliberately deceive others; it also applies to anyone of weak or uncertain belief.

al-Munafiqun. Title of surah 63, 'the Hypocrites'; a Madinan surah of 11 verses warning that Allah is well aware of all the thoughts of our minds. Revealed after the battle of Uhud, it deals with the problems of hypocrisy. The Prophet said: 'There are four qualities in a hypocrite—when they are trusted they cheat; when they talk, they lie; when they give promises, they break them; when they argue, they are abusive.'

Munkar. 'Unusual'. A tradition narrated by a weak transmitter which disagrees with what is generally reported.

Munkar and Nadir. The angels that question souls after death.

Munqatl'. 'Disconnected'. A tradition having an *isnad* (chain) with a link missing at the beginning, middle or end.

Muqallad. A jurist who employs taqlid, that is, who relies upon the teachings of a master or of a school without question and without employing independent investigation of the reasons for these teachings.

Muqarnas. Term used in architecture to denote the honeycomb or hanging decoration which often appears in domes or over mihrabs. Decorative moulding with a web of miniature vaults. A particular feature in Moorish architecture in Andalusia, Spain.

al-Muqatta'at. Single or 'disjointed' letters that appear at the start of a number of surahs, for example Alif Lam Mim, Ya Sin, Ta Ha and Nun. About 25% of the surahs start with disjointed letters;

of the 28 letters of the Arabic alphabet, 14 are used in this way. They are always pronounced singly. There is no record of the Prophet ever referring to them in his recorded hadiths, and commentators have offered various meanings or reasons for them. They might have been abbreviations of words, or have some relation to the numerological value of the letter.

All surahs prefixed in this way open with reference to revelation, and some scholars conclude they are meant in some way to illustrate the inimitable nature of Qur'anic revelation. However, this is conjucture—a solution still remains beyond our grasp.

Muqawqis. See Negus al-Muqawqis.

Murabitin. See Almoravids.

Muraqabah. Lit. 'watchfulness'. The Sufi practice of becoming aware of one's own self; the development of sensitivity, resulting in the ability to 'open' that which is within. Mainly practised during spiritual retreats, when the seeker recognises the vast emptiness and timelessness within himself/herself; it is the culmination of self-awareness, and the begninning of awakening and enlightenment.

Murder. See Qatl.

Murid. An initiate in a Sufi tariqah.

Murji'ites. Those who adhere to a belief in 'postponement' (irja'). They agree that a Muslim who commits a grave sin does not cease to be a Muslim (contrary to the view of the Kharijites). They say any decision about such sinners must be postponed, and left to Allah.

Mursal. A tradition free from the link of the Companion. A tradition having an *isnad* (chain) where a person in the generation following that of the Prophet's Companions quotes the Prophet directly. In other words, a chain where the link of a Companion is missing, and a Successor relates a tradition directly from the Prophet.

al-Mursalat. Title of surah 77, 'Those who have been sent'; a Makkan surah of 50 verses, on the gradual revelation of the Qur'an.

Murshid. A saintly person. See Pir.

Murtadd. An apostate. Someone who turns back from the faith. See Irtidad.

Muruwwah. The central notion of the pre-Islamic value system, meaning 'virtue' or 'manliness;' it included the qualities of loyalty, courage and hospitality.

Musa. Arabic name for the Prophet Moses, the chief prophet of the Old Testament. The Qur'an tells how he was raised as an

Egyptian prince, but called by the One True God to lead the Israelites out of slavery. He received the revelation known to Muslims as the Tawrah, the best known part of which is the Ten Commandments (2:51-61; 5:22-29; 6:84; 7:103-145; 10:75-92; 11:96-110, 17:101-103; 18:60-82; 19:51-53; 20:9-98; 23:45-49; 25:35-36; 26:10-69; 27:7-14; 28:4-42; 37:114-122; 40:23-46; 43:46-56; 51:38-40; 53:36; 79:15-26; 87:19). See Asiyah.

Musa al-Kazim (c 128/745-183/799). The seventh Shi'ite Imam for the Ithna Asharis, a younger son of Ja'far. He encountered considerable hostility from the Abbasids, and was eventually poisoned.

Musallah. A place for praying that is not a masjid.

Musannaf. A comprehensive collection of hadiths in which various topics are collected and arranged in various 'books' or 'chapters', each dealing with a particular topic. (The Muwatta of Imam Malik belongs to this category, for example).

Musaylima (d. 12/633). An Arab who claimed to be a rival prophet to the Prophet. His real name was Maslama—Musaylima was a name of contempt given to him by the Muslims. He claimed to have received revelations from God like the Prophet. He was defeated and killed at the Battle of 'Aqraba (the Scorpions) by a Muslim force led by Khalid. The Prophet used to call him 'the Liar'.

Mushriq. (pl. mushriqun), a person who practices or believes in shirk. A polytheist, idolater; one who commits the sin of shirk, the association or worship of something other than Allah; one who holds that there are realities independent of Allah.

Music. Some Muslims take a very extreme view about music, claiming that it is forbidden in Islam. This is nowhere stated in the Qur'an, and there are several hadiths reporting that the Prophet allowed and listened to music. The only music which is really haram in Islam falls into three categories; that which leads to lust and uncontrolled sexual urges (much modern pop music), that which incites nationalistic fervour (military music and things like 'Rule Britannia' etc.), and that which encourages people to show off and become conceited. Some of the most beautiful Islamic music includes religious songs and devotional chants. Music can lift the heart, move one's emotions, and help to being a person nearer to God.

Muslim. Any person who has accepted Islam by submitting his or her life to the will of Allah.

Muslim Brotherhood. A reform movement started in Egypt by

Hassan al-Banna in 1928. It demands total dedication to God, extreme religious discipline, and unwillingness to compromise. Followers have tended to become extremist in tendency. An assassination attempt on Nasser in 1954 failed; the attempt on Sadat in 1981 succeeded. The Muslim Brotherhood is particularly feared by Islamic countries whose governments have become lax, corrupt, or over-westernized.

Muslim ibn al-Hajjaj, Abu'l Husayn (c 202/817-261/875). A very famous compiler of hadith, whose collection is known as the Sahih Muslim, and ranks among the six major collections.

Muslim World League. An international Muslim organisation with a particular interest in education. It opened an office in London in 1984.

Musnad. Literally, 'supported'. The hadiths which were supported by a single uninterrupted chain of authorities going back to the Prophet via a Companion. Later, the term came to mean reliable or authoritative. More technically, it means the collections of hadiths whose material is arranged according to the names of their original narrating authorities, irrespective of subject matter. Examples are the Musnads of Abu Dawud al-Tayalisi (d. 204 AH/819 CE), Ahmad ibn Hanbal (d. 233 AH/847 CE); Abdullah ibn Shayba (d. 235 AH/849 CE), and Abu Khaythama (d. 234 AH/844 CE), and many others. Ibn Hanbal's contains more than 30,000 hadiths narrated by some 700 Companions. Abd al-Rahman's contains traditions related by 1,300 Companions.

Mustadrak. A compilation of hadiths in which the compiler adds other hadiths which fulfil the conditions of a previous compiler, which he missed out. For example, the Mustadrak of al-Nisaburi adds the hadiths which fulfilled the conditions laid down by al-Bukhari and Muslim, but were not included in their Sahihs.

Mustakhraj. Collections of hadiths in which a later compiler collects fresh and additional isnads to add to those cited by an original compiler. To this class belongs the mustakhraj of Abu Nu'aym al-Isfahani on the Sahihs of Bukhari and Muslim. He gives new isnads for some of the traditions they related, thereby reinforcing the authority still further.

Musta'lians. A branch of the Isma'ilis. In 487/1094, the wazir al-Afdal supported the younger son of al-Mustansir instead of the older son Nizar as candidate for the Egyptian caliphate. This split the Isma'ilis. Today Musta'lians exist mainly in the Yemen and also in India under the name of Bohras.

al-Mustansir (420/1029-487/1094). The eighth caliph of the Fatimid dynasty, who ruled in Egypt from the age of seven. His reign was notable for a terrible famine, for which he sought aid from the Byzantines. He also reigned in Baghdad, but was defeated by the Seljuqs.

Mut'a. Temporary marriage under strict conditions, allowed in the early part of Islam but later cancelled. Originally sanctioned by the Prophet as an honourable means of satisfying the urges of his warriors when they were away from home, Allah soon revealed that this practice was unacceptable and insulting to women, and it was banned. However, it is still practised in some Islamic societies, notably in Iran, where some Muslim men claim that it is justified, but most women regard it as little more than allowed prostitution (24:33).

al-Mutaffifin. Title of surah 83, 'Those who give short measure'; a Makkan surah of 36 verses which condemns unfair trading practices.

Mu'takif. A person in i'tikaf isolation.

Mutashabihat. The verses in the Qur'an are difficult to understand and that should be interpreted allegorically. The 'clear' verses are mukhamat.

al-Mutawakkil (206/821-247/861). An Abbasid caliph who renounced the Mu'tazila, and tried to reform the army. He was murdered.

Mutawatir. 'Continuous'. A tradition which has been handed down by a number of different channels of transmitters or authorities, hence supposedly ruling out the possibility of its having been forged.

Mutawwif. A resident of Makkah who welcomes pilgrims, feeds them, shelters them, and if necessary teaches them the courtesies and meanings of the rites of Hajj and 'Umrah.

al-Mutayyabun. See Quraysh.

Mu'tazila. A theological school of thought particularly in the C8th-9th, which stressed human free will and the unity and justice of Allah; it embraced Greek rationalist modes of argumentation. In modern times, certain thinkers (eg. Muhammad Abdul are sometimes considered Neo-Mu'tazilites because of their reintroduction of some of these ideas.

Mu'tazilis. (Lit. 'those who keep themselves apart from dispute') believed that truth could be reached by applying reason to what was revealed in the Qur'an. God being just, and having no human attributes, the Qur'an was specifically created in order to be subjected to human reason to find answers.

Muttafaq 'Alayh. 'Agreed upon'. A tradition accepted both by Imam Bukhari and Imam Muslim and included in their respective collections.

Muttaqi. One who leads a life of taqwa.

al-Muwatta. Lit. the well-trodden path, or the 'many times agreed upon,' because it was agreed upon by seventy of the learned men of Madinah. The early law manual compiled by Imam Malik (d. 179 AH/795 CE). A brief but authoritative collection; originally between 4,000-10,000 but reduced by Imam Malik to around 1,000.

Mu'wwidhat. i.e., the surah al-Falaq (113) and surah an-Nas (114).

Muzdalifah. After the Stand before God at Mount Arafat and the asr prayer, pilgrims on Hajj head back towards Makkah. They stop at Muzdalifah and spend a night in the open between the ninth and tenth day of Dhu'l-Hijjah after performing the Maghrib and 'Isha prayers there. (See 'Arafa, Dhu'l-Hijjah, 'Isha, Maghrib, Mina). They collect 49 small pebbles to 'hurl at the Devil'.

al-Muzzammil. The Enwrapped One; the title of surah 73, the fourth to be revealed. It refers to the Prophet either literally wrapped or enfolded in his cloak, or wrapped up in sleep. A call to heightened consciousness and deeper spiritual awareness.

Mysticism. Inner spiritual knowledge and awareness. In Islam, mysticism includes Sufism.

Naas. Humanity, the peoples of mankind.

an-Naba'. The Tidings; the title given to surah 78, with the theme of continuing life after death.

Nabi. Prophet, or messenger of God. A person who surrenders his or her entire being to God, and who receives revelations from Him. This name is used mainly for prophets who did not leave a written revelation.

Nabidh. A drink made by soaking grapes, raisins, dates etc. in water without allowing them to ferment.

Nafl, pl. Nawafil. Lit. 'a gift', from the same root as al-anfal, booty taken in war, it means a voluntary act of 'ibadah. Voluntary prayers.

Nafisah. (d. 208/824) A famous Sufi saint, the great grand-daughter of Imam Hasan. She was married to the son of Imam Ja'far as-Sadiq (see Seveners), and moved to Cairo in Egypt where she was renowned for her asceticism, night vigils and mystical insights. Imam Shafi'i (see Madhdhab) was one of many scholars who consulted her, and when he died his body was taken to her house so that she might recite the funeral prayer for him. She dug her own grave in the village of Fustat, and was said to have recited the complete Qur'an 6000 times while sitting in it. A mausoleum and mosque now marks the site.

Nafs. Nafs means self, soul, mind, being, and is connected to the word 'nafusa,'to be precious or valuable. the concept includes a person's character, inherited predispositions, and the results of conditioned behaviour. See Rouh.

Nafr (The Day of). The 12th or 13th of Dhul-Hijjah when the pilgrims leave Mina after performing all the ceremonies of Hajj at 'Arafat, Al-Muzdalifah and Mina.

Nahda. The renaissance of the Muslim world in general that was pictured by reformers as resulting from the cultural renewal which would take place in modern times.

an-Nahl. Title of surah 16, 'the Bees'; a Makkan surah of 128 verses, based on the reference in vv. 68-69 to Allah's creativeness in the instincts of the bee. This surah is notable for containing the food laws.

Nahr. (Lit. slaughtering of the camels only done by cutting the carotid artery at the root of the neck); the day of Nahr is the tenth day of Dhu'l-Hijjah on which pilgrims slaughter their sacrifice. However, the ritual is only a symbol. The meat slaughtered feeds the poor and the slaughter is a symbol of the self-sacrifice in our hearts. 'It is not their meat nor their blood that reaches Allah; it is your piety that reaches Him' (22:37). See Sacrifice.

al-Najaf. The Iraqi city where Ali lies buried, according to Shi'ite tradition.

Najasah. Impurity. An impure thing is najas. If any part of body or clothing becomes soiled with something najas, it should be made clean again as soon as possible and certainly before prayer. The following things are considered najas: urine and faeces of humans and animals; blood; the saliva, mucus and tears of dogs and pigs; dead bodies. Parts of the body and clothing can be washed with water, and water poured over any ground soiled by najasah. See Wudu, Istanaja, Ghusl, Taharah.

Najd. The region around Riyadh.

an-Najm. Title of surah 53, a Makkan surah of 62 verses containing the major source of details about the Miraj.

It mentions the Prophet's experience of an ascension to heaven. (See Laylat ul-Miraj) The title os the surah has been given by various commentators either as 'the Star' or 'the Unfolding', depending on whether the first line is translated as 'Consider the star when it sets' or 'Consider the unfolding (of God's message), as it comes down from on high.' Najm is derived from 'najama'—it appeared, began, ensued, proceeded or unfolded. The Qur'an revelation was 'nujum'—that is, gradually revealed.

Najsh. Offering a high price for something without having the intention to buy it but just to cheat somebody else who really wants to buy it. Such a person may agree with the seller to offer high prices before the buyers to cheat them, in which case both this man and the seller are sinful. The seller may falsely tell the buyer that he (i.e. the seller) has previously bought the goods at a certain price which is in reality higher than the actual price.

Najwa. Secret consultation, disapproved in Islam (58:7-10).

Namaz. The Urdu word for salah.

Names. A Muslim's name should be honourable and encouraging, but not conceited or false. One should not name an infant 'beautiful one' or 'strong in generosity' because the child might turn out to be no such thing. Muslims should never use hurtful nicknames like 'Fatty' or 'Spotty' etc. The best names include a 'servant of God' name, which has the words Abd-al (meaning 'Servant of') followed by one of the attributes or names of God (e.g. Rahman—'mercy', Karim 'beloved'). To use the name Abdal (or Abdul) followed by Muhammad would not be thought flattering to the Prophet but quite incorrect; similarly Abdal should not be followed by any other person's name either. The Prophet frequently changed people's names if he disapproved of them.

Names of God. See Beautiful Names.

al-Naml. Title of surah 27, 'the Ants'; a Makkan surah of 93 verses, which portrays an ant advising its fellows to seek refuge and not be crushed by Sulayman and his army. The surah used to be referred to as Ta Sin from the Letter symbols given at the start. An-Naml is taken from v. 18. The surah gives the spiritual truths underlying the old legends of Musa and Sulayman; Salih and Lut.

Namrud. Nimrod, who, in the Qur'an is the king who cast Ibrahim into a blazing fire.

Naqib. A person heading a group of six persons in an expedition.

Naqshbandis. The Naqshbandi Order of Sufis takes its name from Shaikh Baha ad-Din Naqshband of Bukhara (d. 1390). It has spread widely in central Asia, the Volga, the Caucasus, China, Indonesia, India and Pakistan, Turkey, Europe, North America and the United Kingdom. It is the only known Sufi order that traces its lineage of transmission back through the first Muslim ruler, Abu Bakr, unlike the rest of the known Sufi orders which trace their origins to Shi'ite spiritual leaders. The present Shaikh is Nazim Adil al-Haqqani, a Turk, and the 40th in descent from Abu Bakr.

an-Nar. Lit. 'the fire'; the most common name of Hell or Jahannam, the final destination and place of torment of the kafirun and munafiqun once the Last Day is over.

an-Nas Title of surah 114, 'the People'; a Makkan surah of 6 verses. This is the last surah of the Qur'an, and refers to Allah, the Lord of Mankind. A declaration of seeking refuge with Allah from evil.

al-Nasa'i. (d. 303/915). Compiler of one of the six major collections of hadiths. He travelled widely, lived mainly in Damascus and Egypt, and is buried in Makkah.

Nasara. Christians.

Nasib. A share, usually referring to a person's 'fortune' or share in the blessings allocated to him or her.

Nasiha. Good advice, sincere conduct.

Nasikh and Mansukh. The doctrine of abrogation, according to which a verse revealed late in the Qur'an may abrogate one revealed earlier; this resolves the problem of any apparent conflict. The word nasikh designates the abrogating verse, and mansukh indicates that the verse has been abrogated. The Qur'an refers to this principle in 2:106. However, the abrogated verses still remain part of the Qur'an.

an-Nasr. Title of surah 110, 'the Help'; a Madinan surah of 3 verses, the last Quranic surah to be revealed to the Prophet, during the Hajj al-Wida. Even if people do accept Islam in large numbers, no-one should ever be complacent.

Nasr. This is the favour of Allah in helping His servants, according to His will. He helps the oppressed, the depressed, the victim of warfare or catastrophe. Although the unpleasant circumstances are not always removed, Allah is beside us through all our sufferings and trials. He is with us when we face the enemy in battle, so long as our cause is for the right. The greatest of all the help of Allah, is the awareness that He does surely exist, and is aware of us, and beside us. This is the greatest of comforts when all else fails. (See 2:107,120; 3:13,126; 4:45,123,173; 8:10,26,40,62; 9:14,25,116; 11:113; 22:39,78; 25:31; 29:22; 30:5; 40:51; 42:31; 47:7; 48:3.) His help is ever near (2:214); if Allah helps you, you will not be overcome (3:160).

Nass. The Shi'ah doctrine that each Imam was designated by his predecessor, the first Imam—Ali—having been designated by Allah through the Prophet.

Nass. Statements and ordinances that are self-evident with words that do not permit any other interpretation.

Natiq. Lit. 'speaker.' In Isma'ili thought, each of the seven eras began with a prophetic 'speaker'.

Nawafil. (Sing. nafl, lit. 'a gift.') A voluntary act of ibadah, for example, prayers over and above the compulsory ones.

an-Nawawi (631/1233-676/1277). A Syrian scholar from Nawa famous for his short collection of hadiths. He was held in particular regard by the Shafi'is.

Nawraz. The Persian New Year.

Nazala. ('sent down'). This word is used over 200 times in the Qur'an to distinguish it from other forms of revelation.

an-Nazi'at. Title of surah 79, 'the Removers'; a Makkan surah of 46 verses, referring to the angels who remove the evil in people's souls and their activities with regard to the souls of the dying.

Necklace. Many women wear necklaces of decorative design; some of them have their names in Arabic; some have the word Allah. Arabic writing and characters are the same as any other language; the fact that Allah chose to reveal His message in Arabic does not impart any sanctity to the language itself or the way it is written. The idea that Arabic is sacred is held by well-meaning people, but this is incorrect. A necklace with a name is simply a piece of jewellery. However, if the inscription includes Allah's name, she should not wear it in unclean places, such as the toilet. She should take it off, or keep it under her clothing. If a man wears a necklace, it should not be of gold. See Arabic.

Neckties. It is not true that it is forbidden for Muslim to wear a necktie during prayer as is frequently said, the reason given because it is in the form of a cross, the Christian symbol. However, no-one, Christian or otherwise, is thinking of a cross when he wears a necktie. Large areas of the Muslim world wear western dress, including ties. It is perfectly permissible to wear them during salah.

Negus, the. The Christian ruler of Abyssinia/Ethiopia was a man called Ashamah, and his title was the Negus. When the early Muslims were cruelly persecuted, many emigrated to Abyssinia for refuge, including Prophet's cousin Ja'far b. Abu Talib. The Quraysh led by Amr ibn al-As pursued them, but after Ja'far recited the Quranic passages about Isa and Maryam, the Negus felt this was so close to his own beliefs that he would not abandon them. He became their guardian and protector. When the emigrant Ubaydallah died, the Negus arranged the marriage of his widow Umm Habibah to the Prophet, and performed it for him by proxy. After the Hijrah many Muslims in Abyssinia decided to join the Prophet in Madinah. The Negus provided their transport. Amr b. al-As tried to take refuge with him when the Prophet captured in Makkah, but the Negus informed him that he would only find favour in Abyssinia if he accepted the Prophet, which he then did. The Negus died the year after the Fall of Makkah, and the Prophet prayed the funeral prayer for him in Madinah. There were reports of a light shining over his grave.

Negus al-Muqawqis. The name of the ruler of Egypt who sent two Coptic Christian girls to the Prophet after the Prophet wrote to him inviting him to accept Islam. (See Maryam Qibtiyyah). He also sent the Prophet the white mule, called Duldul (the Porcupine), which the Prophet rode in the Battle of Hunayn.

Nifaq. Hypocrisy. See Munafiq.

Night of Ascent. See Laylat ul-Miraj.

Night of Power. See Laylat ul-Qadr.

Nikah. The marriage ceremony, consisting of the reciting of readings from the Qur'an, the agreement to the terms of the dowry, the exchange of vows in front of witnesses, and the signing of the agreement to the specific details of the marriage contract. For example, if a bride does not wish to give permission for later wives, it is sensible to make this clear in the nikah certificate. The bride does not have to have a special dress, or even be present if she does not wish to, so long as she sends her 'wali' or marriage representative and two genuine witnesses to her willingness to the marriage and the terms. The scarlet and gold dresses, henna pattern-painting, and huge parties are of cultural origin and have nothing to do with Islam. In fact, the Prophet strongly disapproved of such ostentation, particularly if it caused a financial burden to the people concerned.

The couple are legally married once the contract has been signed, but because of their age or personal circumstances they may decide not to live together until later (like the Prophet and Aishah, or the parents of the Prophet Jesus). A walimah serves the function of announcing publicly that the couple are legally married and entitled to live together.

Ni'matullah Order. A Shi'ite Sufi order named after Shaykh Nur ad-Din Muhammad Ni'matullah Wali (730/1330-834/1431) in Mahan near Kirman in South-west Iran. His followers are now found mostly in Iran and India.

Niqab. A type of hijab that covers the entire face. A woman should never be forced to wear this, since the Prophet specifically stated that face and hands need not be covered. Indeed, many hadiths confirm that the women who were his companions never wore this sort of covering.

an-Nisa. 'Woman'. The title of surah 4, dealing with many of the rights of women.

Nisab. The minimum amount of wealth of whatever kind that zakat can be deducted from. See Zakah.

Niyyah. Deliberate intention. The intention of a person to do something is all important, and in many cases counts as much as the action itself. If you intended to do a particular thing, but were prevented by your circumstances, it would count for you as if you did it (i.e. wished to help a sick person but they died before you got there). If you did a good deed as it were by accident, without the intention of it being so, it would not count for you. Similarly, if you did a bad deed without that being the intention, it would not count against you (e.g. you killed someone in an accident).

Nizamuddin Awliya (1238-1325). A Sufi saint of the Chisti order,

Hazrat Nizamuddin's shrine in New Delhi.

whose tomb is at Delhi in the region named after him. The saint is believed to have lived for about 100 years, preaching love, compassion, tolerance, and self-control, all of which paved the way to communal harmony and Hindu-Muslim unity. After the death of Hazrat Nizamuddin in 1325, the area around his *dargah* became the burial ground of Muslim nobles. Around the shrine are the tombs of the poets, Amir Khusro (1325) and Mirza Ghalib (1869) as also of the Mughal princess, Jahanara (1681) and the Mughal Emperor, Muhammad Shah (1784).

Noah. See Nuh.

Nubuwwah. The means of gaining Divine Guidance through revelation. See Nabi.

Nudity. Appearing naked. This is disapproved of in Islam. Modesty is the more natural attitude of a Muslim, even in intimate sexual relationships between husband and wife.

Nuh. Noah. (i) One of the chief named prophets in the Qur'an and Old Testaments. He lived in a very corrupt society, which was warned about its behaviour, but refused to listen. They were then warned of a catastrophe to come, and refused to believe. In the end, they were wiped out by a great flood, and only the believers in Nuh's family were saved by building a huge ship, or Ark (7:59-64). In the Qur'an version, one of Nuh's wives and sons refused to believe or enter the Ark, and consequently were drowned (11:45-47; 66:10). The main lesson was the hard one for Nuh that he could not plead for or have spared even close members of his family—each person is responsible for his or her own judgement. See Deluge.

(ii) The title of surah 71 which gives the story of Nuh (Noah), and every conscious believer's struggle against blind materialism and lack of spiritual values.

an-Nur. Title of surah 24, 'the Light'; a Madinan surah of 64 verses describing God as the light of the Heavens. Most of the surah deals with ethical rules and legal injunctions concerning personal relationships between the sexes. It includes teaching on the penalties for illicit sexual intercourse and the individual's right to privacy.

Nur Muhammadi. The technical term for the doctrine of the pre-existence of the soul of the Prophet Muhammad. This was an early doctrine in Shi'ite Islam and was found in Sunni Islam from the third century AH.

Nusaybah bint Ka'b. Also called Umm Umarah. A woman of Khazraj, one of the two women who took the Second Pledge of Aqabah. She was an example of the women who fought as warriors alongside the Prophet. She was at his side in the Battle of Uhud when he was attacked by Ibn Qamiah. The Prophet's friend Shammas was cut down, and then Nusaybah sustained a deep shoulder wound saving the Prophet's life. At the Treaty of Hudaybiyah, when the Muslims shaved their hair after the sacrifice, she collected the Prophet's hair and preserved it until she died (a practice he actually disapproved of!) She tended the wounded and provided water at the Battle of Khaybar. In the Caliphate of Abu Bakr she fought against the rival 'Prophet' Musaylimah in the Battle of Yamana, a battle in which her son Khalid was slain. She sustained 12 injuries, and fought until her hand was cut off. Eventually Musaylimah was brought down by Wahshi (the same javelin expert who killed the Prophet's uncle Hamzah) and finished off by another of her sons, Abdullah. She transmitted many hadiths.

Nusayris. Members of a group also called 'Alawis (i.e. those who follow Ali). Their name derives from one of their early leaders, Muhammad ibn Nusayr. They exist in Syria, Turkey and Lebanon, and in Turkey are also known as Alevis.

Nushuz. Rebellion or ill-will. It means any kind of deliberate bad behaviour of a wife towards her husband, or husband towards his wife, including mental cruelty and deliberate persistent breach of marital obligations. See Wife-beating.

Nusuk. A sacrifice. A religious act of worship.

Oil sheikhs. Many Muslim leaders have become exceedingly rich in this century due to the discovery of oil. Some Muslims believe this was warned of centuries ago, when the Prophet stated that the biggest test of the faith of his people would be that of possessing wealth, and making the right use of it. Others, however, point out that 'The Prophet's people' includes Muslims of every race, and not just Arabs.

Old age. Old people should be cherished and valued in Islam, for their wisdom and experience. It is the duty of children to look after and take care of their parents when that becomes necessary, in partial repayment of the care taken of them when they were helpless children (17:23-24). Old people should always be treated with respect, even if their mental faculties are no longer clear and sharp. The Prophet once made an old lady cry when he told her there were no old people in Heaven; but her grief turned to joy when he explained that all the inhabitants of that blessed place were given renewed youth and vigour. See Huri.

Omnipresence. One of the chief characteristics of Allah; it means that He is present everywhere, from the most minute scale even smaller than the atomic level, to the vastest reaches of existence. 'To God belong the east and the west; wherever you turn, there is the Presence of God; for God is All-Pervading, All-Knowing.' (2:115, 142) 'Most certainly We shall relate to them with knowledge, for We were never absent (at any time or from any place).' (7:7) See Witness.

Omnipotence. One of the chief characteristics of Allah; it means to have power over all things, absolute control over all affairs. 'Whatever God grants to humanity out of His mercy, no-one can withhold; and what he withholds no-one can grant apart from Him. He is the (source of) Power, the All-Knowing.' (35:2).

Omniscience. One of the chief characteristics of Allah, it means that He knows everything in every sphere of existence, no matter how great or small, universal or intimate. 'God has the key to the Unseen, the treasures none know but He. he knows whatever is on land or in the sea; no leaf falls without His knowning it; there is not a grain in the darkness of earth, or a green or dry thing, but it is carefully noted.' (6:69). See also 31:16; 67:14; Witness, Khabar.

Oneness of God. See Tawhid.

Option, verses of. 33:28-29 are known as the verses of the Option. The Prophet was allowed to offer to his wives the choice of remaining in marriage with him, which involved a highly austere and self-sacrificing form of life, or of being released from him and well provided for. They all emphatically rejected thoughts of separation and declared that they had chosen God and His Apostle and the Life to Come. Many early scholars held that the subsequent revelation of v. 52 constituted God's reward for their choice, and attitude.

Organisations. A good case of good and evil coming from the same plant! When people organise themselves in order to do good, it adds to individual strength and can produce amazing results. However, one of the big problems faced by Muslims today is the proliferation of all sorts of organisations whose aims are twofold—to be recognised as the 'best' way of being a Muslim, and to 'represent' Islam in their society. Unfortunately, the value of these organisations depends to a large extent on the calibre of the leaders, and the groups have largely proved divisive and destructive. The Prophet disapproved of anything that divided up the followers into cliques or groups (2:176; 3:105).

Orphans. See Yatim.

Ottomans. A dynasty of Muslim Caliphs in Turkey, whose fortunes commenced with the capture of Constantinople. In the C13, the Mamelukes ruled Egypt, but North Africa and the East had Mongol rulers, who had settled down and become Muslims. When they attacked Anatolia, the Seljuks of Anatolia appealed to the Turks for help. The warrior Othman successfully captured Anatolia, and his descendants—the Ottomans—went on to make almost all of the old Arab and Byzantine Empires their own. The line lasted through 36 Caliphs, from 1295 to 1925, reaching its heights under such as Salim the Grim (1512-1520) who defeated the Safavids and Mamelukes, and Suleiman the Magnificent (1520-1566) who conquered Egypt, Syria, Iraq, North Africa and the Balkans. In the 19th century the decline of Turkish power set in, and Turkey was known as the 'sick man of Europe'. Revolutions followed, and the Caliphate was abolished in 1924 by Mustafa Kamal (known as Ataturk), who set up a Socialist Republic and deposed the last Ottoman. Since then there has been no official Caliphate, although many Muslims wish to restore the office.

Pacifism. The notion that one should not fight, or do military service. Muslims, although peace-loving, are not total pacifists because it is felt that there are certain circumstances in which it would be wrong *not* to fight. Muslims dislike cowardice, or attempts to brush off responsibility or 'hide things under the carpet'. It is a Muslim's duty to defend the weak, the oppressed, the exploited, the downtrodden, and those persecuted for their religion. It is particularly important for Muslims not to allow those who have previously claimed to be Muslim to spread false notions about the faith in order to engender hatred. A 'double-danger' is that frequently those who do the most damage to Islam are themselves highly religious and devout Muslims who have rather intolerant and inflexible natures, who believe their distorted and extreme views really are the true Islam. The most effective way to counter this kind of unpleasantness is to show the true teachings and way of life set out by the Prophet, so that the grounds for criticism are removed.

Palestinian Problem. See PLO.

Pan-Arabism. The idea of unification of all Arab states into one United Arab Republic (UAR) on the lines of the United States of America (USA) or Union of Soviet Socialist Republics (USSR—now broken up). Problems include considering who might qualify—those who are born Arabs, or those to whom Arabic is the natural language?

Pan-Islam. A more Muslim idea than Pan-Arabism; the idea of the unification of all Muslim states, Unfortunately, one of the main failings of those whose Islam is only skin-deep is divisiveness and nationalist fervour, so a political Islamic Union is unlikely. Many Muslims, however, favour the idea of a return to the Madinah ideal, the creation of a Kingdom of Islam, which would be led by a Caliph and would include all Muslims, no matter what nationality.

Paraclete. In 61:6 the Prophet Isa (Jesus) mentioned a messenger to come after him, whose name would be Ahmad. There are several references in St. John's Gospel (14:16, 15:26, 16:7) to the Parakletos (usually translated as 'Comforter') who was to come. Christians interpret this to mean that after Isa's ascension to heaven, the third person of the Holy Trinity, known as the Holy Spirit, would come. However, many people feel that the Holy Spirit had long been active in the world, as the activity of God Almighty, and that these references were really to the Prophet Muhammad. It is suggested that parakletos was a corruption of Periklytos (lit. the 'much praised') which is a Greek translation of the Aramaic term or name Mawhamana. Periklytos and Mawhamana have the same meaning as Muhammad or Ahmad, both of which derive from the verb 'hamida'—'he praised', and the noun 'hamd'—'praise'. If this theory is true, it means that Isa predicated the next Prophet, Muhammad. Moreover, Isa's many references to the 'Son of Man' who was to come might also refer to him.

Paradise. The Muslim name for Heaven. It comes from the Persian word for garden, paradisa, and its imagery usually includes peaceful scenes of trees, plants and water—much cherished by inhabitants of land which would be desert unless artificially watered and cared for. Descriptions are given in detail in the Qur'an (e.g.: 37:43-48; 38:50-52; 43:70-73; 48:5; 56:11-26 etc.), but most scholars take the point of view that these are to be interpreted symbolically, since the Qur'an states clearly that the true nature of the Afterlife lies beyond human knowledge and understanding (32:17).

Parvez. Ghulam Ahmad Parvez (1903-1985) aimed to promote a pure Islam without the centuries of foreign influence. He was a prolific writer, and in 1938 started publishing the magazine 'Tulu'-i-Islam' (The Dawn of Islam) which has remained the main vehicle for his ideas since then, and is now published in Karachi. He was a fervent opposer of Pakistan's religious classes, whom he saw as the protectors of elite interests and not of true Islam and true rationality. He saw the dangers of false hadith and the shari'ah being viewed as sources of revealed knowledge, and considered that all the Muslim past, with the exception of the time of the Prophet and the first four caliphs must be rejected as a corruption of true Islam, since foreign influences, especially Byzantine and Persian, had become fully embedded in them. For Parvez, the Qur'an alone was absolute, and he hoped to restructure society on its foundations and halt the decline of Muslim civilisation. See Pervayzi.

PBUH. Stands for 'Peace be upon him', the words of respect added by Muslims when speaking about the Prophet Muhammad. Many Muslims also add this phrase when speaking of any other prophet, saint, or noble companion of the Prophet Muhammad—male or female. Sometimes the letters 'saw' are added (this is the same phrase in Arabic—'salaam alaihim wa-salaam') or 'saaw' ('salla Allahu 'Alayhi wa-salaam'—'May the Peace, blessings of Allah be upon him').

People of the Book. (Ahl al-Kitab). The people before the coming of the Prophet Muhammad who believed in One True God through His previous revelations through the many called prophets; in other words, the Jews and Christians (3:64, 70; 29:46).

People of the Cave. See Ashab al-Kahf.

Persecution. The deliberate hurt and abuse of those who are disliked or unwanted for any particular reason. The early Muslims faced enormous persecution for their beliefs, often including physical torture and possible death as well as ridicule and abuse. The Prophet set the example of not retaliating, but acting nobly and with dignity when abused, and forgiving his tormentors when he was in a position to do so. Needless to say, no Muslim should ever persecute any other person, either a person of a different race, culture or belief, or member of their own community or family (22:40).

Pervayzi. A reformist movement that believes in the authority of the Qur'an, without the hadith. They were a splinter group from the Ahl-i-Hadith led by Abdallah Chakralwi, who named his movement the Ahl-al-Qur'an. Two chief exponents were Allama Inayat al-Mashriqi (1888-1960) and Ghulam Ahmad Parvez (1903-1985).

Pharaoh. See Firawn.

Pharaoh's wife. 28:8-9 tells how the Prophet Musa (Moses) was hidden as a baby from the Egyptians, but was cast into the river Nile and discovered by 'Pharaoh's household', identified in v. 9 as Pharaoh's wife. She adopted him as her own son, allowing his own mother to suckle him. See Asiyah.

Photographs. These are allowed in Islam so long as they follow the general rules of Islam; they should not be pornographic or inciting to lust; idolatrous or inciting to leader-worship; or in any way encouraging feelings that are contrary to Islam. Many Muslims do not display photographs of people or animals just as they do not display paintings of them. (See Art in Islam). Some tourist books say Muslims are frightened the photos will take their souls; they should rather say that some primitive peoples might be frightened of that; the idea is impossible in Islam. However, many Muslim women prefer not to have their images recorded by people outside their own family, even when decently dressed, as they do not know how the photograph will be used.

Pilgrimage. The setting out on a special journey with the intention to visit a particular holy place or shrine. See Hajj.

Pilgrimage, the Final. This refers to the only true Hajj performed by the Prophet, the pilgrimage to Makkah after its capture and restoration of the Ka'bah to the worship of the One True God by people who were all committed Muslims. It was on this occasion that he gave his famous Final Sermon.

Pillars of Islam. See Five Pillars.

Pir. The Persian word for spiritual master.

Pishtaq. Monumental gateway, usually decorated with coloured tiles. A feature of Central Asian modiassahs.

PLO. The Palestine Liberation Organisation; a resistance movement set up after the creation of the State of Israel in 1948 which ignored the existence of the Palestinians as owners of the land. The Palestinian Problem began with the rise of the Zionist Movement at the turn of the 20th century, in which many Jews, suffering and persecuted throughout the world, dreamed of having the land of 'Israel' restored to them, although it had been dwelt in by Palestinian Arabs for longer than any Jewish occupation. (See Jerusalem). People and governments were manipulated by politicians for their own ends, and much bitterness resulted. Support for Zionism increased after the Holocaust of the Second World War. The Muslim view was that Jews should be compensated by being given good land in Germany, but in 1948 the British granted them the right to live in Palestine. Many Arab refugees fled to Jordan and their properties were seized. New Jewish settlements sprang up everywhere. Individuals known as the Fedayeen swore to die rather than let Jewish immigrants take their land, and the PLO was one resistance group formed, under the leadership of Yasser Arafat. After decades of violence, peace plans are now in progress to solve the problem.

Polyandry. The practice of a woman being able to marry more than one husband. This is forbidden in Islam, mainly because it is believed that a child has the right to know who its father is, and also because societies usually have far more women than men without partners over the age of 35 (e.g. the USA has nearly 8 million 'surplus' older women, the UK c4 million, Germany c5 million, etc.). See Polygamy.

Polygamy. The practice of allowing more than one spouse to an individual, usually taken to mean a man having more than one wife. Practised widely in pre-Islamic times, polygamy was condoned in Islam like slavery—but it was drastically limited to only certain conditions. Islam really encouraged the removal of both slavery and polygamy. However, polygamy was still allowed, so long as the man had the permission and certain knowledge that his first wife would not be hurt by this (or subsequent wives if he married more than two!) One of the first principles of Muslim behaviour is that one Muslim should not deliberately hurt another, of whatever sex. If a man did take polygamous marriage, he should not marry more than four; he must be able to deal justly with all of them (4:3). He should have sufficient financial resources to look after all their needs (and possible children), must do equal justice to them all, and must have enough energy to satisfy their physical needs (this does not necessarily mean equal sex, of course, which would not be desired or possible!). Polygamy was accepted as a solution to various social problems—the large numbers of widows and orphans left after a battle; when the marriage with the first wife has broken down but neither party wishes to divorce; if the wife suffers from serious illness such as paralysis, when she would appreciate a helper and is also sympathetic to her husband's physical needs; when the wife has become mentally ill, or is so aged, weak and infirm that she cannot manage the household; when a wife's character becomes unacceptable, or she leaves Islam, or has deserted the home and family (for her own fault, not his!); and if the husband has fallen desperately in love with someone else and the marriage would have broken down with a divorce to follow, but the existing wife does not wish to be divorced. It is a gross abuse of Islam when men bend the rules in order to 'trade in an old model for a new one', or try to excuse their own moral weaknesses, or act cruelly. If they hurt a fellow Muslim or wrong them, they will have to face Judgement for it one Day. Islam tries to balance the needs of all concerned. Many Muslim couples suffer from all sorts of misfortunes including serious illness and inability to produce children and so forth, but they try to accept such trials when they come, and may find that their love and marriage relationship is actually strengthened by their compassion for each other.

Polygyny. The literal technical term for a husband taking more than one wife.

Pork. Pork, or flesh of the pig, is a meat declared haram by Allah (2:173; 5:3). This follows the law given in the Tawrat to Musa (see Leviticus 11:7-8; Deuteronomy 14:8 in the Old Testament). The same law was followed by the Prophet Jesus and the first Christians (see St. Matthew's Gospel 5:19) but relaxed by later Christians (see Acts 10:3-7).

Apart from the fact that Allah forbade eating this flesh, it seems to be a meat which has the greatest content of germs and parasites, most of which are contagious and some of which are fatal. The pork tapeworm (balantidium coli) is the largest protozoan affecting humans. It lodges in the intestine. Trichina roundworms (Trichinella Spiralis) are now very common in Europe and the USA.

Muslims living in non-Muslim communities should be aware that any product including 'shortening' or 'animal fat' probably means pork lard. Gelatine can be made from the skin or bones of the pig; insulin is sometimes made from pigs' pancreas; pepsin in cheese-making is usually derived from pig.

The Christian dismissal of the rule against pork was based on a dream experienced by St. Peter. Muslims maintain that no dream, no matter how pious the dreamer, should be used as basis for legislation opposed to God's revealed law. See Food Laws.

Postmortems. Examination of corpses to determine the cause of death is permitted, especially when a crime is suspected or to enable medical students and their teachers to learn about the effects of certain diseases. It is forbidden to show disrespect to the dead body. Islam forbids the disfigurement of those who die in battle, and does not allow the cutting up of bodies for no good reason.

Prayer. The practice of speaking to God. In Islam, five daily prayers are regarded as compulsory (the salah or namaz), and all other prayers are voluntary (nawafil). A person's private requests and supplications to God for help and guidance are known as du'a prayers. Muslims believe that God's angels draw especially close to people when they are praying, and that some times of day are particularly blessed—for example, the end of the night, just before dawn. See Rakah.

Prayer-cap. Covering the head for prayer is always compulsory for a woman. For a man, it is not compulsory, but many Muslims like to wear a cap, turban or ethnic hat.

Prayer-mat. Little carpets used during the salah. These are by no means compulsory; a Muslim may pray anywhere, providing the place is free of impurity. One can pray on footpaths, courtyards, in open fields, etc. It is not necessary to have a mat, cloth, sheet of paper, etc., although these things might make the prayer more comfortable. A prayer-mat has no significance.

Prayer of Light. A famous prayer of the Prophet: 'O Lord! Illumine my heart with light, my sight with light and my hearing with light. Let there be light on my right hand and on my left, and light behind me, and light going before me.'

Pre-destination, see al-Qadrs.

Priests. Servants of shrines who generally fulfil the function of making sacrifices and interceding between God and the believers. The concept is forbidden in Islam; each person stands before God as an individual, and has no priest (22:37). The Imam or prayer leader is not a priest; it has sometimes become a paid job because of circumstances and expediency, but this is not the ideal.

Prophecy. The concept of risalah. If God is to judge us on our actions and lives, then it is only fair that He must provide the rules to guide us, so that we may know His will and choose whether to obey it or not. Prophecy is the function of revealing this will to humanity.

Prophet. A person specially chosen by God to receive insights and messages, to pass them on to humanity for their guidance. (See Nabi, Rasul). when Muslims speak of *the* Prophet, they are referring to the Prophet Muhammad.

Prophet's family. The immediate family of the Prophet included his wife Khadijah and their six children (Qasim and Tayib who died in infancy, Zaynab, Ruqaiyyah, Umm Kulthum and Fatimah); his subsequent twelve wives and Maryam's child Ibrahim; his fostered sons Ali and Zayd ibn Haritha; the husbands and children of his daughters (especially Hasan and Husayn and Zaynab, Fatimah's children; and Umamah, Zaynab's daughter by Abu al-As); his father Abdallah (died before he was born) and mother Aminah (died when he was six); his grandfather Abd al-Muttalib; the sons and daughters of Abd al-Muttalib, including Abu Talib, Abu Lahab, Abbas, Hamzah and seven aunts; his cousins the children of these uncles and aunts; he also included his Bedouin wet-nurse Halimah and his childhood nurse Umm Ayman and her son by Zayd, Usamah.

Prophet's wives. There is some dispute over the exact number. Most contemporary books state that he had nine wives living when he died, which would mean that Rayhanah the Jewess and Maryam Qibtiyyah were only concubines. Other authorities maintain that these ladies definitely had the status of wife. His certain wives were Khadijah bint Khuwaylid, Sawdah bint Zam'a, Aishah bint Abu Bakr, Hafsah bint Umar, Zaynab bint Khuzaymah, Hind bint Abu Umayyah (renamed Umm Salamah), Zaynab bint Jahsh (the Prophet's cousin, previously married to his foster-son Zayd), Juwayriyyah bint al-Harith (an Arab chieftain's daughter), Ramlah bint Abu Sufyan (renamed Umm Habibah), Safiyyah bint Huyayy, and Maymunah bint al-Harith. Khadijah and Zaynab bint Khuzaymah were the two wives who died before the Prophet himself. All were given the title—'Mother of the Faithful' (33:28-34).

Prophets in the Qur'an. 25 are mentioned in the Qur'an by name, but Islam teaches that there were thousands sent before Muhammad—messenger to every age and society. The 'major prophets' were Nuh, Ibrahim, Musa, Sulayman and Isa. Only three are not mentioned in the

Bible—Hud, Salih and Shu'ayb (who was possibly the father-in-law of Musa called Jethro in the Bible). The full list is: Adam, Idris, (Enoch), Nuh (Noah), Hud, Salih, Ibrahim (Abraham), Isma'il (Ishmael), Ishaq (Isaac), Lut (Lot), Yaqub (Jacob), Yusuf (Joseph), Shu'ayb (Jethro), Ayyub (Job), Musa (Moses), Harun (Aaron), Dhulkifl (Ezekiel), Dawud (David), Sulayman (Solomon), Ilyas (Elijah), Al-Yas'a (Elisha), Yunus (Jonah), Zakariyyah (Zechariah), Yahya (John the Baptist), Isa (Jesus), Muhammad. Muhammad was the last prophet in this line. There have been no further prophets since the revelation of the Qur'an.

Punishment. This should be fair and just in Islam. It becomes meaningless if it is so soft that it does not affect the offender or satisfy the sense of justice of the wronged person. It is savage if it is unnecessarily cruel or vindictive. Allah taught that 'the reward for an injury is an equal injury back; but if a person forgives instead, and is reconciled, that will earn reward from Allah' (42:40). No person should be above the law, or able to corrupt the law, or feel unprotected by the law. Some Islamic punishments (hudood) are seen as very harsh by the West, where the crimes concerned are now so common as to appear trivial; they include flogging for public drunkenness and adultery, and amputation of the hand for theft (5:41; 17:32; 24:2-5). The real punishment for a true Muslim is to know that Allah has noted your dishonourable act and you will face judgement for it in Akhirah; this acts not so much as a deterrent as a wiper-out of any such antisocial desire or weakness.

Purdah. An Urdu word referring to the practice of complete social separation of men from women unless they are members of their immediate family, an extreme extension of the sensible requirements that women should never be left alone with men who might take advantage of them. Many Muslim women achieve purdah when out in public by dressing in such a way that they cannot be seen. Islam requires modest dress, but does not lay down the style—this is frequently a matter of local custom. Purdah can be oppressive and an abuse of Islam when it is forced upon women who do not wish to dress in this manner, sometimes by law backed up with a police force! See Hijab.

Purity. See Taharah.

Qabil and Habil. The Qur'an names for Cain and Abel, the sons of Adam.

Qabr. The grave, experienced as a place of peace and light by the rouh of the Mu'min, and as a place of torment and darkness and no space by the rouh of the kafir.

Qabt. Lit. 'contraction,' 'gripping'; the Sufi equivalent of the 'dark night of the soul,' spiritual desolation. See 2:245.

Qada. The unchangeable Divine decree ordained by Allah for the entire universe.

Qada wa Qadar. Decree and destiny. Cannot be changed, but the inidivdual fates of any of His creatures may be altered by His will under certain circumstances.

Qadhf. A false accusation of unchastity. See Slander.

Qadi (pl. qudah). A judge; appointed by the ruler to settle disputes according to the Shari'ah. These should be people of deep insight, profound knowledge of the Shari'ah, and also honest and sincere people of integrity. The Prophet said: 'Qadis are of three types—one type will go to Paradise and the other two to hell. The one that will go to Paradise is the one who understood the truth and judged accordingly. Those who will go to hell are those who judged unjustly after understanding the truth and those who judged in ignorance.' (Abu Dawud, Ibn Majah). See Judge.

Qadiris. See al-Gilani.

al-Qadisiyya, Battle of. Major battle which took place in 15/636 near al-Najaf between the Muslim army under Sa'd ibn Abi Waqqas and the Persians of King Yazdgird III led by Rustam, who was killed.

al-Qadr. (i) The key Muslim doctrine of Allah's complete and final control over the fulfilment of events, or Destiny. This is famous for being one of the most difficult of all theological problems. How does one balance the idea of God knowing absolutely everything with the idea that a human being has freewill? If God knows in advance everything that will happen to a person, then that person's life must be entirely predestined. Furthermore, if God does not intervene to stop particular courses of action or their outcomes, then one can say He alone is responsible for them. This leads to such cases as a thief pleading innocence, because he was predestined to steal, and so forth. No human brain has been able to untangle this problem satisfactorily—but it is a mistake to assume that Islam is a fatalistic religion. Fatalism is an abuse of

Islam, and not true practice. The entire system of a God sending revelations to humanity through the mediation of chosen prophets indicates that humans are expected to listen and make choices, and adjust their lives accordingly (6:91; 23:73). The whole concept of future judgement in Islam depends on personal responsibility. Even if a scholar argues that God always knows from the outset what the ultimate fate of each individual soul will be, but allows that soul a lifetime as a human in order to prove it to himself/herself, it does not answer the question of why God should choose to go through the exercise. The most satisfactory conclusion is that God knows everything and every possibility, but humans do not. Therefore, if a human chooses to do a particular thing, then there will be a particular outcome leading to one conclusion. If the human chooses a different course of action, then the outcome and conclusion will also be different. For example, if you choose to walk in front of the next lorry, you will die this afternoon; but if you choose to look before you step out into the road, you will not be hit by the lorry, and so on. The full answer to the riddle is part of al-Ghayb, the Unknown.

(ii) Destiny; the title of surah 97. One of the earliest revelations. A Makkan surah of 5 verses.

Qaf. Title of surah 50, one of the letters of the Arabic alphabet; a Makkan surah of 45 verses, the most famous of which is the declaration that Allah is closer to us than our jugular veins (v. 16). It deals with the subjects of death and resurrection

al-Qalam. 'The Pen'; the title of surah 68, one of the earliest revelations. It alludes to those who taunted and ridiculed the Prophet. It mentions the patience of the Prophet Yunus (Jonah). A Makkan surah of 52 verses which reassures the Prophet that he has not gone mad.

al-Qamar. Title of surah 54, 'the Moon'; mainly Makkan, with 55 verses; it refers to the approaching Hour of Judgement, and refers to signs of the Last Hours. See Moon-splitting, Miracles.

Qard Hasan. Lit. 'goodly loan.' Spending generously or doing selfless good deeds for the sake of Allah.

Qari. Lit. 'a reader' (2:245). One who can recite correctly and is acquainted with the science of tajwid. Singular of Qurra'; a well-versed person in the knowledge of Qur'an. One who memorizes and recites the Qur'an.

al-Qari'ah. Title of surah 101, 'the Sudden Misfortune'; a Makkan surah of 11 verses, referring to Judgement, and the coming of the Last Hour.

Qasama. The oath taken by some people (50 men) of a tribe of a person who is being accused of killing somebody.

al-Qasas. Title of surah 28, 'the Story'; a Makkan surah of 88 verses, about half of which tells the story of Musa (Moses).

Qasida. A verse from the diwan of a Sufi shaikh.

al-Qasim. Son of the Prophet and Khadijah, who died aged c 2.

Qatl. Killing, putting to death. Life is sacred and Allah's gift. All forms of unlawful killing are forbidden in the Qur'an (17:31f; 6:151; 25:68f). The penalty for murder is death, but the sentence is tempered with mercy. the fate of the murderer is placed in the hands of the victim's family. They may choose some other penalty for the murderer, for example, money compensation. The Prophet said the best way i.e. the way most pleasing to Allah, was to forgive the murderer. See Qisas, Diyyah.

Qaum al-Fasikin. People who insist on committing sins even though they are consciously aware that they are sins. They transgress deliberately, perhaps mistakenly confident that there is no God and His witnessing of everything is not real. (5:111; 9:24, 80; 61:5; 63:6).

Qaum al-Kafirun. Unbelieving people. These are people who have seen all the evidence of God's goodness and the way of life that is honourable and compassionate, but who still cannot bring themselves to believe in the existence of God, or any realm other than that of the material. They are therefore in a state of refusal of His guidance (2:264; 5:70; 9:37; 16:107). See Kufr.

Qaum az-Zalimin. Unjust people. These are people who do not wish to follow the gentle and kind ways of Allah, and therefore have refused His guidance. (2:258; 3:86; 5:54; 6:144; 9:19,109; 28:50; 46:10; 61:7; 62:5).

Qayamah. See Judgement Day.

Qaynuqa. Major Jewish clan in Madinah, ultimately expelled from that city. It is said they went to Syria.

Qayrawan. Tunisian city of Kairouan, founded in 43/663 or 50/760 by Uqba ibn Nafi. It became a great cultural centre under the Aghlabids and the focus of Maliki jurisprudence.

Qiblah. The direction of Makkah. All Muslims try to face in this direction while praying. Mosques usually have a qiblah niche showing the direction; prayer mats sometimes have a compass (and a little booklet with instructions on how to use it); streets and prominent places in Muslim societies often have an arrow to point the direction.

Qirad. Wealth put by an investor in the trust of an agent for use in commercial purposes, the agent receiving no wage, but taking a designated share of the profits.

Qisas. The notion of exact revenge, or 'an eye for an eye'; this was laid down by God in order to *limit* revenge not to encourage it (42:40). It is always better to forgive, and leave the punishment to Allah. See Judgement Day.

Qitfir. Potiphar in the Bible, the purchaser of Yusuf (Joseph). He is not actually named in the Qur'an.

Qiyam. The position of standing upright, halfway through the salah prayer. See Rakah.

al-Qiyamah. Title of surah 75, 'the Resurrection'; a Makkan surah of 40 verses, in which some of the signs of the Day of Resurrection are itemized.

Qiyam-ul-Layl. Voluntary extra prayers performed during the night.

Qiyas. (from Qasa—measure, compare, correlate). The principle of working out new rulings or decisions for modern society by way of analogy with the principles of rules given in Qur'an or hadith. See Ijtihad.

Quba. A village on the outskirts of Madinah.

Qubbah. A dome or cupola.

Qubbat al-Sakhra. The Dome of the Rock in Jerusalem.

Qudrah. A person's freewill to act by his/her own capacity. Power, with the sense of determining one's own existence. See al-Qadr.

Qudrat. Allah's power and dominion. (2:20, 106, 109, 148, 259, 284; 3:26, 29, 165, 189; 5:19, 21, 43, 123; 6:17; 8:41; 9:39; 11:4; 16:77; 18:45; 2:6; 25:45; 29:20; 30:50; 33:27; 35:1; 41:39; 42:9; 46:33; 48:21; 57:1; 59:6; 64:1; 65:12; 66:8; 67:1.) He has only to say to a non-existing thing 'Be,' and it is so. (2:117; 3:47, 59; 6:73; 16:40; 19:35; 36:82; 40:68) See Malakut, Omnipotence, Omni-science.

Queen of Sheba. See Bilqis.

Qul ceremony. A ceremony of remembrance and mourning held on the third, tenth or fortieth day after the death of a person. Although widely practised in some Muslim societies, there is actually no justification for this practice in Islam; it is an innovation. There is nothing wrong in remembering and praying for dead loved ones, at any time. Qul ceremonies, however, tend to become occasions which can be burdensome to many concerned, and can make people feel guilty. The burden and feelings of guilt are unnecessary. See Urs.

Qunut. Special supplications made during the salah prayer particularly in the standing position after ruku' in the subh prayer.

Qur'an. The 'Mother of Books' (Umm al-Kitab); the collection of messages Allah revealed to the Prophet Muhammad over a period of 23 years (10:37). 'This is the Book, there is no doubt in it, a guide for those who are consciously aware' (2:2). One verse is called an ayah or 'sign' (pl. ayat), one chapter is called a surah or 'step up'. The complete Qur'an contains 114 surahs, all except surah 9 which begin 'In the name of Allah, the Compassionate, the Merciful'. The surahs are not given in the order the Prophet received them, but the order fixed shortly before he died. The first surah now is called al-Fatihah, the Opener. The first revelation given was the first part of Surah 96, and the last was the first part of Surah 5. When not in use, the Qur'an should be stored in a respectful manner that keeps it clean and protected; before handling or using it a person should be in state of wudu, and in a suitable frame of mind. While it is being read, people should not chat, eat or drink, make a noise or behave in a disrespectful manner. It should not be placed on the floor—Muslims often use a wooden stand called a kursi or rehl. It would not be suitable to read it while a TV programme or video was in the background, or in an unsuitable

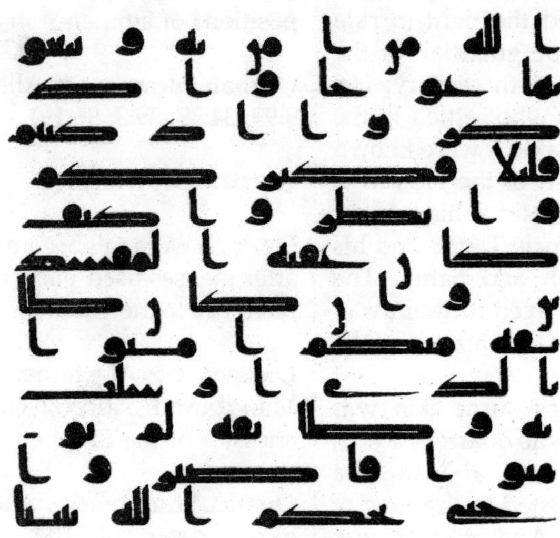

A page of the Qur'an in early Kufic style

place such as a pub (where a Muslim should not be anyway). The handling of Qur'ans in public places such as shops, libraries and schools has upset some Muslims, but they should consider the niyyah behind the use of the Holy Book. If it is being offered for sale or studied by the public at large, it is impossible to expect them to be in wudu or even to accept the principle. That comes later, for practising Muslims.

Qur'an, eternal tablet. See Tablet

Quraysh. Title of surah 106, a continuation of surah 105, al-Fil. It is a Makkan surah of 4 verses, and orders the Quraysh to serve Allah who has fed and protected them.

Quraysh. One of the great tribes in Arabia. The Messenger of Allah belonged to this tribe. The chief Qusayy gained the right to rule Makkah and be guardian of the Ka'bah in the fifth century. His close relatives who settled in the valley near Makkah were known as the Quraysh of the Hollow—the tribes of Qusayy, his brother Zuhrah, his uncle Taym, and his cousins Jumah and Sahm. The Quraysh who lived further away were known as the Quraysh of the Outskirts.

Qusayy's favourite son was Abd ad-Dar, who quarrelled with his brother Abd al-Manaf—a conflict that lasted to the time of the Prophet. Abd ad-Dar was supported by Makhzum, Sahm, Jumah, Adi and their families. These became known as the Confederates. Abd al-Manaf was supported by Asad, Zuhrah, Taym and Harith ibn Fihr. They sealed their pact by bathing their hands in a bowl of perfume at the Ka'bah, and thus became known as al-Mutayyabun—the Scented Ones.

The Quraysh were badly split by Islam, many becoming converts and many becoming bitter enemies. Individual members of families were set against each other. Once the Muslims began to make eminent converts, such as Umar ibn al-Khattab and Hamzah ibn Abd al-Muttalib, the Quraysh placed a boycott on the entire clan of Hashim until the Hashimites themselves outlawed the Prophet. The clan of Muttalib refused to sign, and was included in the ban.

In due course, the Quraysh were converted and rose to positions of eminence in Islam.

Qurbah. Nearness to Allah (5:27; 9:99; 34:37; 39:3; 96:19).

Qurban. See Sacrifice.

Quru'. A woman's becoming pure after menses used particularly in reference to the 'iddah of divorce.

Qusayy. C5 AD father of Abd Manaf and Abd al-Uzza, an ancestor of the Prophet.

Qussas. Story-tellers, who, in the early days of the Muslim community, transmitted religious knowledge in a popular manner to the general public.

Qutb. 'Pole', 'axis;' in Sufism, it means the head of an invisible hierarchy of saints upon whom depends the proper order of the universe. Most Sunni jurists would allocate this function to the angels.

Qutb. Sayyid Qutb, born 1906 and executed in 1966 for his role in the plot against the Egyptian president Nasser. Spokesman for the Radical Islamist Egypt Muslim Brotherhood, al-Ikhhwan al-Muslimun. His main aim was to purify Islam of the corruption of Western morals and influence in general, through revolutionary social action. Islam should regulate life totally, and with its full acceptance, social justice and political freedom would follow. Reason and public welfare should work within the moral principles of Islam, an order which rested on three principles—the justice of the ruler, the obedience of the ruled, and the shura or consultation by which the ruler is elected, controlled, and if need be, deposed. All political parties would be outlawed. Qutb's tafsir was called 'Fi zilal al-Qur'an' (In the shade of the Qur'an).

Quwwat. The might and invincibility of Allah (2:165; 6:18; 12:39; 18:39; 22:74; 28:78; 40:16; 51:58; 85:12). See Omnipotence, Malakut.

Rabb. The title 'Master', used for Allah. In Arabic, Rabb has a wide complex of meanings. It is perhaps best translated by the word Sustainer. It includes the ideas of having just claim to the possession of something and consequently having authority and power over it. It also included rearing, sustaining and fostering anything from its original plan or first stage to its completion. One who enables a thing or person to grow and develop, and eventually fulfil all its potential. Nothing in the universe comes into being in a state of perfection or fulfilment; in its origin it has certain potentialities which, when developed and actualised, enable the object concerned to become what it was designed to be. Humans also have an enormous number of potential skills and qualities, which, if properly realised, enable them to rise from the animal to the human level. Allah wishes every human to develop all his or her latent potential, for good.

Rabia al-Adawiyyah. (d. 801) A famous Muslim woman teacher and mystic, who preached the way of divine love. She lived a life of extreme self-denial and prayer in Basrah, Iraq.

Rabi' al-Akhir. The fourth month of the Muslim calendar.

Rabi' al-Awwal. The third month of the Muslim calendar.

Racism. The persecution, either verbal or physical, of people of a different race, frequently practised when someone arrogantly feels that another person's racial origin, colour, accent or physical appearance is inferior or funny. Forbidden in Islam (5:9).

ar-Ra'd. Title of surah 13, 'the Thunder'; a Madinan surah of 43 verses, in which the thunder is described as praising God. The main theme is the revelation of fundamental moral truths which we may not neglect without suffering the consequences.

Rada. The good pleasure of Allah towards those who make an effort to serve and please Him.

Rafidi. (pl. arfad or rawafid). A rejector, the general term used by Sunnis of Shi'ites, especially in mediaeval times. The Shi'ites rejected the legitimacy of the caliphs Abu Bakr, Umar and Uthman.

Rahbaniyyah. The concept of monastic life with its exaggerated asceticism, often denying any value to life in this world. This attitude was common amongst early Christians, but disapproved of in Islam (2:143; 57:27). Muslims are expected to live and work within their community and not to withdraw from the world. The Muslim way involves marriage and family relationships, and not celibacy.

Allah requested His followers to be a 'community of the middle way, so that (with your lives) you might bear witness to the truth before all humanity, and that the Messenger might bear witness to it before you' (2:143).

Rahib. A Monk. Monks were Christians who lived separately from other people, either alone as hermits, or in communities. Islam disapproves of such withdrawal from the community, which is a permanent state. Short-term withdrawal for meditation is approved (see i'tikaf). Spiritual people should live and work as part of general society, not withdraw with a 'holier-than-thou' mentality. Monks were criticised in 9:34 for living at the expense of others. This was particularly true of hermits and those who did not support themselves by their own toil.

Rahila. A fast racing camel.

Rahim. The Merciful. One of the many epithets for Allah given in the Qur'an. Both Rahim and Rahman are derived from the noun Rahmah, which means mercy, compassion, loving tenderness and grace.

ar-Rahman. Title of surah 55, 'the Merciful'; a Madinan surah of 78 verses, it refers to one of the Allah's most frequently used titles. It deals with the Last Day and the life to come.

Rajab. The seventh month. One of the four sacred months, in which fighting is prohibited.

ar-Rajim. An epithet of Iblis or Shaytan—translated as 'the Accursed'; 'the Stoned' and 'the Outcast'.

Rakah. (literally 'bowing') one complete unit of movements and words during the salah prayer. It consists of 8 separate acts of devotion; (i) takbir—the shutting out of the world and its distractions; (ii) placing hands on the chest and praising God, reciting the Fatihah and another prayer; (iii) ruku—the bowing at the hips to show respect for Allah; (iv) qiyam—the straightening up again and acknowledging awareness of God's presence; (v) sujud or sajdah—the prostration on the ground, touching the earth with forehead, nose, palms, knees and toes; (vi) kneeling up again; (vii) sujud repeated; (viii) sitting up again and either preparing to repeat the rakah or finishing it. At the end of the rakahs, the Muslim performs the salam, turning the head to right and left to greet the angels. The number of compulsory rakahs is two for fajr, four for zuhr, four for asr, three for maghrib and four for isha. Most Muslims perform many more than this set number, usually completing enough to end in an odd number (witr). It is considered polite and normal to offer two rakahs when entering a mosque, as a 'greeting to the mosque'.

Ramadan. The month of fasting (see Fasting). The ninth month of the Islamic calendar.

Ramal. 'Hastening'; Fast walking accompanied by the movements of the arms and legs to show one's physical strength. This is to be observed in the first three rounds of the Tawaf around the Ka'bah, and is to be done by the men only and not the women.

Rami. Throwing the pebbles at the jamras at Mina. See Jamras, Mina.

Raml. See Ramal.

Rasul. A Prophet who has been granted a revelation which has been written down. Usually used as a name by Muslims for the Prophet Muhammad.

Ratiba muwakkada. Voluntary prayers which the Prophet stressed as being very important, as opposed to casual prayers.

Rawdah. A remembrance feast or service, usually taking place 40 days after the death of a person. It is based on culture, and is not compulsory nor normal in Islam. See Qul.

Rawi. (pl. ruwat). A story-teller, transmitter of hadith or of old Arab poetry.

Ra'y (pl. ara). Opinion, idea. In Islamic jurisprudence it has the sense of personal opinion, individual judgement or speculation not based on a recognised source of Law. A judge's decision based on his own discretion.

Rayhanah. A Nadirite Jewess, who had married a man of Bani Qurayzah. She was a woman of great beauty, and was taken by the Prophet after the execution of her husband following the Battle of the Trench in 627. At first she was put in the care of his aunt Salmah, along with other Jews who had converted to Islam, and she also converted. Her status as regards the Prophet is not known for certain; he either married her, or kept her as a protected concubine. See Prophet's Wives.

ar-Razi. He was a great physician who ran the hospital in Baghdad in the 9th century AD. He wrote a medical encyclopaedia in which he discussed measles, smallpox, kidney stones and skin diseases, amongst other things. He was the first scientist to tell the difference between smallpox and measles. Muslims in Turkey practised vaccination from smallpox in 1679, and the knowledge was brought to Europe through Lady Montague, the wife of the British Ambassador who had a great admiration for Islam. Ar-Razi wrote some 200 medical works which were translated into Latin. He died in 925 AD.

Record of Deeds. The work of your two recording angels, the creation of your 'book' on which your judgement will be based (Surah 82:10-11). Any good deed remains as a permanent entry, but bad deeds can be obliterated if the offender is genuinely sorry and seeks God's forgiveness, and also the forgiveness of the offended party.

Rehl. Another name for 'kursi', the little thrones on which Qur'ans are placed.

Reincarnation. The doctrine (common to Hinduism and Buddhism) that a soul does not live once on earth, but after the death of a particular body, leaves that body and comes back to earth in another body—either immediately, or after a period of time. The soul may also enter animal or plant forms.

In Islam, this theory is part of al-Ghayb. The Qur'an teaches that after one's earthly life, the soul of each individual will face a judgement on that life in due course, at a time known only to Allah. However, Allah only has to say to a thing 'Be!' and it is so. If Allah willed a soul to live in more than one earthly host-body, it would certainly not be impossible for Him to achieve this. We can only say it is not part of Islamic teaching as given in the Qur'an, and Allah knows best the truth of the matter.

Relics of the Prophet (e.g. hair, garments etc.). Many mosques claim to preserve hairs from the Prophet's beard, and so on, and even pay homage to them. These may be curiosities, but there are no guarantees that they are genuine, and should not be revered as objects of shirk. Venerating relics of the Prophet, or any other saintly person, is not the right way to show love for the Prophet—no reverence to his hair or any other part of his body will be of use to a Muslim on the Day of Judgement. See Nusaybah.

Repentance. (Tawbah). Repentance means being genuinely sorry for the things we have done wrong, or for not doing the things we ought to have done. Returning to correct action after error. When we truly repent, Allah forgives us, even if the persons we have wronged may not be able to; but the repentance must be before our death (2:161; 39:53). See Kaffarah.

Resurrection. To rise from the dead. Muslims believe that the whole of humanity will be resurrected at a time when God wills, and face Judgement Day. Non-believers point out that there is no scientific evidence for this, and that dead bodies decompose and rot away. Perhaps the only element of a human being that survives is the soul? However, Allah points out that the renewed creation of a body that has died is no more difficult than the creation of a human's first body; a time will come when each person will be resurrected 'even to the tips of their fingers'—that is, even the individual finger prints! (75:4). However, our resurrected bodies will bear no resemblance to our present ones. Allah said: 'I will create you in forms you know not of' (56:61). The ultimate fate of any person or body is a matter not known by anyone except Allah. See Akhirah.

Revelation. Truths that come from beyond the human mind; messages from God. See Nazala.

Rhazes. See ar-Razi.

Riba. Making interest on loaned money. In its general sense this term denotes an addition to or increase of a particular thing over and above its original size or amount. It becomes immoral and against the will of Allah when it signifies unlawful addition, by way of interest, to money or goods lent by one person or group to another. According to Ibn Abbas, the last revelation granted to the Prophet before he died a few days later was 2:275-281 on the subject of riba, in which he made clear that on the Day of Judgement every human being will be repaid in full for what they had earned, and none would be wronged. The Companions had no opportunity to ask about the shari'ah implications of the injunction. The main offence of riba is the exploitation of those who are economically weak by those who are strong and have the resources. See Usury.

Ribat. A fortress, or Muslim stronghold, or hospice—usually on the frontiers of Islam. (From ribata—to bind or post).

Rida. Rashid Rida (1865-1935) was an associate of Muhammad Abduh and helped to publish the modernist journal al-Manar. He argued that following all the traditional hadith sciences was simple taqlid. The sunnah, based on hadith, therefore needed severe examination.

Riddah. Apostasy from Islam. An apostate, or one who leaves Islam and turns against it, is called a murtadd.

Ridwan. An angel in charge of Paradise; he will set out robes of honour for the Prophet at the Last Day. He will also feed the blessed fasters as they rise from their graves.

Ridwan Allah. The approval and pleasure of Allah. The sublime serenity of contentment that fills the heart.

Rifa'iyyah. A Sufi order named after Shaykh Ahmad ibn Ali al-Rifa'i (499/1106-577/1182). He lived mainly in the marshland of southern Iraq, and had many disciples famous for their extreme practices such as eating live snakes and various feats with fire. Ibn Battuta encountered a large group of Rifa'i dervishes and commented with fascination on their practices. It was a widespred order, found in Egypt, Syria, Palestine, Asia Minor and the Maldives. The Order has spread to Eastern Europe and the Caucasus, and more recently in North America.

Righteousness. In the Qur'an, surah 2:177, righteousness is defined as follows: 'It is not righteousness to turn your faces towards east or west, but this is righteousness—to believe in Allah and the Day of Judgement, and the Angels, and the Book, and the Messengers; to give from your wealth out of love for God to your family, to those without family, to the needy, to the wayfarer, to those who ask, and for the freeing of slaves; to be steadfast in prayer, and practise regular giving; to fulfil all the promises which you have made; to be firm and patient in suffering and adversity, and through all periods of panic. Such are the people of truth, the God-fearing.'

Rihlah. 'Journey' for the purpose of pilgrimage to Makkah, or to study and gather knowledge from scholars elsewhere. One famous hadith urges Muslims to seek knowledge even as far as China. Many scholars spent their lifetimes in travel. The best known Muslim travelogue is that of Ibn Battuta.

Risala. A Collection of hadiths which deals with one particular topic selected from the eight topics into which the contents of the Jami' books of hadiths are generally classified; these include belief, laws and rules on all the subjects of fiqh from ritual purity to legacies, piety and asceticism, manners in eating drinking etc. Qur'anic commentary, historical and biographical matters, crises anticipated towards the end of the world, and the virtues and defects of various people, places, etc.

Risalah. Arabic name for Prophecy.

Riwaq (pl. arwiqa). Lit. 'tent', 'tent-flap', 'porch'; the word has the specialist sense of living and working areas for students. The cloister bordering the courtyard of a mosque. Each riwaq might be named after a particular nationality or region, as at al-Azhar.

Riwaya. A reading or transmission of the Qur'an or another text.

Rububiyyah. The process by which a person or object fulfils what it (or he/she) is designed to be. The process is one of the ultimate purposes of Islam. See Rabb.

Ruh. The soul. The exact nature of the soul is not known by humans, and many do not believe it exists. It is like the concept of mind—you cannot extract a mind from a body and examine it in the operating theatre! However, to a Muslim, the soul is far more important than the body; it is the real person, the abiding essence of any individual which persists through all the stages and changes of human life, and endures beyond the death of the human body. Theories about souls are numerous and impossible to prove; for example, certain people claim to be able to see them; souls can leave the body while it still lives, and frequently do so during sleep (32:16; 10:44). At death, Muslims believe that the soul of a good person, although still linked to the body that will resurrect in due course, can range infinite distances and will enjoy its experiences while waiting for the Day of Judgement; whereas the souls of bad people will be earthbound, confined to the grave, and have a time of torment and despair.

Ruku. The bowing position during salah (see Rakah).

ar-Rum. Title of surah 30, 'the Byzantine Greeks'; a Makkan surah of 60 verse, referring to the capture of Jerusalem by rhe Persians. The central theme is the wonder of God's creation and his constant bringing forth of the living from the dead. See Byzantines.

Ruman. An interrogating angel who, according to some traditions, visits the deceased in the grave even before Munkar and Nadir, and tells them to write down their good and evil acts. His face is said to be bright like the sun.

Rumi. The Sufi mystic Jalal ud-Din Rumi of Qonya, founder of the so-called Whirling Dervishes.

Ruqayyah. The second daughter of the Prophet and Khadijah. She married his companion Uthman. They were deeply in love, and famous as a couple of extra-ordinary beauty and grace. She died during the Battle of Uhud. Later Uthman married her sister Umm Kulthum also.

Ruqya. A superstitious charm, things like horseshoes, hare's feet, and so on. They are forbidden in Islam; even pious charms like miniature Qur'ans are disapproved of, for they encourage the unwary to believe they have power in themselves.

Ruqya. Recitation of verses of the Qur'an for treatment of, and protection against illness. It is a rather superstitious kind of treatment, i.e. to recite *Surah al-Fatihah* or any other surah of the Qur'an and then to blow one's breath or touch with saliva the affected part of a sick person.

Rusulullah. Belief in the Messengers of Allah.

Ru'yat Allah. The vision or sight of Allah, in Paradise—an idea vehemently opposed by the Mutazilites who denied that God could ever be visible in a literal sense.

as-Sa'ah. An hour; usually used to denote 'the Hour' when the world ends and the Last Day begins. The Hour, the Last Day, the Day of Resurrection; it will take the unwary believer by surprise, although there will be many signs before its coming. It can also mean 'time' in the absolute sense, or any part of it, large or small. In 7:34 it is used in the sense of the least fraction of time, a single moment.

Saba. Title of surah 34, the place name 'Sheba'; a Makkan surah of 54 verses referring to the major seat of Arabian civilisation in ancient times. The story of the Queen of Sheba gives an example of the impermanence of all human power, wealth and glory. It reminds humanity of how little is their real knowledge of the universe. See Bilqis.

SAAW. Letters standing for 'Sall-Allahu 'Alayhi Wasallam' meaning 'May the peace and blessings of Allah be upon him.' The phrase is often written or spoken after saying the name of the Prophet Muhammad. It is by no means compulsory, but an act of piety and courtesy. See PBUH.

Saba. The kingdom of the Queen of Sheba (27:22-44), which reached its heyday in Yemen in 800-700 BC. They worshipped the Sun, Moon and planet Venus. Their capital was near San'a.

Sabaeans. (i) the pagan Neoplatonic sect which flourished in Harran in Northern Syria; (ii) the inhabitants of the Arabian kingdom of Sheba; (iii) mentioned in surahs al-Baqarah, al-Hajj and al-Ma'ida and probably referring to the Mandaeans of southern Iraq, a sect named in the Qur'an along with Jews and Christians as those who believe in God and the Last Day, and who work righteousness (Surah 2:62). It is believed that they were followers of the prophet John the Baptist. A community still survives near Basra in Lower Iraq. See Yahya.

Sab'a al-Mathani. The seven repeatedly recited verses, i.e. surah al-Fatihah.

Sabil. A public drinking fountain, usually paid for by endowment.

Sabiya. The Shi'ite sects of Seveners; those who believe in the first seven Shi'ite Imams, the seventh of whom went into occlusion.

Sabr. The attitude of patience or acceptance. Not complaining about one's lot in life, but making the best of any situation and seeking to do God's will (3:17).

Sacrifice. Killing an animal while dedicating it to God. On the 10th Dhu'l-Hijjah the pilgrims on Hajj sacrifice an animal in memory of Ibrahim's test of obedience. The animal is usually a sheep, goat, cow or camel. Even Muslims not on Hajj may do this. The feast that follows is known as Eid ul-Adha or Qurban. This sacrifice is not to appease God, bribe Him, or try to please Him with an innocent creature's blood—all ridiculous notions (22:37). It is submitting one's meat by dedicating it to God, from the moment of killing the animal in a halal way to the sharing of food with the poor and needy, and the awareness of belonging to the family of all mankind. See Nahr, Slaughter.

Sad. The title of surah 38—the letter S. The surah deals with divine guidance and those who reject it. A Makkan surah of 88 verses which surveys some of the people who disbelieved the messages sent to them.

Sadaqah. Charity; acts of voluntary giving or kindness. The Prophet stated that every little act done to please God or to make life more pleasant for others was sadaqah, and brought blessing upon the person who did them. Specific examples of sadaqah that he gave himself were moving obstacles from people's paths; planting trees and fields to provide food; cheering people up by smiling, speaking comfortingly to them, helping them; reconciling people who are arguing; having a loving and considerate relationship (including sexual relationship) with your partner; giving little gifts to people, and so on.

Safa. Small hill in Makkah, near the hill of Marwa, between which the Prophet Ibrahim's wife Hajar ran looking for a caravan carrying water. (see Sa'i)

Safavids. The Shi'ite Empire founded by Shah Isma'il that ruled Persia from 1500-1722 CE. It peaked under Shah Abbas in 1587-1629, and was eventually destroyed by continuous border warfare with the Russians and the rise of the militant Qajar dynasty.

as-Safar. The second month of the Muslim lunar calendar.

as-Saff. Title of surah 61, 'the Row' or 'Rank'; a Madinan surah of 14 verses referring to those who fight for Allah in ranks. It is a call to believers to practice what they preach.

as-Saffah (d. 136/754). The first ruler of the Abbasid dynasty, full name Abdallah ibn Muhammad Abu'l Abbas. As-Saffah means both 'the generous' and 'the bloodthirsty'.

as-Saffat. Those Ranged in Ranks; the title of surah 37, a Makkan surah of 182 verses, refering to the angels ranged in front of Allah. It includes many stories of previous prophets. It deals mainly with the prospect of resurrection and judgement.

Safiyyah. Daughter of Huyayy ibn Akhtab, the chief of the Jewish tribe of the Banu Nadir defeated by the Muslims at the Battle of Khaybar and one of the Prophet's most persistent enemies. She could trace her ancestry back to the Prophet Harun (Aaron). After the battle, Bilal brought Safiyyah, stunned with shock, and her screaming cousin, before the Prophet. He ordered his friend to aid the cousin, and himself took off his cloak and placed it round Safiyyah's shoulders. Later, although her father had hoped to assassinate him, he invited her to embrace Islam, and then married her. She was 17, and the Prophet 60. When some of the wives spoke unkindly about her, calling her the 'daughter of a Jew!', the Prophet reminded her that she was the descendant of a prophet and the wife of a prophet. When he became ill, she declared that she wished it had been possible to suffer instead of him. Only 21 when the Prophet died, she lived to the age of 60.

Sahabah. A Companion, or close friend of the Prophet.

Sahifa. Lit. 'page', 'paper'. (i) It designates any revealed writings of the prophetic predecessors of the Prophet.

(ii) A collection of sayings of the Prophet which were written down by one of his companions during his lifetime, or by their successors of the next generation. One such collection was assembled by Abu Hurayrah and handed down to his student Hamman ibn Munabbih. The most important is the sahifa collected by Abdullah ibn Amr ibn al-'As (d. 65 AH/684 CE), who gave it the title al-Sahifa al-Sadiqa. It contained around a thousand traditions. See Hadith.

Sahih. 'Sound' or 'valid'. This name is given to the absolutely faultless hadith, in which there is no weakness either in the chain of transmission (*Isnad*) or in the text (*Matn*) and in which there is no tendency to contradict any established doctrine of Islam. The Sahih al-Bukhari and Sahih Muslim were the collections of hadiths vouched for by the Sunni scholars Imam Muhammad ibn Ismail al-Bukhari and Abul Husayn Muslim ibn al-Hajjaj—two collections regarded by all Muslims as reliable. See Hadith.

Sahir. Magician or sorcerer.

Sahn. Dish, yard, courtyard. Usually the central courtyard of a mosque.

Sahu. 'Forgetting' (here it means forgetting how many Rak'at a person has prayed, in which case one should perform two prostrations of Sahu).

Sahur. The early morning meal taken before first light when fasting.

Sa'i (or Say). The second ritual of Hajj. After circling the Ka'bah and praying, pilgrims walk briskly between the small hills of Safa and Marwa, now an enclosed passageway. Invalids have a wheelchair path down the middle.

Pilgrims performing the Sa'i

It commemorates the desperate search of Ibrahim's wife Hajar for water, and symbolises the soul's search for that which gives true spiritual life.

Saint. This is not an Islamic term. It implies that a particular person, male or female, is especially holy, or beloved of Allah. Allah loves all His created beings, even those afflicted by evil, and it is correct to pray for their improvement. It is not for us to make any judgement on a person's destiny in the life to come; even if a person lived a life which could be described as saintly, how can we judge his or her intentions and motives? These are known only to Allah, and it is He Who judges us. People who pray to saints at their tombs wrongly believe that that person has an influence with Allah, which he or she does not have. It is ignorance of Islam to worship saints. One may, however, respect their graves and pray *for* them.

Sa'ir. One of the seven ranks of Hell, used 16 times in the Qur'an.

Sajdah. See Sujud.

al-Sajda. Title of surah 32, 'the Prostration' taken from v.15; a Makkan surah of 30 verses referring to those who believe in Allah's signs and prostrate themselves. The main theme is the divine origin of the revelation granted to Muhammad, the same as that granted to Moses and all the Prophets.

Sajdah sahev. Prayers to make up for something done incorrectly in the salah (e.g. you forgot how many rakahs you had done).

Sajjada. Carpet, prayer rug, prayer carpet. In Sufism, the head of a tariqa might have the title 'Master of the Prayer Rug' (Shaykh al-Sajjada); i.e. prayer rug previously owned by the order's founder.

Sakinah. The presence of Allah sometimes made clear by a sign; also the feeling of peace of mind and security that comes from a heart at peace. Tranquillity, calmness, etc.

as-Salaamu alaikum wa rahmatullah wa barakatuhu. 'Peace on you and the mercy of Allah and His blessing.'

Saladin. (Saleh al-Din ibn Ayyub, 1138-1193), a military leader of Kurdish origin who became ruler of Egypt and Syria, and defeated the Crusaders in Palestine. He was the warrior who fought Richard the Lionheart, and was famous for his chivalry. When Richard's horse was killed, he sent him two of his own, and when Richard was ill he sent him cold water and fresh fruit. Richard married his sister, but Richard's sister, Joan, would not marry Saladin in return. He postponed his siege of Kerak when Reynald de Chatillon's son Hugh was getting married, but later Reynald broke his truce with him. At the Battle of Hattin in Galilee, Saladin captured and killed the treacherous Reynald, but spared the Crusader King Guy of Jerusalem. Saladin's dynasty, known as the Ayyubids, ruled in Syria from 1169-1260.

Salafiyyah. (i) Adjective from as-salaf, the 'early years,' and used generally to describe the early generations of the Muslims, particularly the sahabah, the companions of the Messenger of Allah. 'ancestors', 'predecessors'; the early generation after the Prophet.

(ii) The name of an Egyptian reformist movement founded by Muhammad Abduh and al-Afghani; they tried to steer a middle way between the stricter tenets of Islam and the ideas of secular society and modern science. (Al-salaf al-salih)

Salah. The ritual compulsory prayer, made five times per day under special conditions in the manner taught by the Prophet in the Arabic language (20:130). See Rakah.

Salat ul-Istiqsa. This is a prayer for rain, a prayer of two rakahs.

Salat ul-Janaza. The funeral prayer said for a dead person. It consists of two rakahs, but there is no bowing to earth.

Salat ul-Jum'ah. The 'Friday Prayer'; the one occasion during the week when all male Muslims are urged to try to come together in the mosque to pray. It takes the place of the Friday zuhur prayer, and consists of the double khutbah and two rakahs (62:9).

Salat al-Khawf. Prayer 'in danger'

(4:101). This means praying in shifts at times when one needs to be on the alert for an attacking enemy. The group praying is guarded and protected by the armed fighters who remain on the alert and take their turn when the praying ranks have finished.

Salat al-Khusuf. Salah prayed during solar and lunar eclipses—a prayer of two rakahs, with two rukus in each rakah.

Salat ul-Layl. Voluntary prayers said during the hours of darkness.

Salat al-Musafir. Salah prayed whilst travelling. As a gift of Allah, it is permitted to be shortened, with the four rakahs of zuhr, asr and isha reduced to two. The sunnah rakahs may all be dropped with the exception of those offered at fajr.

Salih. The Prophet sent to the Thamud. One of the three Messengers of Allah mentioned in the Qur'an but not in the Bible (7:73-78; 11:61-7; 17:59; 26:141-155; 27:45, 157; 51:43-44; 54:24-28; 69:4).

Salih (pl. salihun). A spiritually developed person. One who is in the right place at the right time.

Salik. A Sufi engaged on the suluk, or spiritual journey, to Allah.

Salman. Originally a Persian Zoroastrian from Jayy near Isfahan. He became a Christian, and worked as acolyte (helper) to several Christian bishops, including the Bishop of Mosul in Iraq. One of them told him that the Prophet of the Arabs was about to appear, so he set off for Makkah, but was captured and ended up as a slave of the Bani Qurayzah, a Jewish tribe in and around Madinah. He was offered his freedom for 40 ounces of gold, and to plant 300 date palms. The Prophet rallied support, and the Muslims dug the date palms. The Prophet rallied support, and the Muslims dug the holes and donated the shoots, which the Prophet planted with his own hands, and the money was paid from a nugget of gold sent to the Prophet.

In 627, when a huge army of 10,000 came against the Prophet under Abu Sufyan, Salman told the Prophet that in Persia, when they feared cavalry attack, they surrounded themselves with a trench. The Prophet took his advice, and a huge trench was dug; hence the battle was called the Battle of Trench. The Muslims successfuly held off the Makkans.

Sama'. Heaven or sky. It applies to anything spread like a canopy above another thing.

Sama'at. Allah's characteristic of hearing all things. See Omniscience, Witness.

Samad. The Real, the source of creative energy by which the whole universe of endless forms emerges from the possible to the existent. Allah is in need of nothing, and everything is in need of Him.

Samarra. A city founded in 221/836 by the Abbasid caliph al-Mutasim, some 60 miles north of Baghdad. The 10th and 11th Shi'ite Imams are buried there in two shrines called the Askarayn.

Samawati. The heavens.

Sanusiyya. A major Sufi sect named after Sayyid Muhammad ibn al-Sanusi (1202/1787-1276/1859), often referred to as the Grand Sanusi. He was born at al-Wasita, Algeria, but his order really grew in Libya. He was much influenced by the thought of Ibn Taymiyya despite his hostility towards dhikr. Sanusi dhikr does not seek to induce any kind of ecstatic state. The grandson of the Grand Sanusi, Sayyid Idris, became the king of independent Libya from 1371/1951 until 1389/1969, when he was overthrown by Colonel Qaddafi (Gadafi).

Saqar. One of the seven ranks of Hell, meaning place of scorching.

Saqim. Lit. 'sick', 'infirm'—a technical term used in the hadith criticism to indicate the lowest level of trustworthiness in a tradition.

Sariqah. See Theft.

Sassanians. Dynasty of kings who ruled Persia prior to the Arab conquests. The last king was Yazdird III, who was assassinated in 31/651.

Satanic Verses. This was the title of a book, highly offensive to Muslims, written by the author Salman Rushdie. The book became all the more notorious because of a death sentence placed on Rushdie by the Ayatollah Khomeini of Iran.

The real issue of the Satanic Verses is not this novel, but the question of whether or not it would have been possible for the Prophet to have been duped by Shaytan, so that verses were included in the Qur'an which were not true revelations from Allah. If this was possible, it undermines confidence in the authenticity of the whole and therefore the whole faith of Islam.

It was claimed that in 53:19 the Prophet recited the words: 'Al-Lat, al-Uzza and Manat are the exalted birds (gharaniq) whose intercession may be counted on.' These words delighted the Makkans, who believed these goddesses to be daughters of Allah (see Goddess, Gharaniq). With this concession to their beliefs, the Makkans could have been won over to Islam. However, in Islam—God is One, Alone and has no partners or family.

The Prophet asserted that the goddesses were no more than names, and the Makkans, who had been almost ready to accept Islam if it could be seen as a 'reform movement' of their ancestral religion, immediately realised there was going to be no compromise, and renewed their anger. It was shortly after this that both Khadijah and Abu Talib died and the Prophet withdrew to Taif, where he was rudely rejected.

Many critics have tried to discredit the whole episode by pointing out that it was not in the earliest biography (Ibn Ishaq) and questioning the honesty of those early Muslim authorities who reported the story (Ibn Sa'd and Tabari)—but in fact the incident is the strongest possible testimony to the Prophet's utter and absolute sincerity.

Jibril revealed to the Prophet 22:51 'Never have We sent messenger or prophet before you, but when he has allowed his own wishes to predominate Shaytan interjected (words) into his desires; but Allah cancels what Shaytan interjects.'

SAW. Letters standing for 'Sallallahu Alayhi Wasallam' meaning 'peace be upon him and more peace,' a phrase often spoken or written after the name of the Prophet. It is not compulsory, but a mark of courtesy and piety. See PBUH, SAAW.

Sawdah. Second wife of the Prophet; previously married to Sakran, brother of the Arab chief Suhayl; she was one of the very first converts to Islam, and a member of the group that emigrated to Abyssinia in 616 during the time of persecution at Makkah. When they returned to Makkah Sakran died, and she lived with her father Zam'a. Although the Prophet had possibly not intended to remarry after Khadijah's death, for he struggled for a long time to bring up his daughters alone, his relatives felt sorry for him, and his aunt Khawlah negotiated his marriage to the motherly widow Sawdah. Opinions vary as to her age; some say she was around 30, others that she was 55, a little older than the Prophet. She was a large lady both in size and in kindness, very much loved by everyone, and she not only 'mothered' the Prophet's daughters but also his little wife Aishah. She was the Prophet's dear friend. Later, when physical love grew between the Prophet and Aishah, she gave up 'her' night with him, so that Aishah could be with him more often. She died in 644 CE.

Sawm. Abstinence or self-denial. To keep away from something. See Fasting.

Sawma'a (pl. sawami). A minaret; popularly used for the square minarets of Spain and the Maghreb.

Sayyid. Master. It is also used as a title name of the descendants of the Prophet Muhammad.

Sayyidi. My master.

Sayyidna. 'Our master,' a term of respect.

Scented Ones. See Quraysh.

School. The school at the mosque is known as the madrassah. This is for training Muslims in Islamic subjects, perhaps such things as Arabic, and how to recite and understand the Qur'an; how to carry out Muslim practices, and the general principles of Islam. Many Muslim youngsters attend a mosque school for around two hours every day, after their normal school.

School of Thought in Islam. Each of the four scholars who founded the schools of thought after them in Sunni Islam, (Imams Malik, Abu Hanifa, Al-Shafi'i and Ahmad ibn Hanbal) was simply a great scholar. They did not aspire to any higher position. There was nothing special about the number four—there were many other eminent scholars, some of whom were contemporaries of those four (e.g. Imam al-Layth ibn Sa'd of Egypt). None of the four made any special claim to be followed. A school of thought is a matter of deductions of rulings and verdicts from Qur'an and hadith statements. The four Imams all drew from the Qur'an, but had different knowledge of and approaches to the hadith. They had eminent disciples who gave a continuity to their 'schools,' but in each school we may find scholars who differed on specific questions. There was no rigidity about following any one Imam in *all* questions and matters. If they had known later generations of Muslims would be divided into narrow 'schools' they would have been horrified—they were the first to admit they were liable to error. A Muslim may choose which of their opinions they agree with, or even not belong to a 'school' at all. See Madhhab.

Seal of the Prophets. The prophet Muhammad was granted this 'title' in 33:40. Just as a seal (khatm) marks the end of a document, so Muhammad was the last of the long chain of messengers from Allah. The term khatam is synonymous with khitam, the end or conclusion of a thing. The revelation granted to Muhammad (i.e. the Qur'an) has therefore to be regarded as the culmination, end of all prophetic revelation.

Segregation/Seclusion of women. It is not true that women are required to be kept at home all the time—and this is not attempted in most of the Muslim world. Women may certainly move within women's circles especially, visiting their friends and relatives and receiving visitors. The notion of complete segregation, leaving women to have their own gatherings away from those of men, is mainly social tradition. What is forbidden in Islam is for a man to be alone in an enclosed area with a woman to whom he may be legally married—including his first cousins. At least one other woman should be present, preferably his mother or sister, in order to prevent any temptation to sexual misconduct. As for men and women being present in the same lecture hall or meeting, this is perfectly permissible in Islam, provided the women are wearing correct Islamic dress. Islam is the middle way between the lax and the too-strict. It was normal, at the time of the Prophet, for women to attend prayers at the mosque. See Purdah, Mahram.

Sema. The sacred dance used in Sufi mysticism, notably by the so-called Whirling Dervishes.

Sermon. See Khutbah.

Sermon, the Last. The speech given by the Prophet on the occasion of the Hajj in 632, to a crowd of some 1,25,000 people. His speech may be summarised as follows: 'O people, listen to my words carefully, for I do not know whether I will meet you again on such an occasion as this. You must live at peace with one another. Everyone must respect the rights and properties of their neighbours. There must be no rivalry or enmity among you. Just as you regard this month as sacred, so regard the life and property of every Muslim in the same way. Remember, you will surely appear before God to answer for your actions. All believers are brothers... you are not allowed to take things

The Summit of Mt. Arafat, the place where the Prophet Muhammad preached the last sermon.

from another Muslim unless it is given to you willingly. You are to look after your families with all your heart, and be kind to the women God has entrusted to you. You have been left God's Book, the Qur'an. If you hold fast to it, and do not let it go, you will not stray from the right path. People, reflect on my words... I leave behind me two things, the Qur'an and the example of my life. If you follow these you will not fail. Listen to me very carefully. Worship God, be steadfast in prayer, fast during Ramadan, pay alms to the less fortunate. People, no prophet or messenger will come after me, and no new faith will emerge. All those who listen to me will pass on my words to others, and those to others again.'

Seven Beliefs. The Iman-i-Mufassal, or 'Faith in Detail.' The seven beliefs of Islam are as follows: I believe in Allah, in His angels, in His revealed books, in all His prophets, in the Day of Judgement, in that everything—both good and evil—comes from Him, and in Life after Death.

Seveners. Shi'ite sects that believe that the Prophet said there would be twelve Imams to lead the Muslim world after he died, but that the seventh Imam went into occultation (disappeared mysteriously, in order to re-appear at the end of time, or to guide the faithful mystically). (See Twelvers). The sixth Shi'ite Imam was Ja'far as-Sadiq (d. 765); his elder son Isma'il died before he did, but Isma'ilis claimed he was the true successor, and had not died but been taken out of the world. See Isma'ilis.

Severe penalties. See Punishment, Hudood.

Sex. Islam teaches that sex is one of God's gifts to humanity; it is not sinful or dirty or degrading, unless it is abused. Sex is supposed to engender deep love and affection between spouses, to teach compassion, cooperation and generosity, and in its heights of feeling and ecstasy to give in a small way a glimpse of the wonderful joys of the ecstasy of being close to God in the Paradise for good people, in the life after death. The practices of celibacy and monasticism were disapproved of as being ungrateful and unnatural, and probably causing dangerous repressions in a person's character. The sort of sex that brought sadaqah was that which put the fulfilment and comfort of the partner before one's own, which was skilled, modest, and generous.

Sex outside marriage. This is totally forbidden to Muslims. Sexual experimentation before marriage has not brought happiness to the societies that condone it—only a weakness of character and resolve when people get used to the idea that they can 'sleep around' that becomes dangerous when the novelty wears off a marriage and the real hard work of building love together really begins—the 'for better, for worse' part of marriage. In Islam, a youngster has the right to enter marriage as a virgin, untouched by anyone, and to learn the ways of love with the chosen life partner. When a marriage is not successful, sex outside marriage (adultery) is still not condoned. One should first have an honourable divorce, then one is free to find a new and more compatible partner. See Zinah.

Sha'ban. The eighth month of the Muslim calendar and one of the four sacred months.

Shadhdh. 'Rare'. A tradition coming from a single transmitter and contradicting another. If the transmitter is a recognised authority, it deserves examination, but if he or she is not, the tradition is to be rejected.

Shadhili (d. 1258). Shaikh Abu'l Hasan ash-Shadhili of Morocco (d. 1273) was the founder of the Shadhiliyyah Sufi order, one of the most important brotherhoods in North Africa. He was born in Tunisia and buried in Egypt. His teachings emphasized ma'rifah (knowledge). Today the Shadhili are found in North Africa, Egypt, Kenya and Tanzania, the Middle East, Sri Lanka and West and North America.

Shafa'ah. Intercession, mediation. While many Muslim theologians disapprove of the idea of the intercession of saints, the idea was never stamped out in popular Islam and many are venerated (wrongly) at their tombs. See Saint.

al-Shafi'i. Muhammad ibn Idris (150/767-205/820). A famous Muslim jurist whose key methodology was founded on four points; Qur'an, sunnah, ijma and qiyas. His principle work was called (the Epistle' (al-Risala); his huge tomb is a focus for visitors in Cairo.

Shahadah. (Lit. 'witnessing'). The first pillar of Islam, the public bearing witness or declaration that a person believes that God really does exist, and that Muhammad really was a true messenger, in the same way that Ibrahim and Musa and Isa had been. The words in Arabic are—'Ash-hadu an la ilaha il-allahu wa Muhammadar rasulullah'—'I believe (or 'I bear witness') that there is no God but Allah and that Muhammad is the Prophet of Allah'. See Seven Beliefs.

Shahid. Lit. 'a witness', a martyr in the way of Allah. This is a person who 'bears witness' to the extent of giving up his or her own life as a martyr. Someone who dies for the faith (2:154; 3:169-170; 22:58-59). See Martyr.

al-Shahrastani, Muhammad ibn Abd al-Karim (479/1086-548/1153). One of the best-known historians of Islam. His most famous work was 'the Book of religions and sects.'

Shaikh. See Shaykh.

ash-Shams. Title of surah 91, 'the Sun'; a Makkan surah of 15 verses. It tells the story fo the Thamud tribe and the prophet Salih.

Shamyl. A Naqshbandi Sufi and tribal leader who led the Muslim tribes in Daghestan against the Russians. He died while on pilgrimage and is buried in Madinah.

ash-Sharh. The title of surah 94, 'the Laying Open' or 'the Expanding'; a Makkan surah of 8 verses referring to the question to the Prophet: 'Did We not open your heart for you?' It refers to the lifting of the burden of past sins. It may refer to an incident that occurred in the Prophet's childhood when his Bedouin milk-brothers saw two angels open up his chest and remove something.

Shariah. (from 'Shari'—a road, and 'shara'a'—to begin, enter, introduce, prescribe). The Way of Islam. 'This is My straight path, so follow it, and do not follow paths which will separate you from this path' (6:153; 57:28). It is the code of behaviour for a Muslim, that determines whether any action or detail of life is halal (right and allowed) or haram (wrong and forbidden). It involves putting faith in God into action (see Iman and Amal); faith is meaningless without the deeds that express it in action.

Sharif (pl. shurafa) persons claiming descent from the Prophet.

Sharr. That which is evil; when people use their faculties and powers against the laws of Allah, it brings about the disintegration of their own personalities and harm the interests of humanity at large. It also includes any human faculties that are not put to any constructive use.

Shawwal. The tenth month of the Muslim calendar.

Shaykh. (Lit. 'Old Man') A Sufi master or teacher; also, a leader of a tribe.

Shaykh Nazim. The leader of the Naqshbandi Sufis, the 40th Shaikh in the chain from Abu Bakr. See Naqsbandis.

Shaytan, pl. Shayatin. A devil, particularly Iblis (Satan). Lit. 'rebellious', 'remote'; from 'shatana' he became remote. This denotes a force remote from, and opposed to, all that is true and good). The Muslim name for the Devil, also called Iblis. The Qur'an does not suggest that Shaytan was a fallen angel (i.e. the Jewish tradition concerning Lucifer, the Angel of Light) for it teaches that angels always do the will of Allah, and do not have free will. The Qur'an states that all the angels obeyed Allah, but not so Iblis, the chief of the jinn, who used his freewill when he refused to bow down to Adam when God requested him to. This may have represented his piety in not wishing to bow down to any other but Allah—but the point is that it showed his disobedience and pride; he questioned God's will. He may also have thought he knew better! It is worth pointing out to those who think of the Devil as being obviously evil, that he was pious and devout and highly placed. The Devil is quite 'at home' amongst deeply religious people, leading them astray. (See Extremism). The word 'Shaytan' implies 'rebellion". Qur'an references to Shaytan are: 2:34-36; 3:36; 4:117-120; 5:94; 7:11-18, 200-201; 8:48; 14:22; 15:17, 31-34; 16:98-100; 17:61-65; 18:50; 20:116-123; 22:53-54; 24:21; 35:6; 36:60; 38:71-85. Shaytan is certainly not regarded as a power equal to God, or the opposite of God as black is to white as in Dualist religious systems.

Sheikh. See Shaykh.

Sherif. A descendant of the Prophet.

Shi'ah. Lit. 'followers.' This usually refers to the Shi'at Ali, or followers of Ali, the Shi'ites.

Shighar. A forbidden form of marriage whereby a man gave his daughter in marriage to another man who gave his daughter to him without there being any bride-price. This practice does not even begin to consider the personal feelings of the young people involved, and can prove disastrous and traumatic, since divorces in these circumstances are virtually impossible without enormous upset.

Shi'ite. Around 90% of Muslims are Sunni and around 10% are Shi'ite. Originally, they were supporters of the Prophet's son-in-law Ali (the party of Ali—Shi'at Ali), and claimed that he had been appointed Successor at the gathering of Ghadir al-Khumm. Ali then nominated his son Hasan to follow him, and then his other son Husayn; Shi'ite nominations remained in the Prophet's family for the next ten generations. However, Sunnis interpreted the Prophet's words as an acknowledgement of Ali's merit rather than a definite political appointment, and accepted the Succession of Abu Bakr as being what the Prophet intended, and he was followed by Umar and Uthman. Ali finally became the fourth Caliph, although Shi'ites still regard him as the first. The quality of the caliphs after Ali varied, and the basic difference between Sunni and Shi'ite stems from this origin—the Sunni stance that peace under an unjust ruler was better than anarchy under a just one, and the Shi'ite opinion that the ruler should be the ultimate spiritual authority, and God would not leave people unguided—hence the series of special Imams. See Seveners, Twelvers, Ghadir al-Khumm.

Shiqq. The qiblah niche made in the centre of a grave.

Shirk. (Lit. 'association, sharing'). The division of the Unity of God, or associating other beings with Allah. Shirk can take many forms—the belief that God is not Supreme or Alone; the belief that some other entity shares His power and has the right to judge, or forgive sins, or to make permissible what is forbidden, or forbid what is permissible (2:116; 6:22-24, 100-101, 133-137, 163; 10:68; 24:35). The opposite of tawhid, affirmation of Divine Unity. See Ruqya, Magic.

Shu'ayb. One of the three prophets mentioned in the Qur'an who was not mentioned in the Bible, although later commentators identify him with the Midianite Jethro, the father-in-law of Moses (Musa). He was sent to the peoples of Madyan (7:85-93; 11:84-95; 26:176-189; 29:36).

ash-Shu'ara. Title of surah 26, 'the Poets'; a Makkan surah of 227 verses, taken from v. 224. It includes the stories of many previous Prophets. It stresses human weakness and tendency towards self-deception, and why people reject the truth.

ash-Shura. Title of surah 42, 'the Counsel'; a Makkan surah of 53 verses based on v. 36; it includes teachings about God's power and omnipotence, and mentions the major prophets of the past. The reality of Divine Revelation, and the consistency of the essential truths. God is beyond definition and human knowledge.

Shurah. The duty of Islamic leaders of any level to consult properly with those they represent, in order to give guidance that is acceptable and reasonable to those who have to accept it.

Shukr. Thankfulness. Our appreciation of the grace and bountiful blessings of Allah. However, this is a two-way blessing—for although our actions neither help nor harm Allah, He appreciates and rewards the good things we try to do. 'If there is a good deed done, Allah doubles it and grants from Himself a great reward.' (4:40). 'Allah does not permit the reward of the righteous to be lost' (3:171; 7:170; 9:120; 11:115; 12:56,90; 18:30). 'Allah gives reward according to the best of His servants' deeds, and grants more out of His grace and bounty,' (24:38; 29:7; 42:26; 2:245; 57:11,18; 64:17).

Siddiq. A person of truth.

as-Siddiq. 'The Truthful,' a name of respect given to Abu Bakr.

Siddiqun. Those who are truthful, sincere (12:46; 19:41, 56).

Sidrat al-Muntaha. 'The lote-tree of the furthest limit,' the place where form ends. Located in Paradise.

Sifat Allah. The attributes of Allah.

Siffin. A significant early battle in the history of Islam between Ali and Mu'awiyah; it lasted three months in 37/657 at the plain of Siffin. The Syrians fixed copies of the Qur'an on their spears, in an effort to gain more talks rather than warfare. The result was arbitration, but in 40/661 Ali was assassinated and the way was open for Mu'awiyah b. Abu Sufyan to inaugurate the Umayyad dynasty.

Sighar. See Shighar.

Sihr. See Magic.

Silsilah. 'Chain;' the Sufi chain of spiritual authority, passing from one shaikh to another.

Sinan Pasha (895/1488-996/1588). The leading architect of the Ottoman age, responsible for many of Turkey's great mosques.

Sirah. The historical study of the Prophet's life. A written 'life' or biography of the Prophet. The earliest were those of Zohri, and Ibn Ishaq, Zohri's disciple.

as-Sirat. Sirat, originally means 'a road.' It also means the bridge that is laid across Hell-Fire for the people to pass over on the Day of Judgement in order to enter the Garden of Paradise. It is described as sharper than a sword and thinner than a hair.

Sirat al-Mustaqim. The 'straight path' of Islam.

Sirri. The daylight compulsory prayers.

Siwak. A piece of a branch or a root of a tree called Al-Arak used as a toothbrush. The last gift given to the Prophet. As he lay dying, Aishah's brother Abd ar-Rahman came in carrying one. Aishah saw that the Prophet wished to use it, and chewed the end to soften it for him. After he had cleaned his teeth, he passed away in her arms.

as-Siyam. See Fasting (also spelled Sawm).

Slander. (Ar. Qadhf). Speaking ill of another, usually behind their back. Malicious gossip is always unpleasant if not dangerous. The Prophet felt that if you couldn't speak well of someone, it was better not to speak at all; he described 'backbiting' as 'eating the flesh' of the subject of the nasty talk (24:19; 49:12). When people 'backbite' and make nasty, unpleasant statements, this may be due to their own unpleasant or suspicious character, and be quite untrue as regards the person spoken of Unfortunately once a 'fact' has been passed on, even if it is a complete lie, some of the 'mud' sticks and the innocent party is damaged. The Prophet's wife Aishah was the subject of unpleasant slander until Allah granted a revelation in her favour and laid down the severe penalties for false witness.

Slaughter. (Arabic dhabihah—lit. 'cutting the throat.') Halal (allowed) slaughter has to be done in a particular way, the object of which is that if the animal has to die it must be killed in the kindest and most humane way possible. The animal should be kindly treated beforehand, and not in any state of fear or discomfort; it should be held for slaughter in as kind a way as possible, and have its throat cut across the jugular vein with a very sharp knife; a prayer dedicating the animal to God should be uttered. The blood is then allowed to drain out swiftly. Many of the slaughter-house practices accepted as normal in the west are regarded with horror by Muslims, who reject firing bolts into animals' brains or electrocution as very cruel methods—not to mention the callous treatment of animals, and their panic in the slaughter-house atmosphere. On the other hand, there are horrendous conditions and cruelty to animals in many so-called Muslim societies too. Muslims involved with killing (or rearing, or using) animals must realise that when they behave cruelly, or kill an animal with a blunt knife, and so on—this is gross abuse of Islam, and any animal made to suffer cannot be said to be halal for a Muslim to eat.

Slaves. Slavery was not directly forbidden in Islam, as at the time of the Prophet it was advantageous to many poor people to use the system in order to pay off their debts. However, a good Muslim would always prefer to forgive a person their debts rather than see them in slavery. The Prophet and his companions were famous for the number of slaves they freed, frequently by paying for their freedom themselves. Islam granted many rights to slaves—such as the right to earn and save money, and not to be forced to accept sex from their masters or their relatives—and many Muslim converts were slaves or ex-slaves. Surah 4:36 enjoins doing good to those whom you possess. The best that can be done to a slave is to grant freedom.

In 9:60 Allah explicitly mentioned freeing human beings from bondage as one of the objectives of zakah.

Smoking. Inhaling tobacco is not directly forbidden in the Qur'an or hadith, since cigarettes belong to a later period; however, one can argue that they should be haram by principle of analogy. Tobacco (nicotine) is a harmful substance, harming not only the smoker but others in the vicinity, and unborn children. Anything harmful is haram.

Solomon. See Sulayman.

Sorcery. Ar. Jibt. Casting lots in an attempt to find out the future (4:52). See Jibt.

Soul. See Rouh.

Star. The five pointed star on many minarets and Islamic flags symbolises the five pillars of Islam, the 'foundation' of the faith of a Muslim.

Steadfastness. Istiqamah. Hanging on, remaining trustworthy, not giving up hope, not breaking promises, keeping loyal. All recommended by Allah (41:30, 72; 46:13).

Stoning the Devil. See Mina, Ibrahim, Isma'il, Jamarat.

Subh. Morning, in particular the dawn prayer which can be prayed at any time between the first light (see fajr) and just before the sun rises.

Subhah. A string of 99 beads. Many Muslims praise God after the daily prayers, using the beads as an 'aid'. Others count using the finger-joints of their right hand. They say 'subhan-Allah' (Glory be to God), 'Alhamdu lillah' (Thanks be to God) and 'Allahu Akbar' (God is great) 33 times each as they pass the beads. There is a large bead dividing each set of 33.

Subhanallah. 'Glory to Allah.'

Successors. See Caliph.

Suffah. A verandah attached to the Prophet's mosque in Madinah where Muslims who had arrived destitute used to sleep. They were cared for by Fatimah and Umm Ayman. See Ahl as-Suffah.

Suffering. A hadith related by Aishah states that 'for any adversity a Muslim suffers, Allah erases some of his/her sins, even though the suffering may be no more than the prick of a thorn.' (Bukhari). Another related by Abu Hurayrah stated: 'Whatever befalls a Muslim of exhaustion, illness, worry, grief, nuisance or trouble, he earns forgiveness by Allah for some of his/her sins.' So, if we are ill or afflicted, we should bear it with patience. See Euthanasia.

Sufism. (Arabic—'tasawwuf', probably derived from 'safa'—purity, or 'suf'—wool, the material of the modest garments of the Prophet and his companions). Sufism is often called Islamic mysticism, but the Muslim never seeks a mystical way of life just for its own sake. Sufis highlight the need for personal purification and piety through constant awareness and love of God, and honest and humble self-knowledge. Sufis often choose a way of life based on asceticism and meditation on the transient nature of all forms of existence as opposed to the Divine Creator. They sometimes make use of such ritualistic practices as the sacred dance, or the chanting of the name of Allah (dhikr) as a means of enhancing inner awareness. Muslims differ greatly in their attitudes towards Sufism; some regard it as the true Islam, the real heart of the faith—the champions of keeping true Islam alive in times of corruption and loss of spirituality; others see it as dangerous emotionalism, and a movement away from the practical humane-ness of the Islamic way of life. The main Sufi orders are: the Chishti in India and Pakistan (founder—Khwaja Abu Ishaq Shami Chishti d. 966); the Qadiri (founder—Shaikh Abd al-Qadir al-Gilani of Baghdad d.1166); the Rifa'i (founder Shaikh Ahmad ar-Rifa'i of Basra d. 1182); the Shadhili (founder—Shaikh Abu'l Hasan ash-Shadhili of Morocco d. 1258); the Mevlavi (founder—Maulana Jalal ud-din Rumi of Qonya d. 1273); the Naqshbandi (founder—Shaikh Baha ud-Din Naqshband of Bukhara d. 1390); the Bektashi (founder—Hajji Bektash of Khurasan d. 1338); the Ni'matullahi (founder—Shaikh Nur ud-Din Muhammad Ni'matullah of Kirman d. 1431); the Jarrahi (founder—Shaikh Nur ud-Din Muhammad al-Jarrah of Istanbul d. 1720); the Tijani (founder—Shaikh Abbas Ahmad at-Tijani of Algeria d. 1815); the Sanusi (founder—Shaikh Sayyid Muhammad as-Sanusi of Algeria d. 1859). The Naqshbandis are the only known Sufi Order, tracing their descent from Abu Bakr. The rest of the known Sufi Orders trace their origins through Shi'ite spiritual leaders to Imam Ali. Some of the most famous Sufis were Rabia al-Adawiya d. 801; Nafisah d. 825; Imam Junayd al-Baghdadi d. 910, Mansur al-Hallaj (crucified in 922 by orthodox Muslims for claiming to be one with God in his statement 'Ana'l Haqq'—'I am the Truth'); Imam Abu Hamid al-Ghazzali d. 1111; Jalal ud-Din Rumi d. 1273, Shah Waliullah d. 1719, and Shaikh Muhiyud-Din ibn Arabi d. 1240.

Suhur. A light breakfast taken before dawn before commencing a day's fasting.

Suhrawardiyya. The Ishraqi Illuminationist school of philosophy in Persia. A major Sufi order whose origins go back to Abd al-Qahir Abu Najib al-Suhrawardi and Shihab al-Din Abu Hafs Umar al-Suhrawardi. He was put to death by Saladin in 1191 on the grounds of heresy. The traveller Ibn Battuta was affilliated to this order in Isfahan.

Suicide. A person putting an end to their own life. This is just as forbidden in Islam as the taking of any other person's life, and regarded as a great sin. Perhaps the worst part of it is the punishment it inflicts on those left behind, who feel that they somehow failed the suicide, or let them down, or perhaps even caused the suicide. The suicide usually does it in order to escape the pressures of life, which seem unbearable to them; unfortunately it does not solve the problem, for they continue to 'live' in the next state of existence, with the added trauma of being aware of the terrible hurt and damage they have caused in taking their own lives, and the inability to put that right. Luckily for all involved, the mercy of God is such that it takes into consideration the state of mind of the suicide. No blame is attached to the person whose mind has been disturbed, or who is no longer capable of rational thought. In any case, we should not presume that we know the extent of Allah's mercy. The kindest thing any bereaved person can do is to pray for the soul of that suicided person, and forgive them the hurt they caused to you, so that the soul can be at peace at least from the torment of awareness of the suffering they caused to their families.

Sujud. Bowing to earth in humility; the position of prostration, particularly in the prayers. Muslims touch the ground with the 'seven bones'—forehead, hands, knees and toes. See Salah, Rakah.

Sukara. See Drunkenness.

Sulayman. Solomon. The son of King David (Nabi Dawud) famous for his great wisdom. The Qur'an records several incidents of his life, notably his conversion of the Queen of Sheba (see Saba). It also records his ability to communicate with animals and birds (2:102; 6:84; 21:79-82; 27:15-44; 34:12-14; 38:30-40).

Sulayman the Magnificent (900-1494-974/1566). The greatest of the Ottoman rulers, the employer of the great architect Sinan.

Sultan. Name for a ruler of a Muslim state. From the Arabic world for 'clear authority,' or empowerment. (See 4:91). A famous modern sultan is the Sultan of Brunei, who is said to be the richest person in the world.

Suluk. Journeying; the Sufi term for a mystic's progress on the way to Allah. It commences with the entrance to a tariqa under the direction of a shaikh. A salik is someone engaged on this spiritual journey.

Summayah. The first Muslim martyr (a lady). Said to have been the seventh convert to Islam, she was the elderly maid-servant of Abu Hudhayfah of Makhzum, the wife of Yasir and mother of Ammar. She was tortured by the Quraysh by being dressed in metal armour and tied up in the blazing sun. She was released, but Abu Jahl went to her house and in a fit of rage stabbed her to death.

Sumud. Taking up position in straight rows, ready for prayer to commence.

Sunan. These are hadith collections which only contain legal-liturgical traditions and omit material relating to historical, spiritual and other matters. For example, the collections of Abu Dawud, al-Nasa'i fall into this class.

Sunnah, pl. Sunan. Lit. 'a form', (from 'sanna'—to shape, form, establish); the customary practice of a person or group of people. It has come to refer almost exclusively to the practice of the Messenger of Allah. The Prophet's example, or way of life. Everything he said, did, approved of or condemned.

The original principle was that those who followed the Prophet's sunnah would be rewarded for it, but there was no punishment or censure for those who did not. The Prophet was very clear that no-one should be coerced into making compulsory anything that was not compulsory. Attempts to preserve his way of life in exact detail in societies that have changed considerably are misguided and extremist. In any case, some Muslims seem rather quaint in which examples of sunnah they accept and which they reject. Many insist on not eating with knife and fork where it is normal to do so, yet think nothing of using a modern toilet instead of crouching over two bricks! The real importance of following sunnah lies not in such trivial details, but in following the Prophet's way of compassion, gentleness, honesty, courage and truth (33:21). At the time that Imam Malik, may Allah be pleased with him, compiled the Muwatta', there was no sense of setting the sunnah of the prophet apart from the sunnah of Madinah, so that the actions of its knowledgeable people were given even more weight than the behaviour of the Prophet related in isolated hadith. This has always characterized the Maliki viewpoint.

Sunni. Mainstream Islam: those who follow the Prophet's sunnah.

Superstition. A form of kufr, or lack of belief or trust in God. No object, charm or incantation can possibly over-rule the will of Allah (7:188; 35:2). See Magic, Ruqya.

Surah. A chapter of the Qur'an, meaning a 'step up'.

Suspicion. Disapproved of in Islam. Although we are not expected to be gullible or foolish, Allah recommends those who do not spoil their lives and characters with suspicious thoughts (49:12).

Sustainer. See Rabb.

Sutrah. A screen or barrier placed in front of a person while they pray, so that they are 'cut off' from the world, and so that people will pass beyond it and not 'break' the qibla and concentration.

Suwari — the practice of praying one prayer so late and the next one so early that they come together. Only approved in emergencies; a gap should be left between them.

SWT. Stands for 'Subhanahu wa Ta'ala'—'May He be praised and His lordship of creation affirmed'—words frequently said after using the name of God.

al-Suyuti, Jalal al-Din (849/1445-911/1505). Famous Egyptian jurist and commentator, who wrote over 500 books.

Swimming. Women should not expose their bodies for men to look at. It is perfectly permissible for women to swim in female-only circumstances, or in mixed circumstances if they are properly covered.

Taawwudh. The prayer said before the start of the rakah, seeking refuge in God from evil.

Tabaqat as-Sufiyya. The earliest collection of biographies of famous Sufis compiled by Abdur Rahman as-Sulami (b. 938) of Nisapur, Iran. It contains the biographies of more than 100 Sufis he encountered in his travels, important for revealing the search for truth and the revival of the inner meaning of the way of Islam, and the continuation of the transformative element of this way of thinking during the 9th and 10th centuries CE.

Tabarakallah. 'Blessed is Allah.'

al-Tabari, Abu Ja'far Muhammad ibn Jarir (224/839-310/923). A major early Islamic historian and exegete; his great commentary is used to this day. He founded a school of Law known as the Jaririyya.

Tabi'un. The disciples, or successors of the Companions of the Prophet. Various authorities divide them up into a different number of categories, including (a) the students of the Companions who accepted Islam before the conquest of Makkah; (b) the students of those who embraced Islam after the conquest of

Makkah; and (c) the students of those Companions who were not yet adults at the time of the Prophet's death.

Tablet. The phrase 'upon a well-guarded tablet (*lawh mahfuz*) as a description of the Qur'an occurs only once, in 85:22. Some commentators take this it its literal sense and understand it to mean an actual 'heavenly tablet' upon which the Qur'an had been inscribed from all eternity. Others give this phrase a metaphorical meaning, namely the imperishable quality of this Divine Writ, relating to Allah's promise that the Qur'an would never be corrupted and would remain free of all arbitrary additions, deletions or textual changes. See also 15:9. There is no other instance of any other book which has been similarly preserved over such a length of time.

Tablighi Jamaat. This is a religious group founded by Maulana Muhammad Ilyas (1885-1944). Originally a student at Deoband, he became disillusioned with their introversion and wanted to project Islam with missionary work. He formulated a six-point programme to achieve it: (i) the profession of faith; (ii) ritually prescribed prayers; (iii) knowledge and remembrance of God; (iv) respect for all Muslims; (v) sincere intentions; (vi) the giving of time. Tablighis travel round in groups on gasht (tours)

Extention of the mosque of Tablighi Jamaat in New Delhi.

to bring other Muslims round to their way of thinking. They often wear a cap, beard, long shirt reaching to below the knees, and pyjamas or trousers shortened to be above the ankles.

Tabuk. A town in northern Arabia close to ash-Sham, some 250 miles from Madinah near the gulf of Aqabah. In the ninth year after Hijrah, the Messenger of Allah hearing that the Byzantines were gathering a large army to march against the Muslims, led a large expedition to Tabuk, only to find the rumours premature. It was his last campaign.

Tadbir. A contract given by a master to a slave that the slave will be freed after the master dies.

Tadhkirah. Warning, admonition, recollection. The world dhikr (remembrance of Allah) is derived from it.

Tadhkiya. Proper slaughter in Allah's name (5:3). See Slaughter, Sacrifice.

Tadlis. Lit. 'fraud,' in hadith terminology it assumes interfering with or disguising defects in the isnad.

Tafsir. Commentary on the Qur'an. From the Arabic word 'fasara'—'to make clear, show the objective, or lift the curtain.' The science though which the Book of Allah can be understood. The earliest scholars of tafsir were the four rightly Guided Caliphs, and then: Abdallah ibn Abbas (d. 68 AH/687 CE), Abdallah ibn Mas'ud (d. 32 AH/653 CE) Ubayy ibn Ka'b (d. 20AH/640 CE), Zayd ibn Thabit (d. 45 AH/665 CE), Abu Musa al-Ashari (d. 44 AH/664 CE), Abdallah ibn al-Zubayr (d. 73 AH/692 CE).

Tafwid. The stipulation in a marriage contract that the wife may terminate the union herself, if need be.

at-Taghabun. Title of surah 64, 'the Mutual Disillusion' or 'Mutual Cheating'; a Makkan surah of 135 verses, based on the word in v. 9, which refers much to Musa (Moses), the rebellion of Iblis and the temptation of Adam. Humanity's denial or acceptance of truth.

Taghut. Evil, the powers of evil. (See, 2:256). At-Taghut primarily denotes anything that is worshipped instead of Allah, and, derived from that, all influences that might turn a person away from God and lead towards evil. See Evil.

Ta Ha. The title of surah 20. Some commentators regard this title as being two single letters, as are prefixed to several of the surahs (see al-Muqatta'at). Many commentators, however, feel 'ta-ha' is synoymous with 'ya rajul'—'O Man' (Sa'id ibn Jubayr, Mujahid, Qatadah, al-Hasan al-Basri, Ikrimah etc.). It does mean 'O Man' in Nabataean and Syriac and the dialect of the Yemenite tribes of 'Akk.

It was this surah that Umar ibn Khattab heard being recited in his sister's house, which led to his dramatic conversion.

Tahajjud. Voluntary prayer in the night between the 'isha prayer and fajr. Lit. 'night vigil' (17:79; 73:2-4).

Tahannuf. The ardent devotions, long vigils and prayers, of those who believed in only One True God in pre-Islamic times. (See Hanif). Devotional or pious practice. The Prophet used to occupy himself with tahannuf in a cave on Mount Hira.

Taharah. Purity, cleanliness. Muslims always pay attention to personal cleanliness and try to wear clean clothes. A full bath or shower must be taken after sexual intercourse, menstruation and childbirth. A ritual wash (wudu) is taken before prayer or handling the Qur'an. The Prophet particularly recommended special cleanliness of hands, mouth, hair and private parts. Of course, couples should also be clean before sexual intercourse if they are considerate.

Tahayyat al-Masjid. Two rakahs prayed on entering a mosque as a 'greeting to the mosque'.

Tahmid. The phrase 'To You, O Lord, be all thanks'.

Tahrif. Corruption, distortion, alteration, especially as applied to sacred texts. Muslims used this to explain, for example, the disparity between the data about Isa (Jesus) in the New Testament and in the Qur'an. Muslims believe that Christian and Jewish editors altered the original texts as revealed to the prophets. Hence, the Injil is not the same thing as the Gospels of the New Testament.

Tahrim. To declare something unlawful.

at-Tahrim. Title of surah 66, 'the Prohibition'; a Madinan surah of 12 verses, which asked the Prophet why he had forbidden himself something allowed in the eyes of God. It referred to his decision to alter his relationship with his last wife, Maryam Qibtiyah, because of the raised feelings of his other wives. See Maryam Qibtiyah.

at-Tahtawi, Rifa'a (1215/1801-1289/1873). An Egyptian translation expert who spent five years as Imam of Paris, and attempted to interpret the West to the East. On his return to Egypt, he directed a school of languages and a translation bureau.

Ta'if. A mountain oasis-town in Saudi Arabia, fifty miles to the east of Makkah where the Prophet was rejected before his migration to Madinah.

Tajalli (pl. tajalliyat). Self-manifestation, the unveiling of spiritual reality; a moment of enlightenment to the inner eye of the seeker.

Tajwid. The art of the correct pronunciation of the Qur'an when reciting. Lit. 'to make better.'

al-Takathur. Title of surah 102, 'the Growth' or 'Greed for More and More'; a Makkan surah of 8 verses; directed at clans that boasted about their numbers.

Takbir tahrim. The pronouncing of the phrase 'Allahu Akbar!', or 'Allah is the Most High (Great)!' Prayer begins with a takbir.

Takfir. This is the practice of accusing others of shirk or being kafirun. It is a symptom of extremism that cannot find tolerance for differences of opinion and expression, and oversteps the bounds of what is permitted. For example, extremists frequently describe Christians and Jews as kafirun (nonbelievers), even though the Qur'an calls them the 'Ahl al-Kitab' or 'People of the Book', and recognises that they have received revelation and believe in the One True God, even though some of their doctrines distorted the faith. (For example, most Christians hold Trinitarian beliefs and regard the Prophet Jesus as Son of God, which the Qur'an calls shirk and a 'denial of truth' (Surah 5:73); yet they are still Ahl al-Kitab and not kuffar, for they are not conscious of shirk—God to them is still One, even though He is said by them to have three 'Persons'. Their error, according to Islam, is in overstepping the bounds of veneration (see Surahs 4:171; 5:77). The Prophet himself regarded all non-Muslims as potential Muslims to be welcomed.

The presence of Takfir can almost be taken as a measure of the extremism of any particular Muslim or group of Muslims. Many exceedingly zealous persons do not seem to realise that there are enormous variations of thought offered by the madhhabs, and that Islam is a religion for all times and all places. Matters need constant interpretation and thoughtful decisions according to Islamic principles and conscience.

In any case, the Prophet's attitude to non-Muslims was not to vilify or abuse them, but to treat them graciously, gently, and with tolerant welcome, viewing them as potential converts. The result was that he made thousands of converts, whereas those who accuse others too readily of takfir usually drive away all who are not of their own type.

Takhayyur. The selection of a particular position from a legal school other than the one to which a jurist belongs.

at-Takwir. Title of surah 81, 'the Winding Up' or 'the Shrouding in Darkness'; a Makkan surah of 29 verses referring to the moment the Sun is darkened on the Day of Resurrection. It also refers to the time the Prophet saw the angel Jibril for the first time.

Talab al-'Ilm. The quest for knowledge, especially religious knowledge.

Talaq. The formal procedure of pronouncing 'I divorce you' three times, once at the end of three consecutive months, during which times the spouses must continue to live in the same house but without resuming a sexual relationship. Family and friends should do their best to reconcile them; if they resume their relationship, the divorce is instantly nullified. The Prophet made it very clear that to pronounce 'I divorce you' three times on one occasion only counted as *one* occasion, so where Muslim men have done this, it is an abuse of Islam.

at-Talaq. Title of surah 65, 'the Divorce': a Madinan surah of 12 verses, concerning the iddah or waiting-period which divorced woman must undergo before remarriage.

Talbiyah. The prayer of arrival at Makkah uttered by each individual among the thousands upon thousands of pilgrims, that they, too, have arrived at God's command. See Labbayka prayer.

Talfiq. Lit. 'concoction', 'fabrication', 'piecing together'—meaning piecing together jurisprudence from different schools of Law to formulate a legal principle or rule.

Tamin. The 'Amin' said at the end or the recitation of al-Fatihah in the first rakah, usually murmured aloud.

Tanzih. Considering God to be above all anthropomorphic elements or description; it stresses the remote and transcendent aspects of God.

Tanzil. Revelation, i.e. of the Qur'an.

Tanzimat. Reforms promulgated by the Ottomans from 1255/1839-1298/1880 which promised to guarantee the basic rights of all subjects regardless of their religion.

Taqdir. Measuring; the realisation of potential. For example, the realisation of the potential of a date stone is the date palm. If the stone does not grow into a palm, it has not fulfilled its potential. On the other hand, no date stone can grow beyond its potential; it has the destiny or fate to be a date palm. However, if the stone is not placed in the soil, looked after and nourished with water, it will not grow. Taqdir is frequently thought of as 'fate' or 'fatalism,' but this is totally contradictory to the concept of human freedom. People have been endowed with millions of potentialities. If they follow the right path in life, and make the right choices and effort, these potentialities will gradually be realised, and their personality become fully developed. The development of each individual is his or her taqdir. See Rabb, Free Will.

Taqiyah. Precautionary dissimula-tion; in Shi'ah practice, concealing one's true religious beliefs for fear of persecution, or simply in order to keep the peace and not cause division in a community.

Taqlid. Garlanding sacrificial

animals. In reference to fiqh (see above), it means the following of previous authorities and and the avoidance of ijtihad.

Taqlid al-mayyit. Reliance upon the teachings of deceased religious leaders alone, and avoiding ijtihad.

Taqwa. Awe of Allah, which inspires a person to be on guard against wrong action and eager for actions which please Him. Consciousness of God, the realisation that God always sees you, even if you cannot see Him. A person who has this quality is called muttaqeen. It brings a deep sense of closeness, serenity, personal responsibility, and becomes the Muslim's total frame of reference (see Surah 3:134-146; 8:2; 21:49; 23:57-61).

Tarawih. ('salat al-tarawih'—'prayer of pauses'). Extra prayers made on a voluntary basis during the nights of the month of Ramadan. Each evening Muslims meet at the mosque for a service that may be as long as 40 rakahs with a pause after every four; during this month the Qur'an is recited in sections, the aim being to get through the whole Revelation. The sunnah of the Prophet was actually either eight rakahs or twenty, according to which tradition one is following.

at-Tariq. Title of surah 86, 'the Night Star'; a Makkan surah of 17 verses, referring to God's power to raise people from the dead on Judgement Day.

Tariqah. (a 'way' or 'path'), a way of applying the teachings of Islam to the realm of inner experience. Used by Sufis to mean the 'science of the self'—the inner aspect of Shariah. In Sufism, it is the combination of Tariqah and Shariah that leads to Haqiqah (Truth), i.e. knowledge of God.

Tarji. The practice of repeating the call to prayer (adhan) to oneself in a low voice, just before commencing salah.

Tasawwuf. The word for spiritual insight. See Sufi.

Tasbih. Another word for Subhah. The praise and glorification of Allah (2:30; 3:41; 13:13; 17:44; 24:41; 57:1; 59:1).

Tasdiq (also called 'tasdiq bil qalb'). The silent assent to one's belief in Allah and His messenger, in the heart.

Tashahhud. Lit. 'to make shahadah.' In the context of prayer it is a formula which includes the shahadah, said in the final sitting position of each two-rakah cycle. It often includes a blessing on the Holy Prophet Muhammad.

Tashbih. Anthropomorphism—describing God in human terminology. See Tanzih.

Tashdid. Bigotry. Extremists believe they are right and cannot be wrong; therefore everyone who differs from them is virtually or actually regarded as an enemy, or at best an ignorant person. A bigot cannot tolerate differences of opinion, and generally has a closed mind impervious to further development. See Takfir.

Tashriq. The Days of Tashriq are the 10th, 11th and 12th of Dhu'l Hijjah, when the pilgrims sacrifice their hadis and stone the jamarat at Mina. Since these are days of feasting, Muslims are not allowed to fast in them. Those who wish to add days of fasting to their Ramadan, must continue after these three days.

Taslim. The saying of 'Peace be with you' or 'Salaam alaykum' at the end of the salah prayer. Muslims turn their heads to right and left, symbollically greeting their recording angels. See Rakah.

Tasmee. Technical term for the phrase 'God always hears those that call upon Him' used when standing upright during the rakah.

Tasmiyah. The recommendation 'In the name of Allah, the Compassionate, the Merciful'—*'Bismillah ar-Rahman ar-Rahim'.*

Taswiya. Bringing something to perfection.

Ta'til. Stripping God of all attributes, the opposite of tashbih.

Tawaf. Circling the Ka'bah, tawaf is done in sets of seven. The first act of pilgrims when arriving at the Ka'bah mosque, no matter what hour of day or night—a procession that has continued unceasing since the time of the Prophet. Pilgrims circle the central shrine in an anti-clockwise procession seven times, trying to run the first three circuits if they are able. Invalids and old people may be carried on special stretcher-chairs. They use the Black Stone to count their circuits, raising their hands in salute each time they pass. Many, if they are able to get to it, touch it or kiss it in their fervour—but they are not worshipping it and it is not compulsory. It is not an idol. When the pilgrims return to the Ka'bah after the Stand at Arafat, they perform another circling. If they circle yet again before going home, it is called tawaf al-wida—the farewell tawaf.

Tawaf al-Ifadah. The tawaf of the Ka'bah that the pilgrims must perform after coming from Mina to Makkah on the tenth day of

Dhu'l Hijjah. It is one of the essential rites of the Hajj.

Tawakkul. See Trust.

Tawarruh. The sitting position for tashahhud, with the right foot upright with the toes on the ground, pointing towards Makkah.

Tawassul. Entreaty, intercession, especially those sung during a Sufi hadra.

Tawatur. A technical term used in hadith criticism to denote the consideration that a tradition is mutawatir.

Tawbah. See Repentance

at-Tawbah. Title of surah 9, 'the Repentance'; a Madinan surah of 129 verses. It is the only surah not preceded by the Invocation 'In the name of God, the Compassionate, the Merciful.' The reason for this is most likely because it is a continuation of al-Anfal (surah 8) and the two are really one surah, even though seven years separated the two revelations (Zaqmakhshani). It concludes the seven long surahs. It refers to God accepting repentance (or otherwise) from His servants.

Tawhid. Lit. 'One Alone.' The doctrine of the One-ness of God. Nothing is remotely like God and nothing can be compared to Him (in any case, our knowledge and capacity for imagination is so limited) (see Surah 6:103, 112). To call God 'He' is only a tradition, God has no human gender. Allah is totally 'other' from His creation, transcendent, outside time, eternal, and can only be known as He chooses to reveal Himself (6:103)—such concepts as absolute Justice, Mercy, Truth, Love, and Compassion. God is the Alone, the Almighty, the Supreme; He is the First Cause, Creator and Sustainer, Judge and Decider of our fates. He is also at the same time immanent, so close to us and intimately involved with us that He is aware of our every thought; He is closer to us than our jugular veins (50:16; 2:186). See Kufr, Takfir, Shirk, First Cause, Tashbih, Beautiful Names.

Tawqif. Limitation. Nothing should be commanded or restricted to a Muslim as compulsory except what Allah has specifically commanded or prohibited. If any authority or person tries to impose a command or a restriction not laid down by Allah, they are making themselves 'partners' with Allah and committing shirk. See 42:21; 10:59; 16:116.

Tawrah. The Muslim name for the Torah, or revelation given to the prophet Musa (Moses). This is not regarded as being the same thing as the collection of writings Jews would call the Torah, however, for Muslims maintain that although those originated with Musa, they have been styled and compiled by later human editors, and are not the revelations just as Musa received them (11:110; 53:36; 87:19).

Tayammum. Purification for prayer with clean dust, earth or stone, when water for ghusl or wudu is either unavailable or would be detrimental to health. (4:43)

Taziyah. Lit. 'consolation.' (i) An expression of condolence for someone suffering from grief. (ii) A passion play performed by Shi'ites mourning the martyrdom of the Prophet's grandson Husayn. (iii) A decorated wagan used in procession in Muharram with a commemmoration of Husayn. See Ashurah.

Tazkiyah. Purification of the soul (2:129, 151; 3:164; 24:30-31; 53:32; 62:2; 91:9-10).

Tekke. The Turkish equivalent of a zawiya.

Temporary marriage. See Mu'tah.

Ten, the. See al-Ashara al-Mubashshara.

Tests. All sorts of circumstances are presented to human beings during their lifetimes; some involve great suffering and distress, some involve luxury and positions of power. The Muslim regards every circumstance as a test, to see if they will be aware of the principles that God requires in each given condition, and act in the best possible way. Allah promised that no person would face a burden that was too much for them to bear (2:155-156, 286; 3:139-142; 23:62).

Test-tube babies. A sperm bank is used to fertilise eggs of women who have remained childless; in surrogate motherhood one woman is employed to bear the child for a woman who cannot have a child of her own, for which she may be paid a fee. The ruling agreed by many scholars is that whatever is used strictly between a married couple to help them have a child of their own is permissible, provided no third party is involved in any way. If her egg is taken out, fertilised in the laboratory with her own husband's sperm, and then replaced, this is acceptable. When the process involves a third party, such as surrogacy, or taking sperm from a bank when the father is not known, this is forbidden. The prohibition is based on the principle that Islam maintains proper family relationships.

Thamud. A Nabataean tribe descended from the tribe of 'Ad, often referred to in pre-Islamic poetry as the 'Second 'Ad'. (7:73). The Prophet Salih was sent to them. The inscription of Sargon of Assyria in 715 BC mentions the

Thamud; the tribes of Thamudae and Thamudenes are mentioned by Aristo, Protemy and Pliny. They were settled in the northernmost Hijaz and many of their rock-inscriptions are still extant.

They were destroyed by an earthquake (7:78)—probably that which laid the extensive black lava-fields of northern Hijaz, particularly around Mada'in Salih.

Tha'r. Blood revenge on any member of the tribe, nullified in Islam by qisas.

Thawab. Reward for an act of merit.

Theft. (al-Sariqah), stealing from another. This is so serious a sin in Islam that a person could really be said to have departed from Islam if he or she stole from another. It is one of the sins that has a hard punishment (see Hudood), the cutting off of a hand (5:41). This is the sentence if the thief is a Muslim, and is adult, sane, was not forced to do it, did not steal out of hunger and the case has been proved beyond doubt. If the thief later repents, he or she can be forgiven and can re-enter Islam. It is worth commenting that it is a very successful deterrent, but the shame of Allah seeing your action, and your loss of Islam is the real deterrent to a Muslim.

Tijani Order. This order of Sufis was founded by Shaikh Abbas Ahmad ibn al-Tijani, an Algerian Berber (1150/1737-1230/1815), born in Algeria, settled in Fez. He saw a vision of the Prophet who bade him begin his Sufi work. It did not stress zuhd and accepted the ownership of wealth. It laid stress on thanksgiving to God. It has spread from Algeria to the south of the Sahara and into Sudan, Egypt, Senegal, West Africa and Northern Nigeria, as well as North and West America.

Tilawah. Reading the Qur'an with intent and concentration.

Time-span. The amount of time one is granted to live on earth as a human being. Allah, Who knows everything, knows a person's exact time-span from their moment of conception or even before. The Muslim regards his or her life as a gift from God, which must be returned when He wills. Although it is only human to feel grief at the loss of loved ones, and be shocked by the circumstances of some deaths, the Muslim should always be ready to return his (or her) life at God's command (3:145; 16:61; 53:42-27), and accepts that they do not know how, when or where they are to die, but Allah knows. (31:34)

at-Tin. Title of surah 95, 'the Fig'; a Makkan surah of 8 verses, which warns unbelievers of what lies ahead for them. The universal validity of moral law.

al-Tirmidhi, Abu 'Isa Muhammad (209/824-died between 270/883 and 279/892). One of the six major compilers of hadiths; he was said to have been blind, which did not limit his vast travels. He came from the area around Balkh, and travelled extensively gathering the hadith which he collected into what became one of the six chief collections.

Tobacco. See Smoking.

Tolerance. Being prepared to listen to and consider the opinions of other people. Allah requested all Muslims to be tolerant of other Muslims and of non-Muslims, and the Prophet pointed out that one was not a Muslim whose neighbour did not feel safe from his or her harm. A Muslim's duty was to show the way of life pleasing to Allah, and to warn—not to try to enforce or dominate or despise (88:21-22). Even when confronted by an evil person, one should continue to love the person, even if hating the evil that had spoiled them. See Takfir, Tashdid.

Transcendence. This is the doctrine that God is totally beyond human perception or understanding. See Latif, Tanzih.

Trench. See al-Khandaq.

Trinity. See Crucifixion.

Trust. Tawakkul. The confidence that Allah sees everything, and no matter what the circumstances of life, everything will work out for good, according to His will, if we trust Him and have patience. It does not imply accepting wrong things, but having faith that Allah 'who never slumbers nor sleeps, knows all our problems, and that He moves in mysterious ways unknown to us to bring about His will. See Istikharah.

Tughyan. The sin of arrogance and tyranny, becoming over-confident and so 'religious' that others are made to feel small and uncomfortable or stupid. Being oppressive and unkind, and fanatical. See Takfir, Tashdid.

Tulunids. See Ibn Tulun.

at-Tur. Title of surah 52, 'the Mountain'; a Makkan surah of 49 verses referring to Mt. Sinai where Allah revealed the Tawrah to the Prophet Musa. It deals with the Day of Judgement and the life to come.

Twelvers. (Also called Ithna 'Ashari and Ja'fari); the mainstream Shi'ite Imams (Ali being the first, followed by the Prophet's grandsons). The twelfth Imam mysteriously disappeared and now follows the course of history in a mystical way as the Hidden Imam. See Mahdi.

Tyranny. The Prophet stated that whoever supported an oppressor, knowing him to be an oppressor, had left Islam; and that the most excellent jihad was to speak the truth in the face of a tyrannical ruler. Tyrants are not always the kings and rulers of the world; some of the worst tyrants might be your own husband or wife, or even a spoiled child or over-domineering parent. Muslims should always be alert to this, and humble, making sure that they themselves never become tyrannical towards others. Tughyan can also apply to the sin of arrogance and becoming over-confident and so 'religious' that others are made to feel small or uncomfortable or stupid. See Tughyan.

'Udwan. One of the Quranic terms to denote crime or transgression of God's Law. It means conduct that stimulates a spirit of defiance that prompts a person to transgress the limits of the law.

Uhud. A mountain just outside of Madinah, much beloved by the Prophet. The site of the second battle against the Makkan idol-worshippers in 625. The Makkans came to avenge their defeat at Badr. This time, the Muslims acted hastily, without waiting for direction from Allah, and were defeated by the Makkans. Many great companions and in particular the uncle of the Prophet, Hamzah, the 'lion of Allah,' were killed in this battle. The Prophet himself was wounded, and lost two teeth. The Prophet used the defeat to teach people that when he or they relied on human judgement they were fallible, and could easily make mistakes; when they waited for Allah's directions and were obedient, they would come to success (3:152).

Ukaz. Town south-east of Makkah where an annual fair was held.

'Ulema. Scholars of Islamic law and jurisprudence. Plural of 'alim.

Umamah. The Prophet's grand-daughter, daughter of Zaynab and Abu'l-'As. She was 'famous' for the occasion when the Prophet once came to the mosque with her sitting on his shoulder, and performed the public prayer while carrying her (only putting her down during the prostration). When her aunt Fatimah died, she married Ali; and when he died, she married Mughira bin Nawfal despite the Caliph Mu'awiyah offering a thousand dirhams for her hand.

Umar. (Caliph 634-644). Famous for his fiery temper, Umar ibn Khattab was originally a fierce enemy of islam, determined to slay the Prophet and put an end to it. To his horror, he discovered his sister Fatimah and her husband were Muslims. He rushed to their house, intending to kill her, but on hearing a surah being recited he was impressed, and then converted. After that, he became one of the Prophet's closest and most devoted companions, although he never lost his tendency to sternness. He became the Prophet's father-in-law when his daughter Hafsah's husband was killed, and the Prophet married her. During his caliphate the Muslims captured Syria and Palestine, and he went to Jerusalem himself and began the repairs at the site of the Jewish temple, and granted a decree of tolerance to the Christian Patriarch Sophronius. He was loved for his humility, fairness, and generosity. He was assassinated by a Persian Christian, Firoz, whose case he had heard but given judgement against. Firoz stabbed him while he was praying the dawn prayer. Before he died, he appointed a six-man committee to elect his successor.

Umayyads. A leading tribe amongst the Quraysh. The third Caliph, Uthman, was an Umayyad, and after his cousin Mu'awiyah became the fifth Caliph, the office remained with that family until the time of the Abbasid rising (661-750). Most famous Umayyads of the time of the Prophet were Abu Sufyan and his wife Hind, and their daughter Umm Habibah who married the Prophet. The Umayyad collapse was due largely to their increase of wealth and power, and decrease of spirituality. Muslims wished to bring back the original purity of the Way.

Ummah. Lit. 'community.' The 'family' of Islam, the community of believers. The word 'ummam' (pl) means 'creatures (6:38). Ummah primarily denotes a group of living beings who have certain characteristics or circumstances in common. Thus, 'ummah' is often synonymous with 'community', 'people,' 'nation,' 'genus,' 'generation' etc.

The Ummah is the word often used to describe the 'brotherhood' of Islam, but to use the word 'brotherhood' is misleading, for there are as many female Muslims as males, probably more. Muslims from an immense diversity of cultures and languages all live by the same faith, doing their best to follow the same sunnah. Islam breaks down all barriers of race, colour, nationality, and social status (see 2:143; 3:103, 110; 9:71; 8:62-63; 49:10 etc.).

The Ummah extends across all places and ethnic groups, and also links people in different historical periods. Each believer is part of a community extending from the past—all the followers of all the Prophets from Adam onwards.

The unity of believers takes precedence over all other relationships, including those of family. It is the unity of faith.

Umm Ayman. Abyssinian maid servant of the Prophet's father. When he died, she served the Prophet's mother Aminah, and was nurse to the Prophet. Her second husband was the Prophet's fostered son Zayd ibn Harithah. Her two children (Ayman from her first husband, and Usamah son of Zayd, were devoted Companions of the Prophet. Usamah was regarded as the Prophet's first grandson. She acted as nurse and water-carrier to the wounded in the Battles of Uhud and Khaybar. She lived to a great age and always acted as a devoted 'grandmother' to the Prophet's family, and died in the Caliphate of Uthman.

Umm Habibah. She married the Prophet by proxy in 1 AH, although she did not live with him until 7 AH when he was sixty and she was thirty-five. She and her first husband, the Prophet's cousin, Ubaydullah ibn Jahsh (a hanif, and the brother of the Prophet's wife Zaynab) were among the very first converts to Islam, although her parents were bitter enemies. She emigrated to Abyssinia, and there Ubaydullah left Islam and became a Christian. At this stage they were divorced, but she did not return to her father. The Negus of Abyssinia took care of her financial needs, and arranged her marriage with the Prophet. Eventually her parents embraced Islam and she was reunited with them. She lived to 44 AH, and died at the age of seventy-two.

Ummi. The term 'unlettered' really denotes a nation or community or person who has not had a revealed scripture of their own. The Prophet was said to have been sent 'unto the unlettered people (ummiyun)' as 'an apostle from among themselves.' This passage was to stress the fact that he, too, was unlettered and could not, therefore, have invented the message of the Qur'an or derived its ideas from earlier scriptures (see 7:157-8).

Most Muslims conclude that the Prophet could neither read nor write, which made the creation of the Qur'an through his revelations an even greater miracle.

Umm al-Kitab. The 'Mother of Books'—the Qur'an.

Umm Kulthum. The third daughter of the Prophet and Khadijah. Her sister Ruqaiyyah had been married to the Prophet's companion Uthman, and when she died, Umm Kulthum married him. The wedding also smoothed over a hurt that occured when Uthman refused to marry Umar's widowed daughter Hafsah; the Prophet married Hafsah, and gave Uthman his daughter. Umm Kulthum also died before the Prophet, childless, in 9 AH.

Umm al-Mu'minin. Lit. 'mother of the believers', an honorary title given to the wives of the Prophet, may Allah bless him and grant him peace.

Umm al-Qur'an. Lit. 'the Mother of the Qur'an', the opening surah of the Qur'an, al-Fatihah. Also said to be its source in the unseen.

Umm Salamah. She married the Prophet in 4 AH at the age of twenty-nine, when her husband Abdallah (known as Abu Salamah) died from wounds received at Uhud. They had both been among the earliest converts in Makkah, and had emigrated to Abyssinia. They returned, and were looked after by Abu Talib. Later, they attempted to join the Prophet at Madinah, but en route Umm Salamah's family seized her and her son and held her captive for a year, until they eventually took pity on her tears, and allowed her to join Abu Salamah in Madinah. She had several children and was pregnant again when her husband died. Both Abu Bakr and Umar offered to marry her, but she refused. When the Prophet offered, she refused him too at first, because she feared she would be unable to accept his other wives, and was worried about her children. The Prophet assured her that Allah would grant her tolerance, and that her children already belonged to Allah and to him. This example brought blessing to others, for many other Muslims then married widows, and brought up their children, instead of seeing them struggle alone. Umm Salamah was a scholar, accompanied the Prophet on many battles, and was granted at least one vision of the angel Gabriel. When she asked why the Qur'an revelations always referred to men, the words of 33:35 were revealed, and it was made clear that all instructions to Muslims were for both men and women, equally. Her daughter Zaynab became a leading scholar and recorder of hadiths. She was the last of the Prophet's wives to die, in 61 AH at the age of eighty-four.

Umm Walad. Lit. 'mother of a son', slave-girl who has given birth to a child by her master.

Umrah. The 'Lesser pilgrimage'—a pilgrimage to Makkah with its connected ritual events made at any time other than 8th—13th Dhu'l-Hijjah.

Unfurling. The Hajj events that take place after the Wuquf or 'Stand' at Mt. Arafat. They include the stoning of the jamarat at Mina, the Feast of Sacrifice (Eid ul-Adha), the shaving of men's heads and cutting of women's hair, the removal of ihram, return to the Ka'bah, visit to Madinah and other Muslim 'tourist' sites.

Unity. Muslims should all form one Ummah. The Prophet likened the community of Islam to one body; when one part of it was hurt, the other parts ached. When a Muslim began to be divisive, he or she was in danger of splitting from Islam. The usual cause of divisivenesss was religious pride and intolerance, which should be carefully guarded against (see Extremism). Muslims should regard every other Muslim as a brother or sister, a worldwide network of those submitted to Allah's will. See Sermon, the Last.

Unlettered. See Ummi.

Unseen. See al-Ghayb.

Urs. The death anniversary of a Muslim saint. Widely celebrated by Sufi Muslims, but disapproved of in strictly orthodox Islam. Those who write leaflets inviting Muslims to make a saint's tomb a place of pilgrimage, to let him know their desires so that he may be able to beseech on their behalf, and who solicit donations, are committing shirk. It is wrong in Islam to beseech a dead man on behalf of a living man, to speak to Allah for him. However, visiting graveyards, and remembering good people is recommended. It is normal to visit the graves of any loved one to pray for them.

Usul al-fiqh. The 'roots' or theoretical bases of Islamic law.

Usury. (riba—exploitation). Muslims are allowed to make money in fair trade, but not from exploiting the needy. A rich person lending money at interest usually gets people deeper into debt. Muslims with wealth are requested to help the needy by lending what they need without interest. (See Allah's earlier revelations to Jews and Christians in the Old Testament Law in Exodus 22:25; Leviticus 25:36-7; and New Testament Law in Luke 6:34-5). Allah said: 'If the debtor is in difficulty, grant him time until it is easy for him to repay... your repayment would be greater if you cancelled the debt altogether' (2:280). For exploitation in trade dealings, see 2:274-5; 3:130; 4:161). The Prophet also forbade needy Muslims from trying to borrow at interest except in case of dire necessity (e.g. life is not possible without food, clothing and medical treatment); even then, the borrowing should be limited to the exact amount (i.e. don't borrow £100 when £90 is what is necessary), and the borrower should constantly seek to escape the predicament, perhaps by taking on extra work, or by fellow Muslims helping out. See Islamic Banking.

Uthman. Third caliph of Islam (644-656), a rich merchant of the Umayyad family of the Quraysh, who had been married to two of the Prophet's daughters—Ruqaiyyah and Umm Kulthum. He was a gentle and kind-hearted man, but his administration was not as disciplined as that of his predecessor Umar, and he was accused of appointing too many friends and relatives to key positions, even though he would have argued that they merited these posts. When he was eighty, he was asked to consider abdication, but he refused. His cousin, the ruler of Egypt, had imposed harsh taxes and Uthman refused to interfere. He was assassinated whilst at prayer by a group of Egyptians. His wife Nailah tried to protect him and her fingers were cut off. She sent them to his cousin Mu'awiyah, Governor of Syria, who became the next Caliph.

al-Uzza. Name of an idol, said by her worshippers to be a 'daughter of God.' Her chief shrine was at Petra. See Goddesses, Gharaniq.

Values. The chief characteristics valued by Muslims are awareness of God and devotion to Him; honesty, compassion, kindness, generosity, courage, patience, justice, tolerance, forgiveness, sincerity, truth, modesty, chastity, fortitude, and responsibility. The chief characteristics most disliked are pride, envy, divisiveness, hypocrisy, lying, cheating, irresponsibility, backbiting, suspicion, intolerance, excess and extremism.

Veiled women. See Hijab and Purdah.

Vivisection. Experimentation with living creatures. Anything which inflicts suffering or cruelty is haram in Islam; anything which promotes the common of individual good is halal. Obviously vivisection harms animals, and therefore is in this case, a haram practice, especially when the experimentation is for the purpose of vanity or luxury goods (such as make-up). One might argue that when it is for medical research it could be for the good of humanity, and therefore halal. This is a highly debatable matter.

Visions. Being granted the gift of 'seeing' something through the 'mind's eye', because God wishes to raise the awareness of the person receiving the vision above the limits of their physical surroundings. For example, certain people have had visions of spiritual beings not normally visible to humans (e.g. angels); or places beyond our normal limits (e.g. the Prophet's journey from Jerusalem through the Heavens); or of events which will take place in the future (e.g. the Prophet Isa prophesied the coming of a Son of Man, or Comforter who would bear witness, who would come after he was raised up); or of details beyond human knowledge (e.g. the Prophet's grandfather Abdal Muttalib was shown the Zam-zam spring, which had been lost to knowledge). The experience of seeing visions is not limited to Islam, of course, but they are recorded for every religion, and for people with no religion also. Like seeing angels, the vision is usually for a specific purpose and not just a random event (perhaps brought on by drugs or indigestion!). It usually changes or influences the recipient's entire future life.

Vizier. Anglicized form of wazir, an officer to whom a ruler delegated the administration of his realm; head of the imperial council in the Ottoman empire.

Wahdat al-Shuhud. Unity of vision of Allah.

Wahdat al-Wujud. Unity of being, feeling of unity with Allah.

Wahhabism. A 'purist' reform movement founded by Muhammad ibn Abd al-Wahhab (1773-1792), now dominant in Saudi Arabia and Qatar. Originally based on the teachings of ibn Hanbal and ibn Taymiyah, al-Wahhab considered that Islam was being eroded on two fronts—by the mass of theology and scholasticism created by the madhhabs, which meant that simple believers despaired of understanding and could be misled by amateur interpretations (a situation that has indeed arisen today!); and the pious over-enthusiasm for saint veneration (which included excesses of Shi'ite fervour for the Prophet's descendants). Wahhabism is criticised for having encouraged religious terrorism, and for distrusting all aspects of inner enlightenment or personal insight into faith, and concentrating on the rigid observance of formal and ritual duties. Originally sponsored by the Emir Muhammad ibn Saud, the Wahhabis captured Makkah and most of Arabia from the Turkish Sultanate in 1803, and still support the continuing dynasty of the ibn Saud family.

Wahy. Prompting, inspiring, or introducing a thought or feeling into a person. It operates at different levels, from inciting a blind urge to inspiring a thought. In the animal world Divine guidance is given through wahy in the directive force of instincts. Everything receives from the Creator all the guidance which it needs; the directive force is at work everywhere in the universe. (For example, a chick and a duckling may be hatched by the same hen, but the duckling will take to water, and not the chick). Divine guidance carries everything from stage to stage until it reaches its full development. Insight, the ability to understand revelation and the inner depths of messages from God.

Wajib. See Fard.

Wala'. The tie of clientage, established between a freed slave and the person who frees him (or her), whereby the freed slave becomes integrated into the family of that person.

Wali (pl. Awlia). From the Ar. 'wala'—'to be near' and waliya 'to govern, rule or protect someone.' A protector, benefactor, companion, friend. A guardian, a person who has responsibility for another person, used particularly for the person who 'gives' a woman in marriage. A woman not present at her wedding agreement ceremony can be represented by her wali. See Nikah.

Wali Allah (pl. awliya' Allah). 'Friend of Allah' or Sufi holy person, who is reckoned to enjoy a particular relationship (wilayah) with Allah.

Walimah. A party, feast, celebration, usually in honour of a wedding, childbirth, or some other success such as passing one's college exams. The party given by the husband's side of the family after a wedding specifically publicises the fact that the couple are legally married and entitled to live together (even if they do not do so until later, for various reasons). See Nikah, Marriage.

Waliullah (1113-1176 AH/1702-1762 CE). An Indian Sufi mystic, of Naqshbandi background, who was acutely aware of the disunity of the Indian Muslim community; between Sunni and Shi'ah, between scholars of the law and traditions, and between these scholars and Sufis. He devoted his life to resolving and reconciling these splits. He particularly objected to the Hindu practice of forbidding Muslim widows to remarry, excessive amounts demanded in dowry, extravagant expense on celebrations, and ceremonies of mourning for the deceased. He hoped the new spirit of ijtihad would liberate Islamic thought from narrow, bitter controversies and restore Muslim solidarity and power to its former glory. He translated the Qur'an into Persian, and his son translated it into Urdu—thus making it directly accessible to the literate, hoping to bypass the scholars and empowering non-Arabic-speaking Muslims to read and study for themselves.

al-Waqi'ah. Title of surah 56, 'that Which Must Come to Pass'; a Makkan surah of 96 verses. It deals with the resurrection and the life to come, describing the delights of Paradise and the pains of Hell.

Waqf. The donation of certain sources of income (e.g. land or property revenue) to the service of a religious community such as a mosque, college, school or hospital, to provide for its upkeep and running costs.

Waraqa ibn Nawfal. The cousin of the Prophet's first wife Khadijah. He was a hanif, had studied Christianity, and tradition suggests he had even translated a Gospel into Arabic. He had concluded from his studies that both Musa (Moses) and Isa (Jesus) had foretold the coming of another Prophet (e.g. Deuteronomy 18:18, and St. John's Gospel 16:13-15). It was to Waraqa, then a hundred years old and blind, that Khadijah turned for advice concerning the Prophet's experience on the Night of Power. Waraqa was overjoyed that he had lived to see the one who would be the new Messenger of God. Waraqa also warned the Prophet that he would face persecution and be rejected by his own people.

Warid (pl. waridat) that which descends on the seeker while performing dhikr or sitting in the company of a saintly person. The first stage of awakening.

al-Wasil. One who is good and kind to his kith and kin.

Wasila. Something which makes something else take place. Also the highest station with Allah on the Last Day, reserved for the Prophet.

Waswas. Agonising doubt; over-fastidious concern with ritual precision, or the validity of personal purity. This can be so destructive that it prevents worshippers from achieving their objectives. We should remember that we are human, and that God loves us even with our faults and weaknesses. We should place our trust in Allah's loving kindness and mercy.

Wealth. The Prophet stated that 'wealth does not lie in the abundance of worldly goods, but true richness is the richness of the soul' (Hadith). He also taught that the real test of his Ummah would be wealth, perhaps foreseeing the time when Muslim nations would have great riches from oil revenues. To own great wealth is a responsibility and a test for Muslims, for they must behave honourably with it, use it to do good, and not waste it on extravagant and selfish luxuries (64:15). Money in itself is not regarded as evil, so long as it is honourably obtained; Muslims are expected to work hard, be thrifty, and enjoy the fruits of their toil—but along with the benefits go the duties of providing for the poor and needy, and looking after the less fortunate.

Wedding. See Marriage, Nikah.

Wet dreams. See Ihtilam.

Wife-beating. Before the coming of Islam, men often felt that they 'owned' their womenfolk, and usually did not grant them equal status unless they were wealthy. A man would obviously hesitate before striking another man, but women were regarded virtually in the same category as children, and men seemed to think it was quite all right to strike them physically. This was banned in Islam except for women whose ill-will husbands had reason to fear (4:36) (See Nushuz). It is obvious from many authentic traditions that the Prophet himself detested the idea of hitting a woman, and forbade it, with the words 'Never beat God's handmaidens' (Abu Dawud, Nisa'i, Ibn Majah, Ahmad ibn Hanbal). In his Farewell Sermon he said a physical rebuke should be resorted to only if the wife had become guilty in an obvious manner of immoral conduct, and in any case done in such a way as not to cause pain. It should be symbolic, done with a miswak (Tabari) or even a folded handkerchief (Razi).

Wilaya. Friendship, in particular with Allah.

Wilayat. The 'befriending' of Allah, of those who love Him. (2:107,120; 4:45,123,173; 9:116; 29:22; 33:17; 42:9,31)

Wird (pl. awrad). A unit of dhikr constructed to contain in it certain patterns of knowledge and self-awakening. Some can last hours, others only a few moments.

Wisal. Continuous fasting from one day to another without breaking for food. A practice disapproved by the Prophet as excessive and unnecessary.

Wishful Thinking. See Gharur.

Witness. Allah is the Witness of everything we do. he is also aware of all our thoughts, and knows our temptations and tests, and the reasons for our actions. He is also aware when we choose to do anything and the reasons for our actions. He is also aware when we choose not to do any particular thing, and rewards all our good with His blessings. (See Shukr). Allah is with you wherever you may be, and sees clearly all that you do (57:4. 'In whatever business you may be engaged, and whatever deed you may be doing, Allah is witness of it,' (10:61). 'There is no secret consultation among three but He is the fourth, nor among five but He is the sixth, nor among fewer or more but He is in their midst wheresoever they may be,' (58:7). Allah always watches over us (4:1; 5:20; 89:14), and sees all things (33:52). See also 4:33,79,166; 10:29,46; 13:43;

17:96; 22:17; 29:52; 33:55; 34:47; 41:53; 57:4; 58:6; 85:9.

Witr. Witr prayer is often mistakenly thought of as part of the 'isha prayer. It is actually a separate prayer that can be offered any time after 'isha right up to the break of dawn. The Prophet allowed witr to follow straight after 'isha if that was convenient for the believers.

In Arabic, witr means 'one.' The Prophet recommended the number one because Allah is One; he also preferred odd numbers, because when divided by two the remainder is always one. 'Night prayer is to be offered in two rakah units. When one of you feels that dawn is near, then he (or she) should offer one rakah which can make all the night prayers offered into an odd number.' (Bukhari, Muslim).

Witr is therefore a final single rakah to make an odd number of rakahs, which is regarded as preferable.

Witr bil fasal. When the final witr rakah is said after the salutation.

Women as equals. As regards value and spirituality, there is no difference between male and female in Islam. ('All people are equal, as the teeth of a comb'). God speaks to all Muslims, whatever their gender. As regards talents and abilities, Islam recognises that it is the duty of every individual of both sexes to study and improve themselves so far as is possible, and to be as useful to the community as possible. As regards the biological nature of the sexes, Islam recognises that women have certain extra burdens such as menstruation and childbearing, and therefore insists that men should be alert to their problems, sympathetic in their dealings with women (especially in the home and the workplace), appreciative of their sacrifices, and supportive with their strength and ability to earn income and provide home bases. In return for protecting and maintaining women, men have the right to expect loyalty, support and (hopefully) love (4:34).

Women warriors. See Nusaybah.

Work. It is the duty of the Muslim to work to earn a living, and the Prophet conferred dignity and honour on the humblest of tasks. However, certain kinds of work are haram for Muslims, for example anything that degrades or exploits, or is dishonest, or immoral, or abusive. Muslims are requested not to beg, unless in very dire circumstances, but to do whatever they can to make a decent living.

Worldliness. See Dunya.

Wrath of God. See Ghazab.

Wrong-doing. See Zulm, Zalim.

Wudu (Wuzu). The ritual wash before prayer or reading of Qur'an. The wash follows a set pattern—the declaration of intention to turn to God (niyyah); washing the hands up to the wrists three times; rinsing the mouth three times; snuffing water into the nostrils three times; washing the face three times; washing the arms up to the elbows three times; passing wet hands over the top of the head and round the back of the neck; wiping out the ears with the index finger and the back of the neck with the thumbs; washing the feet to the ankles three times (5:7). This wash will do for more than one prayer providing that the state of wudu is not broken by anything unclean leaving the body, or unconsciousness. Wudu when no water is available is called tayammum.

Wuquf. This is the Stand before God at Mount Arafat, 24 kms east of Makkah, on the 9th Dhu'l-Hijjah. The stand takes place between noon and dusk, and without it a pilgrim's Hajj is invalid, and becomes an 'Umrah. It commences with the zuhur prayer, and ends with the asr—very moving moments as around two million pilgrims bow down together before God in silence. A time of great spiritual power, it commemorates the forgiveness and reunion of Adam and Eve, and their release from sin. Pilgrims feel a deep emotion as their own sins are 'washed away' and they renew their allegiance to Allah and become 'new'.

Yahya. John the Baptist, the cousin of the Prophet 'Isa (Jesus) and a prophet himself, miraculously born to the Jewish priest Zakariyah (3:38-41; 6:85; 19:2-15; 21:89-90). He died a martyr, beheaded by Herod Antipas, the son of Herod the Great who became the ruler of Galile. His followers were known as Sabians, 'dippers' or 'dyers', from his practice of baptism in the river Jordan (not to be confused with the Sabaeans, the inhabitants of the kingdom of Saba/Yemen). Once 'dipped', the 'fabric' of the convert was completely 'dyed', or changed to the new way of Islam, or submission to Allah, the One True God.

Yalamlama. The miqat of the people of Yemen.

Yarmuk, Battle of. Fight at River Yarmuk, tributary of the Jordan, between invading Arab armies and the Byzantines in 16/637. The Muslims were commanded by Abu Ubaydah ibn al-Jarrah and the Byzantines by Sacellius Theodorus. The battle was the key to the conquest of Syria.

Ya Sin. Title of surah 36, the two letters Y and S; a Makkan surah of 83 verses often recited at times of distress and approaching death; it refers to the joys of Paradise, and stresses that the body will be raised from the dead.

The title could also mean, 'O Thou human being'. 'Sin' is synonymous with 'insan' in the dialogue of Tayy, and is a similar instance to 'Ta Ha' in surah 20. Zamakshari suggests it is unaysin, a diminutive version of insan, and refers to the Prophet. The surah is devoted to the problem of human moral responsibility and the certainty of resurrection and judgement. See al-Muqatta'at.

Yathrib. The ancient name for al-Madinah al-Munawwarah.

Yatim. An Orphan. The Prophet highly recommended any kind person who would foster and raise an orphan as if he or she was their own child. The Prophet was himself an orphan (his father Abdallah died before he was born, and his mother Aminah died when he was six). He was raised first by his grandfather Abd al-Muttalib, and then by his aunt and uncle—Fatimah and Abu Talib. He once commented of Fatimah that she cherished him more than her own children.

There are many verses in the Qur'an regarding the rights of orphans, and the duties of those who look after them (2:83; 4:2, 6, 10; 17:34; 33:4-5; 93:1-6).

The Prophet pointed his two longest fingers and said: 'I and the one who raises an orphan, will be like these two (fingers) in the Garden.'

Yawm al-Din. The Day of Faith, one of the names of the Day of Resurrection.

Yawm al-Qiyamah. The Day of Resurrection, Day of Judgement, Last Day.

Year of Sorrow. This was the year 619-20 when the Prophet was 50; ten years after his call to Prophethood. In this year, his beloved wife Khadijah, and also his guardian uncle, Abu Talib died. The chief of his clan became Abu Lahab, who was very opposed to Islam. The Prophet left Makkah, and sought to carry out his ministry in the oasis town of Taif, but they rejected him also. It was in this year that he experienced the Laylat al-Miraj.

Yemani corner. The corner of the Ka'bah facing south towards the Yemen.

Yunus. The biblical prophet Jonah, also called Zun-nun, the 'companion of the fish'. He was sent by Allah to preach repentance to the people of Assyria, and was swallowed by a huge sea-creature because he was annoyed when they did repent; he had expected them not to, and had been anticipating their punishment from Allah! He did not die, but prayed to Allah for forgiveness, and was restored (4:163; 6:86; 10:98; 21:87; 37:139-148; 68:48-50).

Yunus. Jonah; the title of surah 10, Jonah being mentioned in v. 98. A Makkan surah of 109 verses. The theme is the denial of the suggestion that the Prophet fraudulently composed the revelations.

Yusuf. The Muslim name for the Prophet Joseph, the son of Jacob (Yaqub). Sold by his brothers as a slave, he rose to prominence in Egypt by his gift of foresight and interpretation of dreams. The Qur'an gives the story of Yusuf being sold to the Aziz (the Exalted in Rank), probably the chief eunuch of the Pharaoh, and the desire of Zulaikha, the Aziz's wife. The full story of Yusuf and his imprisonment in Egypt, and the coming of his brothers to Egypt is given in Surah 12, the title of which is 'Yusuf.'

Yusuf. Title of surah 12; a Makkan surah of 111 verses, with the longest section of narrative, about the Prophet Yusuf (Joseph), in the Qur'an.

al-Zabaniyyah. The principal angelic guardians of Hell, 'those who thrust violently' and will cast people into the fire. (66:6; 74:30)

Zabur. Lit. 'scripture' or 'book', a generic term for any book of wisdom. Usually used as the Arabic word for the revelation granted to the Prophet Dawud (David)—usually known as 'the Psalms', but not identical with the Psalms as presented in the Old Testament (4:163).

Zahid. An ascetic (see zuhd). One who does without, no longer needing or desiring what he/she does without, so the avoidance of it is not a struggle or denial.

Zahir. 'Outward' or 'manifest;' the surface or literal aspect of a text or doctrine. Exoteric, outer, on the surface, obvious. Its opposite is batin.

Zahiris. A defunct school of Islamic law which stressed literal interpretation of both Qur'an and Sunnah.

Zakah. Meaning 'to purify' (from 'zakiya'—to grow, be pure, to cleanse). Muslims 'cleanse' their material possessions and money by donating a percentage of it as a compulsory payment of money or possessions to help the poor, needy, sick, imprisoned, or Muslim mission workers. For money, (cash, bank savings and jewellery) it is 2.5% of surplus income (once the Muslim's own and family needs have been taken care of up to a certain limit—the nisab); other zakah examples are 20% of mining produce; 10% harvest from rain-watered land; 5% from irrigated land; 1 cow per 30; 1 sheep or goat per 40; 1 sheep or goat per 5 camels. Zakah is one of the five pillars, a regular annual duty and not merely charity given out of kindness, which is called sadaqah. (See 2:95, 210, 264, 270; 9:60). The object is to limit the withdrawal of money from being circulated in society. If wealth is just 'saved' for an individual, it is not being used and nobody gets the benefit from it.

Zakariyah. Father of Yahya (John the Baptist). Known in the Bible as Zachariah. He had remained childless until his old age, and his wife was considered well past the age of bearing. He was a priest at the Jewish Temple in Jerusalem, and saw the angel Jibril who announced that he would have a son who would be the fore-runner of the Masih (Messiah). He died a martyr. A tomb believed to be his is carved in the hillside opposite the Haram as-Sharif in the Kidron Valley.

Zakat ul-Fitr. A special donation to charity made during or at the end of Ramadan, often enabling poor Muslims to keep the Eid ul-Fitr.

Zalim nafsahu. A wrong against oneself. A person who deliberately commits a sin or a wrong (zulm) has damaged himself or herself spiritually (4:107).

az-Zalzalah. Ttitle of surah 99, 'the Earthquake'; a Madinan surah of 8 verses, referring to the signs of the Last Day.

az-Zamakshari, Abu'l Qasim Mahmud (467/1075-538/1144). major exegete and Qur'anic scholar. His Mutazilite leanings are apparent in his great commentary on the Qur'an called 'the Unveiler' (*al-Kashshaf*).

Zam-zam. The spring of water shown by the angel to Hajar, wife of the Prophet Ibrahim. The Ka'bah temple was built beside it. It was covered up by the predecessors of the Quraysh in Makkah and its location was lost; it was rediscovered as a result of a vision granted to the Prophet's grandfather Abd al-Muttalib, and thereafter his clan (the Hashimites) had the custodianship, and privilege of granting water to pilgrims. Muslims on Hajj usually drink from its water, take water as souvenirs, and some dip their white ihram cloths in it and keep them to act as their shrouds later. These things are not compulsory.

Zandaqah. Free-thinking or heretical beliefs.

Zaqqum tree. The cursed tree of deadly fruit mentioned in 17:60; 37:62; 44:43 and 56;52. Zaqqum denotes any deadly food. The sufferings faced by sinners in the life to come are but the fruit of their evil deeds on earth.

Zawiyah. (literally, 'a corner'). A centre for Sufi activities, where dhikr and meditation takes place, and where Shaikhs may live and train their disciples. Also called khaneqahs, khangahs, tekkes or ribats.

Zayd ibn Harithah. The fostered son of the Prophet. Originally from the northern Arab tribe of Kalb, he had been captured as a slave-boy, and lived in the household of Khadijah. She gave him to the Prophet on their wedding day. When his family traced him and offered to ransom him, he begged to stay with the Prophet, and was granted his freedom. His first wife was a much older lady than himself, the Prophet's nurse Umm Ayman, and their son Usamah (recognised as the Prophet's grandson) was one of the first children born in Islam. His second wife was the Prophet's cousin Zaynab bint Jahsh, but they were not compatible and the marriage ended in divorce. He fought in several battles, and was sent with Ja'far and an army of 3000 to the Syrian border to confront the Byzantine Emperor Heraclius and his army. They were not successful, and both were killed by the Byzantine army at the village of Mu'tah near the Dead Sea, in 8 AH.

Zayd ibn Thabit. A man relied upon by the Prophet as his secretary. He was given the task of writing down all the separate revelations of the Qur'an and compiling them into one book. He was himself a hafiz, and the text he put together contained no editorial comment; nothing was added and nothing removed. The order of the verses was ordained by God Himself and checked by the Prophet and the angel Jibril. When the volume was completed, it was kept in the custody of Umar's daughter Hafsah, and it was copies of this text that were sent to the chief Muslim centres by the Caliph Uthman.

Zaynab bint Ali. The Prophet's granddaughter, her parents being Fatimah and Ali. She was born in 627, and was said to have closely resembled Khadijah in looks. Her first journey was to accompany the Prophet on the Last Pilgrimage, when she was five. She was six when he died, and her mother Fatimah died the same year. She became famous for her knowledge of Qur'an and virtuous life. She aged prematurely when Ali was assassinated in 661, and went to live with her brother Hasan. In 677 she supported her brother

Husayn on the battlefield of Karbala against the Umayyad claimant to the Caliphate (Yazid), and when he was martyred, saved his son Zayn al-Abidin and became leader of the Shi'ite Muslims until her death in 683.

Zaynab bint Harith. After the defeat of the Jewish stronghold of Khaybar, their lives were spared but they were obliged to surrender with all their possessions. The chief of the tribe and his cousin hid their treasure and were executed—the only ones put to death.

A woman, Zaynab bint al-Harith, who had lost all her menfolk in the battle, invited the Prophet and his companions to a meal of lamb. She had poisoned it. The Prophet chewed one mouthful before he realised and spat it out but his companion Bishr had swallowed some. The Prophet was seized with violent cramps and pain, and although he did not die then, he complained of the effects of that poison until his dying day. Bishr did die of it. Zaynab confessed, but challenged him by saying 'if he is a king, I shall be rid of him; if he is a Prophet, he will be informed (of what I have done).' The Prophet allowed her to live.

Zaynab bint Jahsh. Original name Barrah, the Prophet's cousin, her mother Umaymah being a daughter of Abd al-Muttalib. One of the earliest Muslims, an extremely devout lady. The Prophet arranged her marriage to his foster son Zayd ibn Harithah, who was a freed slave, intending the match to demonstrate that it was not ancestry but virtue in the sight of God that showed worth. Zaynab and her family were disappointed; she had hoped to marry the Prophet himself, and only agreed to marry Zayd when ayah 33:36 was revealed urging the match. The Prophet paid a handsome dowry on Zayd's behalf. However, they were incompatible and the marriage failed. When divorce followed, the Prophet salved the wound by marrying her after all, and she became his seventh wife in 626, when she was 35 and the Prophet 58. He hesitated, until Allah sent the ruling that a fostered son can never be regarded as a natural son, because there was no blood-tie. Muslims who argue that it is sunnah to marry their cousins should reflect on the fact that she was the prophet's seventh wife, not his first choice. It was on the occasion of their marriage that the Verses of the Hijab were revealed (33:53-56) which allowed the Prophet to separate a private space for his wives. Another lesson deriving from her was when the Prophet found a rope tied between pillars at the mosque, and was told she used it to support herself when she felt too faint to continue praying unaided. He commanded that one should stop prayer when one became tired. She died at the age of 50 in 641.

Zaynab bint Khuzaymah. The fourth wife of the Prophet. She married him in 625, when she was 30 and he was 56. She was part of a family of women well-loved by the Prophet, for her half-sister Umm Fadl was the wife of his uncle Abbas, her sister Salmah was the wife of Hamzah and another half-sister Maymunah also became the Prophet's wife later. She became a widow when her husband Abdallah ibn Hajash was killed at Uhud. She made her own proposal to the Prophet (as did Maymunah later). She was so generous to orphans and the poor that she had been known since her childhood as Umm al-Masakin, 'Mother of the Poor'. She died around eight months after her marriage.

Zaynab bint Muhammad. The Prophet's eldest daughter, born when he was 30. She married her cousin, Abu'l-'As, and they had a son Ali and daughter Umamah. Abu'l-'As refused to convert to Islam, and kept Zaynab in Makkah when the Prophet migrated to Madinah. He fought against the Prophet at the Battle of Badr and was captured, but then released on the promise he would divorce Zaynab and let her be reunited with her father. En route, she was shot by an arrow, and lost the child she was carrying. Zaynab never lost her love for Abu-l-'As, and she protected him when he was captured again. At last, he converted to Islam and they were remarried, but sadly she died soon after, in 629.

Zealotry. Zeal generally means enthusiasm; zealotry in religion is where the desire to please God becomes excessive, going beyond the bounds of what is required, from motives of religious pride or unhealthy extremes of humility. Even the genuine desire to please God can become an embarrassment and irritant to others, and drive them away, if it is expressed too publicly. See 5:90; Extremism.

Zenana. Women's quarters in a palace or house.

Zihar. From Zahr, meaning 'back.' In the days of jahiliyyah an Arab could refuse a sexual relationship to his wife by saying: 'You are to me as the back of my mother.' In these cases, the man was reckoned to have divorced the wife, but she could not leave his house and dragged on in a very unhappy existence with him. This practice was forbidden in Islam. Men were not allowed to abandon a sexual relationship with their wives, perhaps because they had grown old and ugly. The revelation came as the result of the sad experience of the Prophet's friend Khawlah bint Tha'labah, whose husband Aws ibn Samit had finished his relationship with her. She begged the Prophet for help, but he said he could not intervene. Then he received the revelation of 58:1-2, which ordered him to do so.

Zinah. This means sex outside marriage. Islam requires all sexual activity to be within the bounds of a marriage relationship, and condemns sex before marriage (fornication) or sex with any person outside the marriage (adultery 17:32), or with any person of the same sex (homosexuality 4:15-16). Zinah was punished by death in many pre-Muslim societies, including Jewish ones; it is on record in the hadith that the Prophet also reluctantly allowed the death penalty in his time. Adultery is regarded as so dishonourable a matter that it still risks the death penalty in some regions. The actual penalty laid down in the Qur'an was a flogging not the death sentence, proved by the ruling that persons who had committed adultery should not be allowed to marry non-adulterers, presumably because they had shown that they could not be trusted (24:2-3). A person had to produce four witnesses to accuse another of adultery, and if they made up false charges, they were flogged for perjury (24:4). Stoning someone without proof would count as murder. If one spouse accused another without witnesses, they had to swear four times that it was true, and the fifth oath brought a curse on themselves if they were lying. The accused person could similarly swear their innocence on oath; the accused should not then be condemned, but divorce would follow (24:6-10).

Zionism. The movement to create a homeland for all Jews in the land of Israel. (See PLO). It is based largely on the notion of Jews as a special chosen race, an idea not accepted in Islam which insists that God has *no* chosen races—people of all races are His 'children'. Zionism is the main cause of enmity between Jews and Muslims; before Zionism people of both faiths lived together in many societies, the Jews usually content to be under the protection of Muslims who respected their faith and their synagogues.

Ziyarah. A visit to a holy place, or tomb of some venerated person. Also used of the Hajj pilgrims visit to Madinah, to pay respects at the grave of the Prophet.

Zubayr ibn al-Awwam (d. 36/656). One of the nephews of the Prophet's wife Khadijah. He opposed Ali at the Battle of the Camel, very soon after which he was killed.

Zuhd. Asceticism; not setting one's heart on worldy things. This usually involves living extremely simply; not clinging to personal possessions such as wealth, fine food or clothing; and perhaps practising various disciplines to strengthen spirituality, such as fasting, long sessions of prayer or study of Qur'an, or dhikr.

Zuhur. The compulsory salah prayer made just after the sun passes its height, but according the actual moment of mid-day in case of association with sun-worship.

Zukhruf. Gold; the title of surah 43 based on the word in v. 35. To attribute divinity to anything or anyone other than god is spiritually destructive and logically inadmissible.

Zulaykha. The wife of Potiphar (Qitfir-) who attempted to seduce Yusuf. The commentator al-Baydawi also suggests the name Ra'il for this lady. See al-Aziz.

Zul-Kifl. See Dhu'l Kifl.

Zulm. Tyranny. Wrongdoing, injustice, denial of a right.

Zulmah. Darkness. Life without God.

al-Zumar. Title of surah 39, 'the Crowds'; derived from vv. 71-73, a Makkan surah of 75 verses referring to the unbelievers being driven into Hell in crowds, and the pious into Paradise in crowds. Only Allah can determine the eternal fate of humans, and it is to Him that humans are responsible.